1250

Occupational Careers

Occupational Careers

A SOCIOLOGICAL PERSPECTIVE

Second Edition

by Walter L. Slocum
WASHINGTON STATE UNIVERSITY

Aldine Publishing Company/Chicago

ABOUT THE AUTHOR

Walter L. Slocum has served as Statistician in the United States Office of Labor, was Associate Chief and Chief of the Research Division of the Office of Vocational Rehabilitation and Education, Veterans' Administration, and was a member of the State Staff, Washington Cooperative Extension Service. Formerly Consultant in Sociology for the United States Department of Agriculture, Professor Slocum served on the department's Panel for Long-Range Social Science Research Plans. Professor Slocum has published over 80 articles in the field of Sociology, and is author of *Agricultural Society*. He is presently Professor of Sociology at Washington State University.

Howard S. Becker,
Consulting Editor

Copyright © 1966 and 1974 by Walter L. Slocum

Published 1974 by
Aldine Publishing Company
529 South Wabash Avenue
Chicago, Illinois 60605

ISBN   0–202–30268–7 clothbound edition
       0–202–30269–5 paperbound edition
Library of Congress Catalog Number 73–84935
Printed in the United States of America

Preface to the Second Edition

Scores of publications dealing with the topics covered in this book have appeared since the first edition. Some, notably those based on the research of sociologists William Sewell, Archie O. Haller, R. M. Hauser, O. D. Duncan, and their students and colleagues, must be regarded as of major significance because they provide quantitative tests of sociological and folk theories concerning the relative importance of such factors as intelligence, socioeconomic status backgrounds, and parental and peer group values and encouragement.

It is not feasible in a book such as this to undertake a comprehensive and critical evaluation of this voluminous literature. What I have sought to do instead is to incorporate new information that I regard as important; important because it provides insights or raises significant questions about the conventional wisdom. With respect to the latter, I have called attention to the thesis of psychologist Arthur Jensen that the intelligence quotient and subsequent educational and occupational achievement are determined to a greater extent by heredity than by environment; this, of course, revives a long dormant controversy. I have also introduced some ideas from such writers as Ivar Berg, Ivan Illich, and Randall Collins, who look at society from a conflict perspective. These men charge that the educational system operates primarily to facilitate the careers of those who have had the good fortune to have been born into white middle- and upper-class families, and that the system tends also to discourage and defeat those who come from culturally different homes.

I have used the latest information available to me. However, it must be recognized that relevant new information appears

almost daily. Consequently, anyone who needs information
that is strictly up-to-date should consult current issues of professional journals and/or current releases from various government agencies.

Although I have continued to make minimal use of sociological jargon, I have made the theoretical framework somewhat more explicit than in the First Edition. Specifically, I
have given greater emphasis to the concept of career as an
integrating idea, and in chapter 11, the reader will find a
sociologically oriented paradigm of career aspirations, choice,
and achievement. This is a synthesis of theories developed
during the past quarter of a century by vocational psychologists, manpower economists, and occupational sociologists.

Chapter 12, "Career Strategies," is primarily directed to the
person who is planning a career. It is not a set of prescriptions
for specific behavior but rather a discussion of alternatives
that have emerged from social scientific studies and theories.

Walter L. Slocum

Preface to the First Edition

In the past few years, a number of sociologists have published articles and monographs reporting research on occupational choice and other aspects of the sociology of occupations. Some of this material has been collected in the form of readers, but, so far as I am able to determine, no one has tried to fit the various pieces together to give an overview of current sociological knowledge relevant to occupational careers. This book represents an attempt to do this. However, it is not to be regarded as an exhaustive digest of all available studies but rather as an eclectic view based on selected works regarded by the writer as representative and illuminating.

While on sabbatical leave, February through July 1964, I devoted most of my time to reviewing the literature in occupational sociology and conferring with leading research workers in the field. Much of this material proved useful in the development of a course at Washington State University in the sociology of occupations. The enthusiastic reactions of my students encouraged me to prepare this book. I hope that it will interest and assist vocational counselors, personnel workers, other sociologists, and young men and women who seek systematic information for personal use in career planning.

I am indebted to the many sociologists and others who have shared their ideas with me, to my students, and to Washington State University. I cannot name all of the persons involved in the development of this book, but I would like to acknowledge helpful suggestions made by George Bowman, editor, Agricultural Research Center, and William P. McDougall, associate professor of education, both at Washington State

University, and Athol Congalton, professor of sociology at the University of New South Wales, Kensington, Australia, who was visiting professor of sociology at Washington State University from February 1965 to February 1966. I wish also to acknowledge the forbearance and assistance of Esther Clark Slocum.

Contents

1. Introduction   1
2. The Meaning of Work   15
3. Scientific and Technological Developments and Occupational Change   37
4. Occupational Career Lines in Work Organizations   75
5. Occupational Status Levels   124
6. Labor Force, Employment and Unemployment Trends   138
7. Occupational Trends and Outlook   149
8. Scientific and Professional Occupations   165
9. Education and Occupation   184
10. Occupational Mobility   211
11. Determinants of Career Aspirations, Decisions and Attainments   240
12. Career Strategies   299
    INDEX

1. Introduction

In this revolutionary age, change is so rapid and so pervasive, not only in the United States but throughout the world, that there may be a tendency on the part of some people to underrate the significance of the past as a stabilizing force in human affairs. This is, of course, unfortunate, because it should be obvious that much can be learned from the past that can help us in the present and in planning for the future. What we need is a balanced perspective. The rapidity of change is a relative matter. We know that man's ways of life have always undergone constant change since the dawn of recorded history, and we are quite sure that changes occurred even in prehistoric times. What makes the present age different is that major changes happen so quickly that unprecedented problems of adapting to them have arisen; and the prospects are that the tempo of change will speed up even more in the future.

What This Book Is About

This book focuses on careers in work organizations. This emphasis stems from the fact that we live in an "employee society." [1] In 1970, only 10 per cent of the U.S. labor force

1. Peter F. Drucker, "The Employee Society," *American Journal of Sociology*, vol. 58 (1953), pp. 358–63.

were classified as self-employed; this included all farm operators, all self-employed lawyers and doctors, and all operators
of independent businesses. Because competition is severe and
bankruptcy rates high among small businesses and because,
for the most part, the large rather than the small farm operators continue in farming, the percentage of self-employed will
probably decrease still further in the future.

Work occupies a central place in the lives of people in industrial societies such as the United States. But, as we shall
see in chapter 2, work has had many meanings for different
societies. The meaning of the same occupation may vary from
one individual to another because of temperament or a different pattern of values or previous experiences. Beyond this,
variation may be due to differences in occupations, differences
in work organizations, or even the demands of nonoccupa-
tional roles performed in other groups or organizations.

The number of different occupational roles pursued by
adults in the United States is almost incredible. The 1965 edition of the *Dictionary of Occupational Titles* is said to contain descriptions of 21,741 separate occupations with 35,550
different occupational titles.[2] This is a far cry from the relatively simple division of labor that characterized earlier societies. Warrior, craftsman, priest, and herdsman were a few of
the more important early occupational roles. Other roles existed, of course, and the situation actually was not simple
except by comparison with the complexity of modern life.

Chapter 3 calls attention to great changes in occupations
that have occurred since the beginning of the Industrial Revolution, about 200 years ago. Most of these changes have accompanied the application of science and technology to industry and agriculture. In a sense, the entire elaborate contemporary industrial establishment rests on improvements in farm
technology, including use of new crop varieties, new breeds
of animals, farm chemicals, and machinery. The application

2. U.S. Department of Labor, Bureau of Employment Security, *Dictionary of Occupational Titles* (Washington, D.C.: U.S. Government
Printing Office, 1965), p. xv.

of scientific knowledge to agriculture has so greatly increased the efficiency of commercial farms that a surplus of farm products has been produced in the United States and a few other advanced countries, although a shortage of food exists in many of the underdeveloped countries.

Parallel developments in industry have increased productive capacity and nonfarm employment has risen. New inventions appear at an ever-increasing rate and each major technological development creates problems. At the present time, the problems associated with automation are of major concern to many thoughtful people. In chapter 3 we will consider in some detail the occupational implications of automation. It is sufficient to note here that the consequences of rapid technological change for career planning are profound.

We will discuss in chapter 4 the occupational requirements of work organizations, a matter of increasing importance for occupational careers. Different types of organizations show many basic similarities in respect to organizational structure including the establishment of career lines for professional, managerial, and technical personnel; yet, at the same time, there are important differences in organizational norms and occupational duties.

Chapter 5 presents a discussion of occupational prestige and other systems for measuring occupational status levels in current use. The concept of occupational stratification is essential for our later consideration of occupational and career mobility and for an adequate interpretation of occupational data from the census.

Chapter 6 reviews some of the important factors affecting the supply of workers. These include changes in length of working life, the upsurge in new workers due to the postwar baby boom, the increasing participation of married women in paid employment, multiple employment, and trends in employment and unemployment.

Chapter 7 deals with recent trends and future prospects in major occupational categories.

Because of their great and growing importance in modern

industrial society, it seems appropriate to consider the characteristics of professional and scientific occupations in some detail in chapter 8.

The discussion in chapter 9 of the relationship between education and occupation pays special attention to the growing importance of education as a means of preparing for occupational roles.

So many sociologists have studied occupational mobility that it is not possible to attempt an exhaustive review of the available data on this topic. Fortunately, much information of great importance for our discussion of the sociological aspects of occupational careers is available in a few major studies. Chapter 10 presents briefly the central findings of selected studies of intergenerational and individual occupational mobility.

In chapter 11 we will present the central findings of selected recent sociological studies of educational and occupational aspirations and decisions. As in the case of occupational mobility, there are now so many such studies that an exhaustive review is not feasible in this book.

The final chapter discusses some aspects of career patterns and strategies in a few elite occupations that have been studied in some depth by occupational sociologists.

Conceptual Overview

What can sociology contribute to the understanding of careers that is useful to individuals and organizations? The answer will be developed in the following pages as we examine, from a sociological perspective, familiar data as well as data and insights from specifically sociological studies. At the outset, however, I would like to introduce the major concepts that will be employed and tie these concepts together into a coherent overview.

First, what is meant by occupation? For our purposes, an *occupation* is defined basically as the kind of work an adult does on a regular basis. Usually it is an activity performed for wages, salary, commissions, or other forms of money income. An important exception to this attribute is the occupation of homemaker. Viewed in this way, it is clear that occupations are restricted to advanced and developing societies. Occupations, as such, are not generally found in primitive tribes.

The term *career* has been used in ordinary, everyday conversation for a very long time, and it carries a favorable connotation. It is considered desirable to have a career and undesirable not to have one; but the concept has been used very loosely—it is applied to occupations, but it is also used in many other ways. For example, one woman is said to make a career of raising a family, while another makes her career in club work. Some sociologists would reserve the term for the professions, whereas others use it to include the entire period of a person's participation in the world of work, regardless of the number and kinds of different occupations in which he or she may have been employed.

An *occupational career* may be defined for this discussion as an orderly sequence of development extending over a period of years and involving progressively more responsible roles within an occupation. With reference to occupational careers in work organizations, the theoretical model involves entry into a position that requires the performance of occupational duties at the lowest rung of the occupational ladder. This is followed by a sequence of promotions into higher-level positions within an organization, leading eventually to the pinnacle, and finally to retirement. Although this generalized model calls for upward progression from the bottom to the top, we know that not every entrant moves through all these steps. There are thus varying degrees of conformity to the model.

What is a work organization? This concept will be used to refer to social systems organized to perform work of various kinds. Industrial corporations, business partnerships, school systems, and government agencies are some types of work organizations.

The work organization is a social system in which members perform specialized work required to produce ideas, goods, or services. Competent performance of occupational skills is essential to the success of a work organization, although other factors are also important. To obtain occupational competence, organizations provide incentives such as wages and salaries plus fringe benefits of various types. Key employees (those who hold the top positions in various career lines) receive the greatest rewards in power, prestige, and money.

Work organizations may be viewed sociologically as networks of relationships among persons who perform work and other activities that are expected because they hold certain positions. The expectations that exist among members of the system with respect to the performance of the incumbent of a *position* will be called an *occupational role*. From an analytical point of view, performance of an occupational role is a dynamic process while the (associated) position is a static or structural component of the work organization.

An occupational role may also be regarded as a component of personality. It is frequently said that the occupational role is the key role for many contemporary American men in the sense that the expectations associated with other roles may be given a secondary order of priority.

Closely related to the concept of occupational career is the concept of *occupational career line* in a work organization. But there is a difference. Only individuals have careers, but they have them as they pursue career lines established by work organizations. Sociologically, a career line may be thought of as a structural aspect of an organization. As such, it consists of hierarchically related occupational positions in the organization that require successively more responsible performance of occupational skills. An example is the career line of professor, which in an American university or college normally consists of four steps: instructor, assistant professor, associate professor, and professor.

Every work organization is characterized by a more or less distinctive organization *culture*, consisting of the values, folkways, and knowledge that guide the work-related attitudes and behavior of members. Each profession and many other occupations have a distinctive *occupational culture*—approved ways of performing occupational roles, such as surgery. In addition, as we will note in the next chapter, some aspects of the *societal culture* pertain to work.

In small work organizations, as in other small groups, all of the employees get to know each other as human beings rather than merely as occupational specialists. Consequently, interpersonal relationships may be affected by the personal attitudes that workers express from time to time. These, in turn, are based on their previous experiences as well as experiences in the work situations. Informal behavior norms develop and become accepted as the right way of doing things. These comprise an aspect of organizational subculture. In addition, the members of a work organization sometimes share a common ideological outlook.

In large bureaucratic organizations, occupational roles tend to be more rigidly prescribed and relationships among workers are somewhat more impersonal. In such organizations an aspect of the subculture includes job descriptions and rules for various types of behavior that are put in writing. However, large organizations do not necessarily function like well-oiled machines in strict compliance with the formal organization chart and the written rules. Industrial sociologists have discovered that small informal groups exist and perform essential functions in all large organizations. These small groups function in much the same ways as primary groups everywhere, providing recognition and mutual support for members and providing means for circumventing organizational rigidities.

Occupational and organizational culture, like other aspects of culture, is learned through informal and/or formal education. Sociologists usually use the concept *socialization* to designate the process of internalization of the cultural imperatives.

Achievement as experienced in educational and occupational histories is developmental in nature: Early school achievement is greatly influenced by preschool experiences; later school achievement is based upon earlier success or failure; occupational placement and early achievement may be greatly affected by education; and subsequent occupational achievement is built upon earlier achievement.

In our society, children receive their early socialization or social training from parents and siblings. This, of course, includes socialization into family value orientations toward education and work, and socialization into family behavior norms governing task performance. The development of educational and occupational aspects of one's self rest, in large measure, upon signals received from others, especially from "significant others," those who are important to us—our parents, friends, and some teachers. W. E. Moore takes the position, which I share, that *normative* aspects of educational and occupational socialization (acceptance of the protestant work ethic, for example) rest upon affective recognition— (praise or punishment)—from these "significant others." [3]

The occupational socialization of an individual begins at an early age, even prior to kindergarten. The preschool boy has sex-typed occupational role models such as his father and the other adult males with whom he interacts or sees on television. When he enters school, and the range of his interpersonal contacts expands, additional role models are encountered.

While the occupational values, norms, and behavior of the individual are influenced by "significant others" with whom he interacts, it should be borne in mind that these "significant others" transmit the values and norms of their social systems. Consequently, it appears to be justifiable to say that group values and norms are internalized as part of the occupational socialization of the individual.

In simple agrarian societies, work is performed within a closely knit social system in which there is little, if any, change in membership except through birth and death. Consequently, there is little disagreement concerning values and behavior norms. Our society is closer to the other polar extreme, with

3. Wilbert E. Moore, "Occupational Socialization" in David A. Goslin, ed., *Handbook of Socialization Theory and Research* (Chicago: Rand McNally & Co., 1969), pp. 877–882.

plural norms. Except for family farms and family businesses, work for pay is performed away from home. But, except for a few occupations such as unskilled agricultural work, a boy does not move directly from his family to a work organization. He has to go to school first. Therefore, an essential part of his occupational socialization occurs in educational systems.

Education involves much more than learning the formal subjects offered by educational systems, including knowledge related to the world of work. A boy must also gain acceptance as a person from other students as well as teachers before he can be regarded as a student in good standing. It is, of course, easier to move from one social system to another if the core values and behavior norms of the two are congruent. Because the public schools are staffed chiefly by teachers from middle-class backgrounds, it is obviously easier for children from middle-class families than for those from working-class families to gain acceptance as scholars and/or peers.

Studies by sociologists have produced convincing evidence that intelligence and socioeconomic status of family of origin are positively correlated with the degree of success of an individual in educational systems.[4] Socioeconomic status is more than a simple index of income or wealth; it is an indicator of diverse culture including linguistic patterns, values, and life-styles.

After leaving school, a young man ordinarily joins a work organization (sometimes after a tour of duty in the armed forces, a special type of work organization). Both initial occupational placement and subsequent achievements are strongly influenced by educational achievements. School systems identify those persons who are academically talented and, by providing suitable recognition (rewards) in the form of high grades and other honors, encourage them to strive for still higher educational attainments.

The step-like nature of the educational system with its age-related classes can be conceptualized as a career line; hence, it makes sense to talk about educational careers.

4. Cf. William H. Sewell and Vimal P. Shah, "Socio-economic Status, Intelligence and the Attainment of Higher Education," *Sociology of Education*, vol. 40, no. 1 (Winter 1967), pp. 1–23.

There is a "pecking order" among educational systems, especially institutions of higher learning; for example, Harvard University, University of Chicago, and the University of California at Berkeley will be among those at the top, and the junior colleges would be at the bottom. There is much evidence that a successful educational career in a high status educational system leads directly to placement in an elite occupation and increases greatly the probability of a successful occupational career in a relevant work organization.[5] Thus, Wall Street lawyers are recruited mainly from Harvard, Columbia, and Yale;[6] apparently few, if any, are recruited from law schools affiliated with universities below the top.

There is another outcome for some students. School systems, beginning with elementary school, screen out and reject those who are unable or unwilling to conform to school standards. The mechanism for this is the grading system. Functional illiterates and others with relatively unsuccessful educational careers (the failures, the dropouts, and so forth) are thereby relegated to low paid, low status occupations. This screening has recently become the source of complaints because of the current salience of education to occupational placement.

In many respects the role of student resembles a work role, especially an occupational role that has an intellectual base or component; for example, definite hours exist for school attendance, students are given assignments (work) that must be completed prior to specified deadlines, quality of oral and written performance is evaluated and rewarded (or punished) by grades and other ways. Learning the student role can be regarded as an important aspect of occupational socialization.

Students who have high motivation for upward mobility take high status persons as role models and high status occupations and work organizations as reference groups.[7] Educa-

5. Cf. Peter Blau and O. D. Duncan, *The American Occupational Structure* (New York: John Wiley & Sons, 1967), p. 402.

6. Erwin O. Smigel, *The Wall Street Lawyer* (New York: Free Press, 1964), p. 59.

7. *See* p. 260 for definition of reference group.

tional preparation to perform high status occupational roles requires performance in accordance with the values and norms of these reference groups and role models. For a student from a working-class family, this may require rejection of some of the values and behavior norms of his family of origin as well as those associated with low status occupations—and ecological settings such as the so-called urban ghettos.

This process has been labeled *anticipatory socialization* by Robert K. Merton.[8] It is most clearly visible for working-class students in professional schools and colleges. Anticipatory socialization of this type may be expected to facilitate movement of a candidate into the desired occupation and/or work organization. It also leads to rejection of working-class norms.

We will be primarily concerned with career mobility which focuses on competition with others for power, promotion, pay increases, and other rewards. However, careers usually also involve entrance into an occupation as a member of a work organization, socialization into the values, roles, and behavior norms of a work system, gaining acceptance as a member, and cooperating with other members to attain personal and system objectives.

Much occupational socialization and virtually all work-organizational socialization occurs within work organizations. Entry (crossing the boundary as a first step toward full membership) is ordinarily accomplished through a voluntary sequence of interaction between candidate and organization. The organization makes known its need for a person or persons qualified to perform specified occupational duties. An individual having the required qualifications, (education, occupational experience, and so forth) makes an application. The application is screened by means of tests, credentials, personal recommendations, and/or interviews. The candidate whose application survives this screening receives an offer, which he either accepts or rejects (perhaps after an attempt

8. Robert K. Merton, *Social Theory and Social Structure* (Glencoe, Ill.: Free Press, 1957), pp. 265–271.

to negotiate more favorable pay and/or perquisites). If the offer is accepted, a formal appointment to a position (frequently probationary) is made by the organization.

A crucial aspect of attaining acceptance in an organization is the adequate performance of the occupational and other roles associated with a position. Some anticipatory occupational socialization may occur prior to entry, but virtually all organizational socialization takes place as one learns the norms of his roles, including the expectations of other members of his work group or role set.[9] These expectations usually include acceptable personal conduct as well as competent performance of occupational duties. Consequently, skill in interpersonal relationships is helpful. Sponsorship by a prestigious member of the system may also be very helpful.

The relationship between worker and work organization is usually contractual. The contract is subject to reexamination by both parties from time to time and either or both may decide to terminate the relationship, subject to certain legal, organizational, occupational, and other rules.

Because the relationship is fundamentally voluntary in nature, because of the well-known history of high occupational and interorganizational mobility in the United States, and because work organizations must have competent occupational specialists to survive, step-like career lines or ladders have been established for executives, professionals, and other specialists. The conceptual model now in vogue is that of the *meritocracy*, a modernized version of bureaucracy.[10]

In a meritocracy, successful upward career mobility is supposed to be based primarily upon high achievement as evaluated in terms of occupational and/or organizational standards. Ability or intelligence is an exceedingly important determinant of performance. But, personal style, sponsorship, and

9. Frederick L. Bates, "Institutions, Organizations and Communities: A General Theory of Complex Structures," *Pacific Sociological Review* (Fall 1960), pp. 59–70

10. Cf. Michael Young, *The Rise of the Meritocracy*, 1870–2033 (Baltimore: Penguin Books Inc., A Pelican Book, 1961) for a humorous treatment of the meritocracy.

interpersonal social skills may sometimes be as important as occupational competence (expressed as intellectual or manual skills) for upward mobility in a particular work organization. The degree of competition among work organizations for competent specialists and executives also affects career progress; persons with scarce skills that are in great demand obviously have greater bargaining power than others.

Most complex work organizations have a well-defined subculture, a set of shared values and norms (both written and unwritten), that governs, or guides, patterns of interaction among occupational specialists, executives, and other workers. At least for managers and professionals, the career ladders established by organizations provide performance incentives. Thus, organizational career socialization is essential for those who become permanent members of the organizational "establishment"; the nonconformists usually either leave voluntarily or are fired if detected prior to gaining tenure.

Work organizations do not exist in a vacuum but have linkages with and are influenced by clients and by other work organizations, including regulatory agencies, unions, and/or professional associations. Work organizations are also influenced by general economic, political, and social developments. Employment opportunities, pay and promotion prospects, and working conditions are affected by the state of the business cycle, by war, and by legislative enactments. Technological change, new forms of business organization such as franchises and conglomerates, and altered work rules demanded by unions or required by legislation, may require profound and/ or frequent changes in the occupational requirements of work organizations. Workers now entering the labor force for the first time may have to be retrained to perform substantially different occupations, not just once but several times during their work lives. Consequently, the *work histories* of most persons, even those who become professionals, executives, or entrepreneurs, are likely to include more than one occupational career in more than one organization.

Thus, it is clear that when we consider work broadly we are dealing with open rather than closed systems. Great changes

have occurred in occupations and in work organizational patterns since the beginning of the Industrial Revolution, some
200 years ago. Both the tempo and the scope of such changes
appear to be accelerating. This means that the ability to adapt
to change is an essential aspect of successful occupational behavior; occupational socialization thus appears to be applicable to the entire work life. Furthermore, resocialization from
the worker role to the retired role is encountered upon retirement.

2. The Meaning of Work

Many important historians, politicians, literary men, as well as persons in other fields, have written about the significance of work to the building of individual character, to the development of the nation's resources, to national survival, and to the fulfillment of self. In every American generation, moralists have criticized young people, and sometimes others, for lack of devotion to work as a way of life. In his autobiography, Benjamin Franklin recommended hard work, especially the appearance of being a hard worker, as a way to success.

Today, there are some indications of change in attitudes toward work. For example, Rev. Robert Lee, professor of Christian social ethics at San Francisco Theological Seminary, recently criticized Protestantism for stressing the central importance of work, to the point that many people are unable to enjoy their leisure. He said, "We feel guilty about anything that is not work. We're a work, work, work culture." [1]

From a sociological perspective, it is important to point out that the sentiments individuals feel toward and express concerning work are largely determined by the values prevalent in the society at a particular time and place. In addition, the views of any particular individual are obviously influenced by his own experiences as a worker and as a member of various groups, organizations, and other social systems, many of which are characterized by configurations of work-related values that may vary somewhat from those thought to be prevalent in the society as a whole.

1. *Daily Oregonian* (14 October, 1965).

The intrinsic meaning of work also varies according to the nature of the occupational role performed. An important aspect of the occupations of managers, officials, and proprietors consists of supervising the work of persons employed in lower-status supervisory occupations such as foremen, craftsmen, inspectors, and junior executives who assign work to and supervise the operations of machine operators, clerks, sales workers, and semiskilled and unskilled workers. Persons occupying positions characterized by close and detailed supervision have much less freedom for the exercise of individual initiative and ingenuity than those who work under general supervision that provides opportunity for the exercise of wider latitude of judgment, ingenuity, and initiative. Persons employed in positions having expectations either for direction or for obedience to orders from higher authority accommodate themselves to these circumstances and tend to internalize these aspects of the occupation as aspects of their self-concepts. Thus, a manager tends eventually to believe that it is his prerogative to direct the activities of others, and the person who occupies a closely supervised position is likely to feel that he has lower capabilities.

These patterns are much less rigid in contemporary industrialized societies than they were in feudal or other preindustrial societies characterized by the existence of a hereditary nobility and monarchy. This is true primarily because modern industrialized societies provide other alternatives for self-expression in addition to those found in work organizations and institutionalized in specific occupational and organizational roles for the exercise of individual initiative. For example, a person who occupies a middle-status occupational position in his work organization may rise to high office in a fraternal organization or other voluntary organization.

Occupational roles reflect other dimensions than those involved in supervision versus obeying orders. Scientists engage in fundamentally intellectual activities that involve the manipulation of symbols of a high degree of abstraction, and, at least ideally, they are dedicated to the pursuit of new knowledge. Engineers have the fundamental mission of working out practical solutions to physical problems by applying the esoteric knowledge developed by such scientists as physicists, chemists, and mathematicians.

Under the direction of professionals, technicians of various types perform somewhat routine operations to produce information useful in the solution of problems of individual patients, business firms, government agencies, or other clients. The list could be expanded almost indefinitely if one attempted to describe the meaning of the activities of any substantial portion of the incredibly large number of occupations in modern industrialized urban society. A fairly objective description of about 22,000 of these occupations is available in the *Dictionary of Occupational Titles,* published by the Bureau of Employment Security of the U.S. Department of Labor. These descriptions do not, for the most part, emphasize the sociologically important aspects of occupational roles, such as the nature of the social systems in which specific occupational roles are formed, the ethical standards developed and applied by professional associations, or the informal norms developed by specific work groups for regulating the occupational performance of specific workers so that they will perform neither more nor less than a "fair day's work." Neither does the *Dictionary of Occupational Titles* deal with the subjective meanings of work to individuals.

Historical Development of Attitudes toward Work [2]

Although information concerning the work-related values of earlier societies is far from complete, it appears from historical sources that the ancient Greeks regarded work as a curse. Physical work was drudgery imposed on men because the gods

2. Information concerning the historical development of attitudes toward work is based primarily on Adriano Tilgher, *Work: What It Has Meant to Men Through the Ages* (New York: Harcourt, Brace & Co., 1930); *see also* "Work Through the Ages," in S. Nosow and W. F. Form, eds., *Man, Work and Society* (New York: Basic Books, 1962), pp. 11–23.

hated them. Agriculture, however, was regarded more highly than other types of manual work, but it was customary for heavy work to be done by slaves.

The views of the ancient Romans were quite similar to those of the Greeks and probably were derived, in part, from Grecian influences. Cicero, the Roman statesman and orator, considered that only two occupations were fit for a free man: agriculture and big business. All other occupations he said were dishonorable and vulgar. His fellow Romans for the most part agreed with him.

The ancient Hebrews also considered work drudgery. They believed that men were required to work in order to atone for their sins. The Hebrews, however, differed from the Greeks and the Romans because they thought work was a way by which man might redeem the sin of his ancestors and gain spiritual dignity for himself. The early Christians, as might be anticipated, held views quite similar to those of the Hebrews; they too, thought of work as punishment for sin. They considered it necessary for people to work to earn a living, but they added the new idea that the fruits of labor might be shared with the needy.

Work was viewed with disdain until after the Reformation which occurred in the Middle Ages. The rise of industrial capitalism in western Europe followed the Reformation. New sects sprang up and some of these, especially Calvinism, emphasized a new attitude toward work, namely that it is the will of God for people to work in order that the fruits of their labor may be used to help establish the kingdom of God on earth. Furthermore, the Calvinists preached frugality and did not scorn business ventures. Although they believed in predestination, they came to believe that success in business indicated that a person was one of the "chosen" few.

Many sociologists, economists, and others have accepted the idea that this basic change in attitudes toward work was responsible for the rise and development of capitalism in Western civilization. The leading exponent of this view was the German sociologist, Max Weber, who considered Benjamin

Franklin a prime example of the influence of the Protestant ethic.[3] Nevertheless, Weber's thesis that the Protestant ethic was a leading cause of the rise of capitalism has been challenged by other scholars.[4] Considering the evidence on both sides, it appears to me that Harold L. Wilensky is probably correct when he suggests that ascetic Protestantism neither obstructed nor encouraged the rise of capitalism but that it did emphasize the importance of work.[5]

American colonists brought with them the work-related culture prevalent in England, but the outlook of the aristocratic Cavaliers who established the plantation system in the South was materially different from that of the New England Puritans.

Although highest prestige was allocated to successful businessmen in early America, unusual prestige was apparently attributed to agriculture and to manual occupations. Unfortunately, occupational prestige ratings prior to the 1920's do not exist, but the general literature suggests that until recently manual occupations were widely regarded as the only wealth-producing occupations, while intellectual occupations were not. Only within the past quarter of a century has there been general public acceptance of the idea that intellectual occupations are really productive; this acceptance rests chiefly upon the impressive and highly visible accomplishments of engineers and physicians, which, in turn, are based upon lesser known achievements of physicists, chemists, and biologists. This early American value position was probably due to the relative impotence of the learned professions, to the necessity for manual work by the settlers, and perhaps in part to the peasant and lower-class origins of most immigrants.

The work imperative (not necessarily focused on manual

3. Max Weber, *The Protestant Ethic and the Spirit of Capitalism* (New York: Charles Scribner's Sons, 1955).

4. Kurt Samuelsson, *Religion and Economic Action, A Critique of Max Weber* (New York: Harper & Row, Publishers, 1964), and Harold L. Wilensky, "Varieties of Work Experience," in Henry Borow, ed., *Man in a World at Work* (Boston: Houghton Mifflin Co., 1964), pp. 125–54.

5. Wilensky, "Varieties of Work Experience."

labor) has been called the "Puritan ethic" in recent public discussions, probably because of the influence of the Puritans on the development of industries in New England.

The Meaning of Work in Contemporary America

There is no doubt that work occupies a central place in the life of modern Americans. Studies made by anthropologists in various parts of the world indicate that this is not universally true in all societies at the present time, and we have just noted that other activities were regarded as more important during the early stages of Western civilization. The development of present-day American attitudes toward work represents a long and gradual evolution.

There is a tendency among economists and sociologists to emphasize the meaning of work in terms of extrinsic rewards such as income, power, and prestige which, in turn, affect life-style and how one is regarded by others. Daniel Patrick Moynihan has even taken the extreme position that occupational achievement is the sole determinant of status—that a person without a job has no standing in our society.[6]

Research by social scientists shows, however, that young men from middle-class American families not only expect to work for wages or salary after leaving school, but are also usually motivated to work hard and generally aspire to move upward toward higher level occupations than those held by their fathers. There is evidence that even high school students regard work as desirable for its own sake rather than merely as a means to an end.[7]

Occupational recognition is supposed to be achieved on the basis of the merits of the individual without regard to his

6. Daniel Patrick Moynihan, "Employment, Income and the Negro Family," *Daedalus* (Fall 1965), p. 747.

7. Walter L. Slocum, *Occupational and Educational Plans of Seniors from Farm and Nonfarm Homes* (Pullman, Wash.: WAES Bulletin 564, 1956).

origin. In its extreme form this is known as the "Horatio Alger myth"—the idea that a boy from a log cabin is likely to rise to fame and fortune. This, of course, has happened in America, but the odds are against it. As we shall see, the evidence from studies of occupational mobility indicates that it happens infrequently.

Some question exists about the extent to which devotion to work, which is believed to characterize typical Americans, is shared by and participated in by manual workers, assembly-line operators, clerks, and others who are employed at unskilled, semiskilled, or routine and repetitive jobs. Nevertheless, no substantial group of able-bodied males between the ages of 25 and 65 in the United States is willingly without work. Unemployment of any substantial length is considered catastrophic not only for the individual but also for his family. Studies indicate that unskilled manual workers and factory workers on assembly-line jobs where the commitment to the job is at a minimum have definite expectations with respect to the performance of occupational roles. Thus, even such work has meaning to the worker. Furthermore, occupational roles, including unskilled roles, have important consequences for the performance of other roles in the family and in the community.

The meaning of work for married women differs from the meaning of work for men or single women because the culture establishes different expectations. For most women, paid occupational roles are supposed to be supplementary to the roles involved in family life. Women are not expected to engage in heavy manual work in the United States, although this appears to be commonplace in the Soviet Union and in some other nations. Women seldom enter the professions or administration, and among those who do, only a few reach the highest positions.

Although there is general agreement that the current generation of American adults tends to regard work as central, especially for men, there are many differences in the meaning of work among different occupations, different communities, and different ethnic groups. There may also be differences between rural and urban residents and between those who live in different regions of the United States. Nevertheless, we may say that the work imperative is very strong among the current generation of adults, especially those in agriculture and in middle-level occupations. Work is regarded as the only honorable way of earning a livelihood. It is required of all men who do not have sufficient means to live comfortably without it; even among the wealthy, laziness and loafing are conspicuous by their absence. As might be expected, these attitudes have been internalized to a considerable extent by young people; they seek employment when they arrive at the proper age.

The pervasive influence of work-related values is such that every little boy is aware that he will "grow up" to have some occupation. Consequently, he starts thinking about it long before he can appraise his future capacity on any realistic basis. With the increasing participation of women in the labor force, girls also play at occupational roles.

Child labor has largely disappeared from the American scene. Even farmers depend little upon their children as a source of labor. This does not mean that a child's time is devoted chiefly to play. On the contrary, from the time a child enters school until his formal education is finished, he is expected to work at his studies. Study, therefore, has many of the same meanings as work for pay. Some students, of course, like their studies better than others do, but the role of student is a key role for the great majority of children. It provides many of the same types of satisfactions and problems as occupational roles provide for adults. Indeed, the role of student can be regarded in many instances as direct preparation for occupational roles.

Bernice Goldstein and Robert L. Eichhorn investigated the extent to which the Protestant ethic continues to be an important guiding principle in the lives of Indiana farmers. The sample consisted of 260 farmers from a total sample of 413 involved in the Purdue Farm Cardiac project, about 40 per cent of whom had heart disease.[8]

8. Berniece Goldstein and Robert Eichhorn, "The Changing Protestant Ethic: Rural Patterns in Health, Work, and Leisure," *American Sociological Review* (August 1961), pp. 557–65.

The following questions or statements were used by the authors to ascertain adherence to the Protestant ethic. In their words, "One of the most crucial elements of the Protestant ethic was chosen as the criterion for division—the importance attached to hard work. We thought that a farmer who agreed with the following four statements placed greater emphasis on the importance of work in his life than a man who disagreed with all four: 1. Even if I were financially able, I wouldn't stop working; 2. I've had to work hard for everything that I have gotten in life; 3. The worst part about being sick is that work doesn't get done; 4. Hard work still counts for more in successful farm operations than all of the new ideas you read in the newspapers." [9]

On the basis of responses to these questions, 71 who agreed with all four statements were termed high work-oriented, 133 who agreed with any three were called middle work-oriented, and 56 who disagreed with any three or all four of the statements were called low work-oriented. This who were characterized as high work-oriented placed strong emphasis on being self reliant. They were more likely to make their own decisions about purchases of cars and farm machinery. They were less likely to follow the advice of their physicians even though more of them had heart disease, and they were more likely to be reluctant to incur debt, which is interpreted as a nonrational procedure for commercial farmers. In addition, they were less likely to follow highly rational procedures with respect to adopting new technology for raising corn. The authors suggest that compliance with the Protestant ethic may not lead to success in commercial agriculture. [10]

John B. Miner, in a study of 44 executives and 41 university professors, tested a hypothesis advanced by William H. Whyte, Jr., that the organization-man point of view, the so-called social ethic, has tended to replace the Protestant ethic of individual independence and nonconformity. Using an adaptation of a projective test (the Tomkins-Horn Picture Arrangement Test), Miner concluded that Whyte is correct in

9. Ibid., p. 558.
10. Ibid.

assuming that the Protestant ethic is strongly adhered to among the executives of large corporations, but he finds him wrong in a companion hypothesis that university professors are more likely to be conformists or organization men. In attempting to explain lack of conformity with the social ethic among distinguished university professors and corporation executives, Miner suggests that lack of conformity may be related to age. In his words,

> "It would seem highly probable that somewhere around the age of 40, perhaps later—perhaps earlier in individual cases—the rewards to be gained by inhibiting one's individuality begin to pale There appears to be less and less to be gained by conforming, as a man's ambitions are satisfied or as he sees that they never will be satisfied. Nonconformity would seem to be an inevitable concomitant of the realization that conformity can no longer bring forth any additional rewards that the group or organization may have to offer—that one's place in life is pretty well set." [11]

Nancy C. Morse and R. S. Weiss, on the basis of information from a nationwide study of employed men, concluded:

> "For most men having a job serves other functions than the one of earning a living. In fact, even if they had enough money to support themselves, they would still want to work. Working gives them a feeling of being tied into the larger society, of having something to do, of having a purpose in life. These other functions which working serves are evidently not seen as available in nonwork activities." [12]

Everett C. Hughes has observed, "A man's work is as good

11. John B. Miner, "Conformity Among University Professors and Business Executives," *Administrative Science Quarterly* (June 1962), pp. 96–109.
12. Nancy C. Morse and R. S. Weiss, "The Function and Meaning of Work and the Job," *American Sociological Review* (April 1955), pp. 191–98.

a clue as any to the course of his life, and to his social being and identity."[13] At another point Hughes says:

"A man's work is one of the most important parts of his social identity, of his self; indeed, of his fate in the one life he has to live, for there is something almost as irrevocable about choice of occupation as there is about choice of a mate and since the language about work is so loaded with value and prestige judgments and with defensive choice of symbols, we should not be astonished that the concepts of social scientists who study work should carry a similar load." [14]

Not every writer has extolled the virtues of work. For example, C. Wright Mills wrote:

"For most employees, work has a generally unpleasant quality. . . . For the white collar masses, as for wage earners generally, work seems to serve neither God nor whatever they may experience as divine in themselves.

"There is no taut will-to-work, and few positive gratifications from their daily round." [15]

Mills asserted that the idea of craftsmanship has largely disappeared, having been relegated to leisure and to intellectuals rather than to work activities. Consequently, he felt that no real psychological satisfactions could be derived from work and that the economic rewards for working "are now its only firm rationale."[16]

Melvin M. Tumin has advanced the opinion that "the emphasis has shifted from the importance of work and striving

13. Everett C. Hughes, *Men and Their Work* (Glencoe, Ill.: Free Press, 1958), p. 7.
14. Ibid., p. 43.
15. C. Wright Mills, *White Collar* (New York: Oxford University Press, 1956), p. 219.
16. Ibid., p. 230.

to the urgency of appearing to be successful . . . as measured by the power and property which one openly consumes." [17]

David Riesman and Warner Bloomberg, Jr., have suggested that work is viewed by an increasing number of workers as less important than leisure:

"The leisure which was once a fringe benefit now threatens to push work itself closer to fringes of consciousness and significance. In many facets of our national life, the anti-Puritan revolution seems to be almost accomplished. . . . We must ask, for instance, whether it is conceivable that, in a culture built on the industrial system, we can and should regard our still obligated work energies as mere payment for our consumer hedonism. . . . The younger workers, high-school trained, become quickly impatient with their slow progress within the plant hierarchy—but this hierarchy is no longer the one they see in front of them. In nonwork activities, they already have more experience and *expertise* than many 'senior' men; and in these, 'around end' as it were, they look for roads to a more personal as well as more portable kind of status. A mill hand today may feel he has it made if, for example, he can afford winter as well as summer vacations. His leisure specialities may bring him income or prestige or both." [18]

The meaning of work cannot fully be appreciated without an understanding of the basic functions of work in modern industrial society:[19]

1. *Work is a source of subsistence.* In a market economy where money is needed to buy food, clothing, and other goods and services, successful participation in the economy requires

17. Melvin M. Tumin, "Some Unapplauded Consequences of Social Mobility in a Mass Society," *Social Forces* (October 1957), p. 34.

18. "Work and Leisure: Fusion or Polarity," in C. N. Arensberg et al., eds., *Research in Industrial and Human Relations* (New York: Harper and Bros., 1957), p. 83.

19. Cf. E. A. Friedmann and R. J. Havighurst, "Work and Retirement," *The Meaning of Work and Retirement* (Chicago: University of Chicago Press, 1954).

a source of money in order to provide purchasing power. For the great majority of the members of the labor force, money is obtained primarily in the form of wages or salaries. Some people also receive income that does not represent direct payment for work. Interest and dividends from investments, rents and royalties, capital gains from sale of stocks or real estate, insurance, pensions, and public welfare grants would fall into this category.

2. *Work regulates activities.* The rhythm of work, including the sequence of activities during the day, the week, the month, and the seasons, affects not only the activities of a worker while employed on the job but also his participation in nonwork activities. To a considerable extent, the patterns of activity of other members of his family are also affected; for example, the family life of a worker on the night shift is obviously affected in a different way from that of a worker on a normal (eight-to-five) day shift. Also, the occupational roles of a professional man have a different impact on his daily round of activities in the nonwork sphere than the roles of an unskilled laborer do on his nonwork activities.

3. *Work provides patterns of association.* Because of the dominant position of work in our society, the personal relationships between a worker and others who occupy related positions in a firm, agency, or organization may take on exceptional importance. In many cases, the favorable sentiments that people develop for each other in the employment system result in a continuation of the interaction into the nonwork sphere. Thus, one's friends and social companions off the job are frequently his associates at work.

4. *Work provides identity.* Work provides one of the principal answers to the insistent question, "Who am I?" Many people respond, "I am a doctor," "I am a farmer," and so forth. Some occupations lead to the development of a higher level of identification than others. Thus, the occupational role of a medical doctor is one in which the participant is almost universally regarded as having great prestige. Even though the personal esteem accorded individuals within the profession

differs, any doctor would be regarded as having higher prestige than any janitor, clerk or manual laborer. Professionals, craftsmen, and persons in some other occupations tend to internalize to a very high degree the values and standards of their occupations, so that they may come to think of themselves first of all as members of a particular occupation. This is part of what we mean when we say that the occupational role has come to be the key role for most men in modern American society.

5. *Work provides meaningful life experience.* Closely related to the function of work in providing identity is its function in providing content and meaning to life. The conscientious executive takes his work home with him. He does not leave his occupational problems at the office. Farmers, of course, work and think about their occupational problems constantly. But even one who does leave his work at the office or in the shop and does not involve himself to the fullest extent in his work finds that his job does give him a point of reference that helps him to interpret other aspects of experience and to integrate his personality.

6. *Work determines social status.* In contemporary industrialized societies, the social standing of most adult males (and that of their families) is largely determined by the prestige of their occupation and the reputations that they establish at work.

Changing Attitudes toward Work

Discussions of general societal values, such as the Protestant work ethic, frequently fail to give adequate attention to the fact that values presumably shared by an entire population are actually shared only by a minority. For example, studies showing widespread alienation from work by workers engaged in routine, repetitive, and/or challenging tasks have been interpreted to mean that all contemporary workers are less interested in their work than their ancestors.[20] In my opinion, sweeping inferences of this kind are based on unwarranted assumptions about the proportions of earlier workers who actually accepted the Protestant work ethic as a prescription for their own behavior. Because there were few social scientists until quite recently, our information about the values of earlier workers is largely based upon impressionistic accounts by creative writers plus interpretations of personal documents and other historical material. Furthermore, most of the people who make history, even in our times, are leaders rather than "common" men. Therefore, we may discount the representativeness of much of the earlier material about work related values. We simply do not have evidence, as many writers seem to assume, that the great majority of earlier workers toiled long hours at hard disagreeable tasks because they were compelled by the Puritan work ethic to do so. There is, of course, reason to believe that men and women who attained positions of leadership in work organizations and/or eminence as occupational specialists in the past put in long hours at their work just as comparable leaders do today.

Even now, we do not have comprehensive empirical data concerning the meaning of work to contemporary workers of all types, but nevertheless some important inferences can be drawn from available research.

The intrinsic meaning of work changed for production workers with the beginning of the industrial Revolution as cottage industries were superseded by factories. With the automation of the assembly line, the remaining factory workers became dial watchers, set-up men, and technicians, and this obviously changed the meaning of their work. Even farming has changed. "The man with the hoe," symbol of the peasant, has disappeared except when needed for seasonal work in harvesting fruits and vegetables, occupations that still provide work for a million migratory laborers in the United

20. Cf. Max Lerner, *America As A Civilization* (New York: Simon & Schuster, 1957), p. 240; Daniel Bell, "Work and Its Discontents," in *The End of Ideology* (New York: Free Press, 1960), p. 262.

States. Most workers on commercial farms are business managers, machine operators, and skilled technicians, and their work is backstopped by professional men (chemists, engineers, agronomists, and others) who work for universities, government agencies, or the great corporations that manufacture fertilizers, farm machinery, or process farm products.

Some writers have deplored the growth of specialization and the substitution of machines for individual craftsmanship. They ask, "What has happened to the 'dignity of work,' the satisfactions that come from completion of the whole task?" This nostalgic view overlooks the sheer drudgery of hand work and the long hours, poor working conditions, and low pay that characterized work in earlier times. Furthermore, it is doubtful if the majority of workers at any time were ever craftsmen.

Craftsmanship survives in other forms. Millions of Americans purchase power tools annually and perform creative work on their own. The rapid growth of the new professional and technical operations provides opportunities for satisfactions similar to those of the craftsman. Also, there are skilled crafts that still exist, especially in the building trades.

Although some changes in the values governing attitudes toward work and leisure are indicated, these changes have not yet had very substantial consequences. More than thirty years ago, Adriano Tilgher wrote that he perceived evidence of a lessening devotion to work,[21] yet business executives, farmers, professional people, and other upwardly mobile persons still work very hard.

There is convincing evidence that the work week for employed workers in many occupations has declined from what was customary a generation ago. Instead of the sixty to seventy hours of work each week that were common one hundred years ago, the typical wage earner works forty hours a week or less for pay, performing fairly light work such as tending a machine, sitting at a desk in an office, clerking in a store, or

21. Ibid.

providing personal or professional services to clients.[22] Thus, in many occupations there has been an increase in the time available daily for nonwork activities. Annual vacations are also more prevalent.

A similar transformation has released American homemakers from much of the drudgery of housekeeping. Instead of long hours spent over a hot wood-burning stove, the modern homemaker is able to do her cooking and baking in a relatively short time on an electric or gas range. She buys most of her bread and uses cake mixes and other semiprocessed foods. If she does her laundry at all, she probably has an automatic washer and dryer. Undeniably, the results of science and technology have materially lightened the housekeeping burden of the modern American homemaker.

In comparison with the past, adolescents appear to have even more leisure than adults. Few do much work for pay, and going to school is an occupation that includes a long summer vacation, several holidays, and numerous extracurricular sports and activities.

There is convincing evidence that substantial differences in psychological orientations toward work exist among different types of workers. Robert Dubin's study of the orientation of industrial workers toward work led him to the conclusion that work is not ordinarily a central life interest for such workers. However, he challenges the idea that this is necessarily a desirable goal. In his opinion, maintaining a level of performance that keeps one from losing his job constitutes adequate performance for industrial workers.[23]

A replication of Dubin's study among nurses by Louis H. Orzack supports the widely held view that work is a central

22. Donald J. Bogue, *The Population of the United States* (Glencoe, Ill.: Free Press, 1959), pp. 449–58.

23. Robert Dubin, "Industrial Workers' Worlds: A Study of the 'Central Life Interests' of Industrial Workers," *Social Problems*, vol. 3, no. 3 (January 1956), pp. 131–42; reprinted in E. O. Smigel, ed., *Work and Leisure* (New Haven, Conn.: College and University Press, 1963), pp. 53–72.

interest among professionals. Orzack properly concludes that Dubin's findings cannot be applied uncritically to all types of occupations.[24]

To an American pioneer or a present-day Pakistani, it might seem that we are living in the promised land, and perhaps we are. However, the picture of the modern American as a leisured person living in idyllic surroundings requires some correction. Sebastian de Grazia, in a study sponsored by the Twentieth Century Fund, has taken a closer look at leisure time. He points out that part of the supposed released time of the male wage earner is utilized in commuting, some of it in "do-it-yourself" activities done to save money, some in doing housework, and some in second jobs (popularly called "moonlighting"). He whittles away the alleged gain in time for the average wage earners (since 1850) to 8.5 hours per week instead of the 25 to 30 hours suggested by the difference in time devoted to paid work. He concludes that "the great and touted gains in free time since the 1850s . . . are largely myth." [25] Many of us are deceived, he says, by the idea that others have a lot of free time, even though we know that we never seem to have any. It is a curious paradox that, with lessened hours of work, Americans nevertheless live at a frenetic pace, their lives geared to the clock, almost always hurried, almost never leisurely even in their pursuit of fun and other "leisure-time" activities. Idleness is not considered an honorable way to use nonwork time.

What are the prospects that leisure pursuits may replace occupation as a source of identity and prestige and other meanings? It is possible that a future style of life, including achievements in leisure activities, may provide some challenge to occupation as the principal determinant of individual esteem and social rank for men. At present, however, nonwork

24. Louis H. Orzack, "Work as a 'Central Life Interest' of Professionals," *Social Problems*, vol. 7, no. 2 (Fall 1959), pp. 125–132; reprinted in E. O. Smigel, ed., *Work and Leisure* (New Haven, Conn.: College and University Press, 1963), pp. 73–84.

25. Sebastian de Grazia, *Of Time, Work, and Leisure* (New York: Twentieth Century Fund, 1962).

activities constitute a supplement rather than a challenge. Conspicuous display of expensive recreational equipment and facilities may be motivated by status anxiety, but such possessions are interpreted as symbols of occupational success. It is highly unlikely that the work imperative will disappear as a central value in the relatively near future even though automation may greatly change many occupations. But it is evident from a review of the existing situation that young people need to prepare not only for work, but also for constructive use of leisure time during their working years.[26] Furthermore, although the working life of Americans has increased greatly (by more than 50 per cent since 1900), most people will spend a number of years in retirement after completion of active participation in the labour force. While this is not a matter of great concern to youth, it is mentioned here to provide perspective.

During the last few years a small proportion of adolescents and young adults, most of them apparently from affluent families, have renounced regular work as a means of supporting themselves. These persons, known as "hippies," have overtly rejected the Protestant work ethic and the idea that regular work is a central and essential part of life. Many of them have become drug addicts. They subsist on welfare, food stamps, and, in some cases, theft; occasionally some of them work at various occupations on a temporary basis to obtain money for specific objectives.

Less extreme, but still a marked departure from traditional attitudes toward work, is the tendency for many college and high school students to do their "own thing," to challenge the formal rules and requirements of the school systems and the "establishment." It seems likely that this questioning attitude and the accompanying search for opportunities for individual expression, which is encouraged by peer groups and tolerated, if not encouraged, by parents and educators, will lead eventually to efforts to restructure the world of work as it has the

26. Donald N. Michael, *The Next Generation* (New York: Alfred A. Knopf and Random House, Vintage Books, 1965), chapter XI, "Leisure."

schools and colleges. As a matter of fact, some of the leaders of the "New Left" are very explicit about this goal. Charles Reich in *The Greening of America* advocates changing the meaning of work and the character of work organizations through what he calls the "noncareer," which is characterized by emphasis on personal interests and rejection of organizational goals and rules, especially the Puritan work ethic. He suggests that work organizations have very little control over workers who are not motivated by the organization's reward system but instead are preoccupied with their own concerns.[27]

How much change will be accomplished by infiltration of work organizations by young radicals remains to be seen. Sociologist Peter Berger of Rutgers University has minimized the threat. He feels that the technical and professional positions that would normally have been filled by these dissident youths from affluent families, if they had obtained the requisite education, will be filled by the upwardly mobile offspring of less prosperous families who still believe in the Puritan work ethic. In his opinion, the threat to societal survival due to possible withdrawal from the world of work of substantial numbers of upper-middle class young people is minimal.[28]

This appears to be a realistic appraisal of the probable outcome. However, it rests on the premise that higher rewards will continue to be allocated to high-status occupations. It should be noted also that this premise is under attack from the "New Left." [29]

The view that all able bodied adults should earn their living by working, was expressed most bluntly by Captain John Smith's dictum in Virginia in 1607: "He who does not work shall not eat." The first major assault on this harsh doctrine came from the Elizabethan Poor Laws. The second attack came during the depression of the 1930s when nearly a quarter of the labor force was unemployed. Acceptance of societal responsibility for providing subsistence and shelter for the

27. Charles Reich, *The Greening of America* (New York: Random House, 1970), p. 369.
28. *U.S. News and World Report* (4 December, 1972), p. 57.
29. Reich, *The Greening of America*, p. 108.

unemployed and for needy persons who are unable to work has led to the establishment of a wide variety of public welfare programs.

In 1964 the Ad Hoc Committee on the Triple Revolution advanced a proposal that all members of the society should be provided with a full share of the products of industry and agriculture without having to work for it. The committee argued that production can now be accomplished by machines and it is no longer possible to judge that the contributions of some workers are worth more than those of others.[30]

Although this proposal was greeted with hostility, it may be regarded as having provided at least part of the stimulus for the so-called negative income tax, proposed by conservative economist Milton Friedman of the University of Chicago, and the proposal advanced by President Richard M. Nixon's administration for a guaranteed minimum annual income. The annual income levels proposed by these schemes are low enough so that the accompanying deprivation would still provide incentives to work. However, several members of the United States Congress have proposed much higher income levels. In fact, recent legislation raising Social Security payments and other benefits makes it highly probable that once enacted the income guarantee would rise. If the amount that is available under such a program should be sufficient to provide food, shelter, clothing, and all other necessities, it may be anticipated, in my opinion, that a substantial number of persons who are now employed would stop working and devote their energies to other activities that they prefer.

Another emerging trend appears to be an increase in the level of interest of women in occupational careers. There have always been some career oriented women in the twentieth century, but the vast majority have been concerned mainly with home and family. When they have entered the labor force, they have done so primarily to earn supplemental incomes rather than to become the main providers. Thus, the

30. Ad Hoc Committee, "The Triple Revolution," *Liberation* (April 1964), pp. 1–7.

Protestant work ethic has had little grip on most women. With the emergence of the Women's Rights Movement stimulated by Betty Friedan's book, *The Feminine Mystique*, in 1963, a vigorous attack on discrimination against females in employment surfaced.

The Civil Rights Act of 1964 provides a legal basis for sex equality in employment conditions, but it will take a long time to change traditional practices. In fact, it is doubtful that the majority of adult women are ready and willing at present to make the occupational role their key role. What women in future generations may do cannot be predicted accurately, but it seems virtually certain that a much higher proportion of them than in the past will opt for careers that will bring them into direct competition with men.

Selected References

de Grazia, Sebastian. *Of Time, Work and Leisure*. New York: The Twentieth Century Fund, 1962. A scholarly review of the impact of technology on work and leisure.

Michael, Donald N. *The Next Generation*. New York: Random House, 1963. This provocative book considers many of the probable social, economic, and psychological effects of automation. The chapters on work and leisure are especially relevant to the ideas introduced in this chapter.

Tilgher, Adriano. "Work Through the Ages," in S. Nosow and W. H. Form, eds., *Man, Work and Society*. New York: Basic Books, 1962. This article presents an historical review of the development of work-related values in Western societies.

3. Scientific and Technological Developments and Occupational Change

Many scientific and technological developments have far-reaching consequences for certain occupations. For example, the blacksmith has been displaced by the welder, and the railroad fireman has been made obsolete by the diesel locomotive. It is no secret that such changes take place and that the duties involved in specific occupational roles may change from time to time.

The objective of this chapter is not to discuss the details of past and present occupational changes that have followed scientific and technological developments, but rather to attempt to provide a basis for a better understanding of the probable implications of emerging developments (including automation) for the occupational requirements of work organizations and for occupational careers.

The culture of science and technology is dominant in contemporary America. Although there are still some criticisms of this culture, these for the most part come from people who would like to change the results of specific technologies. There is really very little opposition to science or technology *per se* in spite of the apprehensions voiced by some scientists when Federal Research and Development appropriations are cut. It is not unrealistic to compare the prestige of scientists and engineers to that of bishops and priests during the long reign of the Church of Rome in the Middle Ages. This status is quite recent and neither individuals, groups, nor society at large have yet learned to cope with many of the consequences of rapid technological change.

Both science and technology include more than tangible

objects. In the case of scientific culture what Thomas S. Kuhn calls the paradigm,[1] a theoretical model, is sociologically most significant. In technological culture the processes and procedures for using machines are fully as important as the machines themselves.

As a basis for evaluating the occupational implications of more recent developments, we will first discuss the burgeoning growth of scientific endeavor—the knowledge explosion. Then we will review briefly the impact of mechanization, electronics, and chemistry upon occupations and look at parallel developments in agricultural technology. Finally, we will consider the implications of automation.

The Expansion of Science

Science is a social activity directed toward understanding nature, man, and society.[2] So conceived, it has a long history. Scientific activities existed in ancient Greece and even earlier. We do not need to trace the historical growth of scientific activity in detail here, but we should note that the foundations of modern science were established in Europe and North America primarily during the last three centuries.

An outstanding feature of the twentieth century, with both direct and indirect occupational consequences, has been a phenomenal increase in scientific activity, which has been accompanied by a corresponding increase in the number and kinds of scientists. The number of scientists listed in *American Men of Science* increased from 4,000 in 1903 to 90,000 in 1955.[3] The 1970 census listed 203,000 natural scientists and 101,000 social scientists. *The great majority of all the scientists*

1. Thomas S. Kuhn, *The Structure of Scientific Revolutions* (Chicago: University of Chicago Press, 1962).

2. For a discussion of the social implications of science, *see* Bernard Barber, *Science and the Social Order* (New York: Collier Books, rev. ed., 1962).

3. Ibid., p. 159.

who have ever lived are now alive. This indicates the rapidity and recency of the expansion of scientific endeavors. We will note some of the characteristics of careers in scientific occupations later.

Scientific work involves systematic efforts to discover principles or laws which explain physical, biological, and social phenomena. Physical scientists stress experiments to verify knowledge in their own fields and within their own scientific traditions. Technology, on the other hand, involves the application of scientific knowledge to create new products or processes. It should be pointed out, however, that the relationships between science and technology are seldom as neat as the foregoing statement might suggest. It is true that the development of new technology by engineers and others utilizes scientific knowledge, but trial and error is also involved in both invention and innovation. A successful major invention, such as the laser, may stimulate scientific research to discover *additional* principles or laws, hitherto unknown, which explain the success of the invention. This may lead to the formulation of new theory.

In the physical and biological sciences, professors who specialize in a particular subdivision of a discipline usually accept a common paradigm. This is a theoretical statement that accounts for what is known, yet is open in the sense that there are gaps which provide opportunities for research. Graduate students learn these paradigms and the culturally approved research methods and relevant scientific values and behavior norms. When they receive their Ph.D. degrees they generally continue their own research and teaching within the paradigm. It has become the core of their scientific subculture. From time to time accepted paradigms are shown by seminal thinkers like Gregor Johann Mendel, Sir Isaac Newton, John Dalton, or Albert Einstein to be inadequate, and eventually new paradigms are developed. Thomas S. Kuhn has aptly described these changes as scientific revolutions.[4] Nobel prizes may be awarded to such scientists but, as the history of

4. Kuhn, *Structure of Scientific Revolutions.*

science demonstrates, the adherents of established paradigms may resist change to the extent of ostracizing those like Joseph Lister, Robert Koch, and Mendel who propose radically new systems of thought.

Although scientific research and theory building is now heavily concentrated in universities, this was not always true. In eighteenth- and nineteenth-century England, most scientists were not university faculty members. Cambridge and Oxford, the two most prestigious English universities, did not establish science departments until the last half of the nineteenth century. They concentrated on classical learning. Engineering and business administration are not considered respectable academic subjects in England or in Europe, even today.

In the United States, self-taught Benjamin Franklin was one of the first scientists. American universities did not pay much attention to science until after the establishment of the Land Grant Colleges in 1862. A major impetus to scientific research came from the Federal Experiment Station Act of 1887, but progress was very slow at first. There were a few great American scientists prior to the twentieth century, but the major expansion in scientific activity and in numbers of American scientists has come in this century, especially in the last twenty-five years.

In the United States, virtually all scientists are now educated in the graduate departments of universities. There is a considerable amount of mobility of scientists between universities and industrial or government laboratories.

Scientific activities are divided into three main categories: physical, biological, and social. Each of these is further subdivided into smaller categories or academic disciplines and subdisciplines. Each discipline and subdiscipline (chemistry and biochemistry, for example) has distinctive traditions, values, and scientific folkways. These are maintained and/or modified by social systems including university departments, professional associations (for example, The American Chemical Society), and informal networks of relationships among scientists who share common interests.

The highly visible successes of physicists and engineers in

developing the atomic bomb and radar, and of chemists and chemical engineers in developing synthetic fibers, petrochemicals, antibiotics, and other immensely important products undoubtedly led to the tremendous post-World War II increase in the support of scientific research and development activities by the federal government. Appropriations for scientific research and development grew from $74 million in 1940 to $16 billion in 1972.

Not until the recent urban riots, the federal government's war on poverty, the civil rights movement, and massive federal aid to education, has there been much interest in social science research on the social consequences of scientific and technological innovations. Even now such work is poorly supported in comparison to the physical and biological sciences.

Early scientists, like early inventors, tended to work alone. This was apparently true of Newton, Charles Darwin, and Einstein and most of the other great men of science. It is, of course, still true to a marked degree of seminal thinkers, the leaders of scientific thought. But a large proportion of scientific research is now conducted in group situations. The largest industrial research and development organization is the Bell Laboratory in New Jersey which has 14,500 scientists, engineers, and other staff members. But there are many other research and development organizations of very substantial size, including Brookhaven, Oak Ridge, and Argonne.

A noted European nuclear engineer has explained that team research appeared in nuclear research and development because of the appearance of large machines which required the assistance of engineers and because the increased complexity of the research required collaboration among physicists, chemists and mathematicians.[5]

The trend toward collaboration among physical scientists is confirmed in a study made by Harriet Zuckerman and reported by Robert K. Merton which showed that during the decade of the 1950s papers published by a single physicist

5. L. Kowarski, "Team Work and Individual Work in Research," in Norman Kaplan, ed., *Science and Society* (Chicago: Rand McNally, 1965), p. 249.

declined to 30 per cent; the study showed the same pattern appeared later in biology.[6] In many cases, papers written by more than a single author report work by *a senior scientist and his students*.

In the social sciences, Zuckerman's study showed a trend toward collaboration in psychology and sociology during the period but not in anthropology, economics, or political science.[7]

Collaboration, however, is nearly always with others in the same discipline. Consequently, it may be assumed that collaborators usually share a common conceptual view. This presents a challenge to the organization of scientific endeavors because it seems clear that the solution of practical problems through research-based innovations increasingly requires the collaboration of engineers with scientists from two or more academic disciplines. In addition, increasing reliance on computers requires either that scientists master and keep abreast of the rapidly changing field of computer programming or that computer programmers become members of scientific research teams.

Except for agricultural scientists, relatively few university based scientists have had much interest in the application of scientific knowledge to practical problems; they have instead preferred to pursue "pure" science. This stricture does not apply with the same force to scientists employed by industry, government, or nonprofit research and development laboratories, although there is some pressure for freedom of choice by individual scientists. It seems to be true, however, that most applied scientists have concentrated their energies on relatively small, specialized problems. Thus, the consequences of scientific and technological developments for the environment and for society have been overlooked by all but a few. This is partially due to career imperatives. A young scientist

6. Robert K. Merton, "Science as a Changing Institution," in Norman Kaplan, ed., *Science and Society* (Chicago: Rand McNally, 1965), p. 129.

7. Ibid.

can achieve professional recognition only from his professional peers, chiefly through publication in scientific journals. It is at least partially due, however, to the cultural norm of science which emphasizes empirical research. This emphasis on minutia in the established sciences casts doubt upon the validity of L. V. Berkner's dictum that one Ph.D. in the sciences creates, on the average, innovations which provide employment for 100 lesser professionals and technicians.[8] There is, of course, no doubt that really seminal discoveries have much greater impact on employment than this, but even in such cases the relationship is indirect. Engineers and other inventors mediate between basic research conducted by scientists and usable inventions which create new occupational roles and additional employment.

M. P. O'Brien, a former engineering dean at the University of California at Berkeley, holds that the director of a project set up to develop a specific technological innovation must be oriented toward creation of a tangible product rather than the discovery of new knowledge. That is, he should have the perspective of an engineer rather than the perspective of a scientist.[9] Where a development unit includes mathematicians, scientists, engineers, and others, it may be difficult to induce the members to work together as a team.[10] In fact, scientists frequently leave such agencies as the National Aeronautics and Space Administration (NASA) and return to universities so as to be able to pursue basic scientific interests.

It would be wrong to minimize the problems of interdisciplinary cooperation in developing new products or processes that are not radically different from existing products or processes. Nevertheless, the problems involved in developing a radical idea are vastly more difficult. O'Brien categorically

8. L. V. Berkner, *The Scientific Age: The Impact of Science on Society* (New Haven, Conn.: Yale University Press, 1964), p. 30.

9. M. P. O'Brien, "Technological Planning aand Mis-planning," in James R. Bright, *Research Development and Technological Innovation* (Homewood, Ill.: Richard D. Irwin, 1964), p. 664.

10. Ibid., p. 664.

states that "separate and autonomous" organizations are required for the development of such ideas.[11] Support for this
position is found in the fact that the telegraph companies did
not develop the telephone; nor did the telegraph companies,
or the telephone companies, develop radio or television. In
each case, new firms with different leaders developed the new
technology. Historically, in capitalist societies, entrepreneurs
who establish new corporations take the leadership in developing radically novel technology, even though established firms
frequently reap the major profits. The single major exception
to this is the atomic bomb. Today, the increasing cost of
developing a commercially successful innovation makes it
much more difficult than in the past for individual inventors
or small corporations to challenge established giant corporations. Furthermore, well-established organizations tend to be
very resistant to radical change.

One solution to the problem of developing radically new
products may be seen in the growth of firms which accept the
development of such innovations as a primary mission. An
example is the Minnesota Mining and Manufacturing Company which started with sandpaper, then developed Scotch
tape, magnetic tape, and other products.[12] Firms which have
followed this route establish new units to develop and promote
the new technology. The leadership role, formerly performed
by the entrepreneur who established his own firm to manufacture a new product, is taken by an entrepreneurial type of
person, an employee of a corporation, designated by Donald
Schon as a "product champion." [13] This favored employee has
access to financial resources (controlled by central management) and is given wide latitude for initiative. In some cases,
the units are semi-independent corporations.[14]

Although research and development units in industrial
organizations contain scientists and other specialists, engi-

11. Ibid., p. 664.
12. Donald A. Schon, *Technology and Change* (New York: Dell Publishing Co., A Delta Book, 1967).
13. Ibid., p. 168.
14. Ibid., p. 123.

neers or persons with the perspective of engineers apparently tend to set the tone.

Scientific investigations are yielding so much new information that it is virtually impossible for a scientist to keep up with new knowledge except in his own specialty. The flood of scientific papers, monographs, and textbooks is so tremendous that the result is almost overwhelming, not only for the graduate student who is attempting to become a professional scientist, but also for the established professional. Consequently, efforts are being made to develop more efficient methods of making results of scientific investigations available without the necessity for a painstaking search of the library by each individual.

To cope with the "information explosion" it will almost certainly be necessary for work organizations that employ scientists and engineers to make provisions for systematic updating of their knowledge. Some large industrial firms and some government agencies with the assistance of the elite universities such as Massachusetts Institute of Technology have already initiated such programs. As we shall note in greater detail later, the armed forces are perhaps furthest advanced of all work organizations in providing occupational retraining for professionals.

The indirect occupational consequences of scientific activities are considerable. Most technological innovations are now based upon scientific discoveries and theories, and new processes and products are systematically sought. Modern science is supported by industry and government, not so much because of its intellectual contributions as because some of the results of scientific activity have led eventually to exceedingly useful and diverse technological applications such as plastics, synthetic fibers, antibiotics, atomic power plants, and new varieties of wheat.

The prospect for the future is continued expansion of scientific activities and many attractive occupational careers in scientific and engineering occupations, with continuous effort required to keep abreast of new developments.

The indirect consequences of the anticipated further growth

of science may be even more profound. As we shall see in our discussion of the implications of automation, some of the potential consequences of technological developments based on scientific discoveries may be quite disturbing.

Mechanization and the Factory[15]

What is known as the Industrial Revolution began in England about 200 years ago. It featured the use of machinery and the appearance of specialized occupations in factories. Prior to that time, clothing, furniture, armaments, and other goods were produced by skilled craftsmen or, as in the case of textiles, by families. Many types of medieval craftsmen were organized in associations known as guilds.

Prior to the Industrial Revolution, high quality consumer goods, such as furniture, were produced chiefly by skilled craftsmen (masters) who operated their own small shops assisted by journeymen, apprentices, and unskilled laborers. In the English cotton cloth industry, prior to 1765, most of the production was accomplished at home by weavers assisted by members of their own families. Most of the weavers were also part-time farmers. Operations such as carding, spinning, and weaving were performed on rather primitive machines powered by human labor. The authority system was that of the family. Hours were long but the family had its recreation while the work proceeded, and the tempo was not set by machines.

There were, however, some groups of weavers who worked together in sheds where the work was supervised by master weavers. A complicated system existed for distribution of orders, supplies, and products.

During the period of 1760–1790, a number of important technological innovations appeared, including the spinning jenny (1764), the water frame (1768), carding machinery (1772),

15. The principal source of the factual information presented in this subsection is Neil Smelser, *Social Change in the Industrial Revolution* (Chicago: University of Chicago Press, 1959).

the spinning mule (1779), and the use of steam as a source of power to operate the machinery (1785–1795).

Concentration of operations in central locations was virtually required because the steam engines were large and expensive, and because power was transmitted from the engines to the production machines by means of shafts, pulleys, and belts. The latter feature required production machines to be near the power source. However, the nature of the authority system and other important aspects of the organization of the factory system were probably attributable, as I have already said, more to the existing work culture and to situational factors than to the machines.

The earliest factories were organized by private entrepreneurs who were profit oriented and accumulated substantial fortunes. The weavers, however, did not benefit much, if any, economically. Venture capitalism was already common, and the pattern of driving sharp bargains for personal gain was an accepted procedure in business relationships.

The long hours already prevalent in the cottage industry were continued in the factories, as was the practice of using child labor for many tasks. The monotonous and arduous labor coupled with extensive use of child labor and transients created problems of worker discipline that frequently led to cruel disciplinary practices. Flogging of children was not uncommon. The factory system, which utilized a cluster of technological innovations, had a number of distinctive consequences for the organization of work. First, because the factory system increased output and reduced costs of production, it became impossible for the hand loom cottage weavers to compete, and this form of work organization eventually disappeared almost completely. Second, the tempo or pace of the work was set by the machines. Third, those who worked in the factories performed their new occupational roles in a work system that was far different from a family; the patterns of reward and discipline that developed were, however, undoubtedly influenced by contemporary authoritarian family practices and by similar patterns followed in other social systems such as the army. Fourth, the private entrepreneur or capitalist became a central figure.

It may be noted that worker dissatisfaction led to organized efforts by the Luddites in 1811–12, 1825–26, and 1829 to destroy the power looms. Later, organized efforts were made to persuade Parliament to regulate wages and working conditions. These activities may be regarded as the origins of the labor union movement in Great Britain.

Migration was another important effect. The centralization of work in factories started the trend of workers to centers of population; thus began the massive shift of population to urban industrial centers which only recently has caused deep concern among public leaders.

Although we do not have specific evidence to test the hypothesis, it seems reasonable to hypothesize, on the basis of recent studies of the diffusion of innovations, that the central features of the factory method of organizing production spread from the first textile factory to other textile factories and eventually to other types of factories. If this is a tenable proposition, we may find in the early textile factories the sources of many of the authority patterns that are still followed in industrial organizations.

The factory system, dominated by an owner-entrepreneur, was the paramount organizational form in nonfarm industry for a very long time, although partnerships and small corporations made their appearance before the twentieth century. Wholesale and retail trade, transportation, and other economic enterprises were also headed by owner-entrepreneurs. Employees were subservient to the proprietor. He could and frequently did fire employees who displeased him. He could and often did give preference to sons and other relatives. Today the balance has shifted. There are still many individual owner-entrepreneurs on the scene but American industry and business is dominated by great corporations. Only 7.7 per cent of nonfarm workers were self-employed in 1970.

Mass Production

Mass production may be regarded as the second phase of the Industrial Revolution. If there is a central theme to the changes that have occurred in the organization of work since the beginning of the twentieth century, it is rationality. Mass production, based upon the use of standardized interchangeable parts and the assembly line with its minute division of labor, time, and motion studies by Frederick Taylor and Frank Gilbreth, and, of course, the bureaucratic form of organization, are all manifestations of a highly rational approach to the organization of work.

Mass production is a technological innovation in the sense that it is a more efficient process of production than was used previously. Although the assembly line is a key element in the innovation, it would be impossible to use an assembly line without an adequate supply of standardized interchangeable parts. By the turn of the century, perhaps earlier, inventors had made so many improvements in machine tools, foundries, and other production machines that it was possible to manufacture many standard mechanical components. Even so, mass production did not automatically emerge. Henry Ford is usually given credit for the innovation even though it is alleged that he got the idea from observing the use of a moving overhead conveyor in butchering plants.[16] He was the first entrepreneur to make successful use of the assembly line (in 1910) on a highly visible and important product, the Model T Ford. This breakthrough reduced the price of automobiles drastically, in spite of the fact that Ford was able later to raise the wages of assembly line workers to $5 a day, an amount regarded as fantastic by his competitors and fabulous by farm and small town men who flocked to Detroit to share in the bonanza. But the workers' euphoria over the high wages did not last; it was followed by boredom and alienation.

Ford, and other entrepreneurs who followed him in adopting mass production methods, proceeded to "improve" the product and the process. They did this partly by quickly adopting new mechanical inventions, such as the storage battery, improved ignition, the electric self-starter, and a long and still continuing list of other inventions. From the standpoint of the organization

16. Cf. Ben B. Seligman, *Most Notorious Victory, Man in an Age of Automation* (New York: Free Press, 1960), p. 28.

of work, the time and motion studies pioneered by Frederick Taylor and his disciple, Frank Gilbreth, were even more important. Taylor conceptualized workers as human machines. Thinking was to be reserved to engineers and managers. He and his followers sought, with considerable success to eliminate "waste" motion so as to make production more efficient and henceforth less expensive. This led to minutely specialized, repetitive, and monotonous operations. One man might insert three bolts, another man start the nuts, and a third tighten them. As in other factory operations, the assembly line was machine paced; it kept moving and the workers had to keep up with it. From an occupational point of view, the early assembly line worker was a low-grade specialist. He found it difficult, if not impossible, to develop much pride in his product. Thus, quality had to be maintained by a system of inspections and subsequent correction of errors.[17]

It is essential that all positions on an assembly line be manned, which means that assembly line workers are required to be at work on time and that they come to work daily; substitute workers must be available when needed.

Many operations previously done by human labor are now automated and some factories now attempt to make the work more attractive by combining several operations and giving workers more responsibility.

Industrial labor unions, of which the United Auto Workers is the largest and most important, were set up to assist industrial blue collar workers to bargain with employers.

Industrial psychologists and sociologists have made numerous studies of assembly line workers. As the assembly line is being phased out by automation, a great deal of information has been accumulated on its effects on personality and social relationships of workers and their families. I will not attempt to summarize this voluminous literature. But, for present purposes, it may suffice to say that, in general, the studies show the existence of substantial alienation; few assembly line work-

---

17. For a discussion of work on the automobile assembly line, *see* Eli Chinoy, *Automobile Workers and The American Dream* (Garden City, N.Y.: Doubleday & Co., 1955), p. 36.

ers regard their jobs as more than a source of necessary income. There is little, if any, occupational identification. Instead, there is organizational identification—for example, "I work at Ford."

Most nonfarm goods are produced in factories, and factories tend to be located with reference to economic considerations. Markets, supply sources, taxes, and transportation are the major factors. Relatively little attention has been given to labor as a factor in plant location.

Factory owners and managers have usually welcomed cost-cutting innovations which reduced the need for human labor. With few exceptions, efficiency in reducing costs of manufacturning has always been regarded as more important than keeping specific individuals employed. Even today few blue collar factory workers have a guaranteed annual wage; they can be laid off when the plant is not working—although now the economic burden is cushioned somewhat by unemployment compensation.

Electronics

It is not feasible here to trace the history of electrical development in detail but it may be of interest to note briefly some of the important inventions that have resulted in organizational and/or occupational changes.

Interest was aroused in colonial times by Benjamin Franklin's famous experiment with a kite during a thunderstorm in 1752. Then, almost a hundred years elapsed before Joseph Henry, a professor at Princeton, invented the electric motor and helped Samuel Morse to invent the telegraph in 1844. The telephone was patented by Alexander Graham Bell in 1876. Thomas A. Edison patented the phonograph in 1877 (although the electrical recording did not occur until 1925).

Using a carbon filament, Edison invented the incandescent lamp in 1879. In 1910 William D. Coolidge of General Electric introduced tungsten as the filament, and in 1913 Irving Langmuir filled the light bulb with an inert gas. Edison and others developed power stations and transmission lines, which have been improved to the extent that it is now possible to generate power in remote areas (such as the great dams on major rivers) and transport it long distances for eventual use in industrialized urban centers.

Heinrich Hertz discovered radio waves in 1888. Guglielmo Marconi, an Italian, sent "wireless" signals for a distance of nine miles in 1896 and then across the Atlantic Ocean five years later. In 1907 the radio tube was invented by Lee De Forest, an American. Although photographs were transmitted by wire between London and Paris in 1907, the first television camera was not patented until 1938, and television was not developed commercially until 1947. Color television was developed during the mid-1950s.

The transistor was invented at the Bell Telephone Laboratory in 1948 by William Shockley, Walter H. Brattain, and John Bardeen. They were awarded a Nobel Prize for this achievement in 1956. Today, transistors are major components of computers, radios, television sets, and other electronic devices. The transistor was one of the keys to space travel. In the words of physicist Alfred Butler ". . . We'd have probably never got to the moon with our old fashioned electrical systems. By the time we'd gotten all the necessary equipment in a spaceship, it would have been far too heavy and awkward to have ever gotten off the ground." [18]

Although there are few electric-powered cars at present, electrical devices are essential components of modern automobiles. Ignition, lights, the electric "self-starter," and many other electrical devices are taken for granted nowadays. Interest in electric-powered automobiles has been renewed recently by the current campaign to reduce air pollution.

Use of electricity as a basic source of power has not resulted in any marked degree of decentralization of industry. Nevertheless, many different occupational roles have been created. As electrical technology has changed, the knowledge and skills involved in specific roles has been altered materially. This is

18. Alfred Butler, *Science in the News*, no. 1150, Washington State University Tape Network Service, Radio Station KWSU, 9 January, 1973. (By permission.)

true not only of electrical engineering but of electronics technicians. The ability to communicate instantly with co-workers by means of "walkie-talkies" and telephones has greatly altered many low-level work relationships in mining, construction, commercial fishing, taxicab operations, and, of course, war. These innovations have also influenced relationships among professionals, managers, and entrepreneurs.

Changes with even greater impact on work and society may be anticipated in the future. For example, a relatively new innovation called "phonovision" will permit people who communicate by telephone to see each other. This may greatly reduce the need for personal conferences between businessmen and thus make greater decentralization of industry feasible.

Industrial Chemistry

Another important unit in the development of modern technology consists of chemical innovations. In fact many of the most important new products during the past century have at least part of their roots in chemistry. In 1970, 32 per cent of all scientists registered with the National Science Foundation were chemists. The scope of chemistry's impact on industry can be gauged roughly by the fact that more than half of all American chemists are employed by industry. Chemistry has been called a bonding science because of its applicability in biology and its close relationship with many aspects of physics. Materials are *shaped* by mechanical processing whereas they are *transformed* by chemical processing.

Although many important chemical innovations had already been developed by Europeans, the American chemical industry was relatively unimportant until about 1920. In the 1920s, however, there was a great upsurge in chemical discovery in the United States and the real beginning of what is now the world's largest chemical industry.

Nylon and other synthetic fibers, many types of plastics, antibiotics and other pharmaceuticals, synthetic rubber, polyunsaturated fats, milk and meat substitutes made from soybeans, detergents, insecticides, pesticides, and chemical fertilizers are only a few of a very long list of innovations created by industrial chemists. Quite similar to industrial chemists are the biochemists who develop antibiotics and other pharmaceuticals.

Most industrial chemists work in industrial laboratories. In fact it would not be far from the mark to say that most research and development laboratories have been established mainly to create chemical innovations. The accomplishments of industrial chemists tend to be judged by economic criteria. Very few receive major recognition for their innovations. The bulk of the so-called fundamental or pure research is carried on in universities.

The Revolution in Transportation

The development of steam engines not only changed manufacturing, as we have already noted, but also transportation. The first successful steam-powered ship was the *Clermont* invented by an American, Robert Fulton, in 1807. By 1830 steam-powered ships were used in cross-Atlantic service. By 1870 sailing ships were superseded by steamships. The first practical steam locomotive was invented by an Englishman, George Stephenson, in 1814; by 1879 railroads spanned the United States from east to west.

The four stroke cycle internal combustion piston engine was invented by a German, Nikolaus Otto, in 1876; and the first four wheel "horseless carriage" was produced by another German, Gottlieb Daimler, in 1886. But it was not until Henry Ford applied the mass production techniques of interchangeable parts and the assembly line that automobiles became a common mode of transportation.

The popularity of the automobile eventually led to the construction of paved streets and highways, the latter culminating in the limited access, divided highway engineered for high speeds. These roads must be ranked with the greatest engineering triumphs of all times.

The almost universal use of the private automobile coupled with the jet airplane have caused the virtual disappearance of long-range passenger trains in the United States, although Japan and some other countries still depend heavily on high-speed passenger trains for intercity transportation. Rising costs of gasoline and automobiles together with problems of parking and pollution may cause a renewal of interest in both mass transit and transcontinental rail service.

For work, the consequences of the revolution in transportation have been extensive; great numbers of new occupations have been created. In addition, rapid transportation via freeway, and in some cities rapid transit, has made it possible for people with good incomes to work in the central city but live in the suburbs. As a result, many of the dwellings in the central cities are now occupied by unskilled migrants, especially Spanish-speaking people from Puerto Rico, Negroes, and poor whites from Appalachia and the southeast states. Few work opportunities for unskilled workers are available there, and large numbers depend (at least in part) on welfare or even petty crime because of the unavailability of low-cost transportation to locations where such workers are needed.

Changes in transportation have also brought about serious consequences for merchants and services in small trade centers. Instead of being restricted to the radius of the "team haul" as their grandfathers were for shopping, rural residents can and do travel great distances to shop, taking advantage of the good roads that have been built. This has been a major factor in the decline of the small shopping centers and many rural employment opportunities.

Medical Technology

The consequences of major advances in medical technology (such as vaccination, blood transfusions, antibiotics and other drugs, early diagnosis of disease, and relatively painless surgery) for the relief of illness and the reduction of mortality are frequently taken for granted. We will not review the historical development of medical technology in detail but it should be noted that, like other forms of modern technology, it is based upon science, much of it upon the germ theory of disease; and it has developed to its present complexity from very small beginnings. Greek and Roman physicians are said to have been servants. Until anesthetics were developed surgery was very painful (ether was first used in 1842 and chloroform in 1847).[19] Millions died from contagious diseases prior to the development of appropriate vaccines, the first of which was the smallpox vaccine invented by Edward Jenner in 1798; and millions of others were afflicted by bacterial infections, which were frequently fatal, prior to the commercial development of penicillin by Sir Alexander Fleming in 1928.

Like other types of technology, many of the dramatic technological advances in the health field were made by specific individuals: Joseph Lister (antiseptics), Marie Curie (radium), Jenner (vaccination), Fleming (penicillin), Wilhelm K. Röentgen (X-rays 1895), Christiaan Barnard, Michael DeBakey (heart transplants). But nowadays most medical research and development is a team effort, involving the cooperative efforts of specialists from various disciplines. Of special interest is the current federally financed "crash" program to find a cure for cancer, which stresses large-scale team effort.

Application of the results of technological development to individual patients also frequently involves a team, the members of which perform specialized roles. Although many physicians and surgeons receive their incomes from fees rather than as salaries, it would be a mistake to think of them as isolated solo performers. Individual practices consisting of a doctor and a few employees; clinics, featuring groups of specialists, nurses, technicians, and other employees; and hospitals, which provide beds, food, and health care, and which employ nurses, medical technicians, and supporting personnel, are the principal work organizations. Although physicians and surgeons are seldom paid by hospitals, their services are in-

19. Virginia S. Thatcher, *History of Anesthesia* (Philadelphia: J. B. Lippincott Co., 1953).

dispensible—they could not treat serious illnesses without access to hospitals.

The impact of the growth of medical technology upon the development of medical occupations is suggested by the following incomplete list of specialties:[20]

anesthesia,	pediatrics,
dermatology,	psychiatry,
internal medicine,	physical medicine,
neurology,	radiology,
obstetric and gynecology,	surgery (several specialties), and
ophthalmology,	urology.
pathology,	

Invention

Considered over the past 200 years, a relatively short span even in recorded history, changes in the occupational requirements of industrial organizations have been almost incredible. Technological developments created thousands of new occupations, while other occupations required by simpler technology became obsolete.

Specific individuals have been credited with the creation of most inventions prior to the beginning of the twentieth century. Since that time, corporations have become more active. In the United States, the percentage of patents awarded to corporations rose from 18 per cent in 1900 to 58 per cent in 1935, and it has remained above 50 per cent since that time.

There is a widespread belief that most early inventors were unlettered mechanical geniuses who worked alone in woodsheds or basements. This may have been true of some of them, but a recent study of inventors and inventions has revealed that even in the nineteenth century most of the men who produced important inventions were well informed concerning relevant scientific principles. Many, in fact, were friends of eminent scientists.[21] It does appear to be true, however, that

20. Cf. Douglas C. Lieberman, *Pre-Med: The Foundation of a Medical Career* (New York: McGraw-Hill Book Co., 1968).

21. John Jewkes, David Sawers, and Richard Stillerman, *The Sources of Invention* (New York: St. Martin's Press, 1958), pp. 27–71.

until recently most inventors were not employed by corporations for the purpose of creating new technology.[22]

Individual inventors have not disappeared, but in the current stage of the industrial development in the advanced nations, the application of rational processes to the problems of production has led to the creation of suborganizations (for example, research and development laboratories) designed to create desired innovations rapidly and efficiently. These suborganizations are found mainly in large corporations, especially those engaged in defense work, and are staffed by scientists, engineers, and technicians who frequently work in interdisciplinary groups and are thus able to bring to bear on the solution of a specific problem the contributions of diverse scientific disciplines as well as engineering principles and business insights.[23]

Essential to the accelerating rate of new technological innovations is the availability in published form of scientific discoveries made by scientists employed by universities and other work organizations.

From a sociological point of view, technological developments can be regarded as a form of culture change. The rate of culture change, insofar as material technology is concerned, has a positive correlation with the size of the base of existing culture traits and complexes. Thus, the bigger the base the higher the rate. It follows from this that continued acceleration of the rate of technological innovations may be anticipated.[24]

Not only has the rate of technological innovations been rising but the time span between the date of discovery or invention of a new machine or process is becoming shorter, both in industry and in agriculture. The National Commission on Technology, Automation, and Economic Progress reports evidence that every step in the process of technological change has accelerated since 1900. Between 1900 and 1965 total time

22. Ibid., pp. 91–126.
23. Ibid., pp. 127–96.
24. Hornell Hart, "Acceleration in Social Change," in Francis H. Allen, Hornell Hart, Delbert C. Miller, William F. Ogburn, and Mayer F. Nimkoff, *Technology and Social Change* (New York: Appleton-Century-Crofts, 1957), pp. 47–55.

from discovery to commercial application shrunk from thirty years to fourteen years for basic technical innovations, with another five years for full diffusion.[25]

The shortened time span between invention and widespread adoption of new technology is perhaps the most disturbing feature of current and prospective innovations. For a long time, these changes occurred rather gradually from the time perspective of an individual. Thus, until quite recently a young man could realistically expect to learn a lifetime occupation as an apprentice or as a student in a professional or graduate school.

The time interval between invention of a new machine or process and its adoption by the majority of the work organizations to which it was applicable was usually long enough for adjustments to be made without creating insurmountable personal or social crises. Occupational retraining due to technological change is a relatively recent concept.

The Agricultural Revolution[26]

Modern large-scale urbanization and nonfarm industrial development rest, in part, upon the availability of adequate food and clothing. Primitive agriculture, which produced little more than enough to feed and clothe the family of the agriculturist, was unable to support large urban populations.

The Agricultural Revolution, which has produced unprecedented surpluses and at the same time released all but a few million American workers from agriculture, bears the label "Made in the USA." It occurred partly because of the establishment of agricultural research and development organizations in the Land Grant universities that applied scientific principles to agricultural problems.

25. *Technology and the American Economy*, Report of the National Commission on Technology, Automation, and Economic Progress (Washington, D.C.: U.S. Government Printing Office, 1966), pp. 3–4.
26. Cf. Walter L. Slocum, *Agricultural Sociology* (New York: Harper and Bros., 1962), pp. 169–86.

The agricultural technology brought from Europe by the colonists was certainly not primitive, but it has been estimated that in 1820 one American farm worker produced enough food and fiber for himself and only three others. By 1971, productivity had more than quadrupled; one farm worker provided food and fiber for himself and 47 others.[27] In much of the world, however, agriculture is still relatively primitive and yields are low.

The rapid strides in applying scientific principles to agricultural production have transformed American agriculture, especially during the past 25 years. This is not the place to describe the development of modern agriculture in detail, but it should be pointed out that this has involved contributions from many scientific disciplines and from industry. The shift from horses to tractors was a major step, but it was followed by chemical fertilizers, insecticides, pesticides, and by new biological innovations including hybrid corn, new crop varieties, and the broad-breasted turkey and other mutations in domesticated birds and animals. At present, mechanical and biological innovations are sought simultaneously. Thus plant breeders have developed new varieties of tomatoes that are harvested by new machines; soon most of California's vast tomato crop will be harvested in this manner.

Many of these new techniques of research and development and some of the improved varieties of plants and breeds of livestock and poultry have been adopted in other countries. In southern and southeastern Asia, the development of new high-yield varieties of wheat, rice, and other crops through the increased use of chemical fertilizers and use of improved farming practices has been called the *Green Revolution*.[28] These developments have made it possible for food deficit areas to become food surplus areas—at least for a time.

One of the important consequences of the changes in agricultural practices has been to place a greater premium on

27. U.S. Department of Agriculture, *Agricultural Statistics*, 1972 (Washington, D.C.: U.S. Government Printing Office), p. 542.
28. U.S. Department of Agriculture, *Contours of Change*, The Yearbook of Agriculture 1970 (Washington, D.C.: USGPO), pp. 244–321.

managerial ability. The inefficient producer cannot compete successfully today. Modern market-oriented agriculture is a high-risk occupation that requires managerial ability as well as long hours and some luck. As noted elsewhere in this book, changes in agriculture have also created new forms of organization such as corporation farms and many new occupational specialties.[29]

The application of science and technology in agricultural production has greatly reduced the need for human labor. This is one of the two principal reasons for the decline in the farm population of the United States from 31,000,000 in 1910 to 10,030,000 in 1970. The second reason is the fact that until recently the expansion of nonfarm industry created a need for great numbers of additional workers, thus luring people from farms. While it is true that the total number of farm workers has declined drastically, many new occupational specialties have been created in production, processing, and marketing.

It appears that the impact of science and technology on the production and processing of food and fiber is far from complete. New discoveries, inventions, and commercial innovations are still being made. Synthetic fibers, such as nylon, polyesters, and acrylics, have captured much of the market formerly dominated by cotton and wool synthetic leather competes with natural leather, synthetic fats and oils have displaced great quantities of animal fats and vegetable oils in soaps and detergents; synthetics are displacing vegetable oils in paint; and synthetic and meat substitutes which look and taste like the real thing are being developed.[30]

These changes affect not only occupations but residential patterns and other aspects of life, and not all of these consequences have been entirely desirable.[31]

---

29. *See* chapters 4 and 7.
30. *Contours of Change*, pp. 66–70.
31. Ibid., pp. 2–31, 182–189; cf. *The Rural to Urban Population Shift, A National Problem*, 17-18 May, 1968, Committee on Government Operations, U.S. Senate, Committee Print, 90th Congress, 2nd Session; and Jim Hightower, "Hard Tomatoes Hard Times; Failure of the Land Grant College Complex," *Society* (Nov.-Dec. 1972), pp. 10–22.

Automation

Perhaps the most important technological development today is automation. You can scarcely pick up a magazine or
newspaper without reading something about it, and there have
been many books written on the subject. To industry it is
apparently very attractive. On the other hand, to organized
labor it appears very threatening, so threatening that a substantial portion of the 1962 AFL-CIO convention was devoted
to its consequences. After three congressional investigations
failed to produced legislation, Congress and President Lyndon
B. Johnson established, in 1964, the National Commission on
Technology, Automation, and Economic Progress, which subsequently made its recommendations in a report entitled
Technology and The American Economy.[32]

What is automation?

Walter Buckingham says that it is a concept of manufacturing that incorporates the principles of mechanization, continuous mass production, and automatic feedback and
control.[33]

Peter F. Drucker says that "it can be defined simply though
superficially as the use of machines to run machines." He goes
on to explain that historically machines have been used "primarily to do things to material," noting that until recently
production machines have been serviced by people who have
performed the following four operations: (1) brought raw
material to it and carried the finished product away; (2) made
routine judgments about the operation of the machine; (3)
changed the setting of the machine for new jobs; and (4) kept
and interpreted records of performance.[34] According to

32. *Technology and the American Economy,* pp. 3–4.
33. Walter Buckingham, "Gains and Costs of Technological Change,"
in Gerald G. Somers et al., eds., Adjusting to Technological Change
(New York: Harper & Row, Publishers, 1963), p. 4.
34. "Cybernation: The Silent Conquest," in Morris Phillipson, ed.,
Automation, Implications for the Future (New York: Vintage Books,
1962), p. 78.

Drucker, under automation, all these tasks are done by machines at lower cost and more rapidly than they can be done by men.

In Donald Michael's view, there are two different kinds of automated devices. The first consists of devices that perform specific tasks automatically, that replace or improve on the capacities of human beings for performing these functions. These devices include various automatic machines—such as vending machines, self-service laundries, and accounting machines—that perform part but not all of a complex process and may be found in factories, in offices, and even in homes. The second kind of automated devices is linked to the use of computers, electronic devices that perform very rapidly "routine or complex logical and decision-making tasks, replacing or improving on human capacities for performing these functions." [35] Computers can be programmed to operate other machines. Thus, when a computer is used to direct and control production machines, we may have a fully automated factory.

Edward B. Shils emphasizes that the contribution of automation to efficient and rapid production by controls involves the instantaneous feedback of information to the computer which then uses it to make necessary corrections resulting in products of more uniform quality and lower cost than would be possible otherwise.[36]

John Diebold, often called the "father of automation," believes that computers will be able, in the future, to learn how to solve increasingly complicated problems. In fact, he indicates that computers have already been created that are able to learn from experience and modify their approaches to problems. Such machines can deal with information processing and solve certain types of problems faster than human beings, thus extending society's capability to deal with complex situations. He holds that such developments are

35. "The Promise of Automation," in Phillipson, *Automation, Implications for the Future*, p. 215.
36. Edward B. Shils, *Automation and Industrial Relations* (New York: Holt, Rinehart and Winston, 1963), pp. 1–14.

harbingers of changes that are more fundamental than employment.[37]

Many degrees of automation exist, ranging from single machines activated by the introduction of the material to be processed to continuous flow operations programmed and controlled by computers. In the following discussion, the major focus is on the more highly developed types of automation.

The accomplishments of automated factory operations can be phenomenal. For example, in one Ford automobile engine plant, 48 men are able to make an engine block every 20 minutes compared to one every 40 minutes previously produced by a work force of 400 men.[38] Petroleum refineries and pipelines are highly automated and controlled by electronic devices. Some office operations—including payrolls, inventory control, and accounting operations—are being automated, permitting some savings in clerical costs and providing current information, in one case reducing inventories 50 per cent even though sales increased.[39]

A more recent example is the use of computers in paper making: Measurex Corporation has developed a system that is said to produce paper more rapidly, with less waste, at lower cost, and with profits that are substantially higher—as much as $1 million per year per system. The first system was sold in 1969, and aggregate sales totaled 110 units by January 1973.[40]

THE OUTLOOK FOR AUTOMATION

What are the growth prospects for automation?

Before attempting to answer this question, let us note the findings of a survey of 8,000 industrial plans made by *Auto-*

37. John Diebold, *Man and the Computer: Technology as an Agent of Social Change* (New York: Frederick A. Praeger, 1969), p. 10.
38. Buckingham, "Gains and Costs of Technological Change", p. 13.
39. Ibid., p. 17.
40. *Business Week* (27 January, 1973), p. 38.

mation Magazine and reported in 1960. The types of equipment reported by 2,693 plants having automatic equipment and controls was as follows[41]:

Type of Automatic Equipment	Per cent of Plants
Drive and speed regulation	72.7
Interlocked controls of operations	59.6
Automatic measuring and gauging	42.6
Automatic weighing	28.3
Process sending and control instruments	41.5
Tape and punch-card control	23.2
Computer control	4.6
Automatic data processing	16.6
Remote control	8.2

This tabulation indicates that the more sophisticated types of automation were not very prevalent in 1960.

The first commercial computer was installed in 1951. By 1965[42] the number in the United States was 27,000. In early 1969, according to John Diebold, there were 56,000, many of them highly sophisticated "third generation" systems, some of which served large numbers of corporations through "remote terminals." [43]

Forecasts made a decade ago of early and radical changes in business due to computers have proved to be exaggerated. There has been reluctance, misunderstanding of potential, and a much more gradual adoption rate than was expected by Diebold and other optimists. Still, there is increasing use and if Diebold is correct in his appraisal of benefits, eventually businesses that could, but do not, make efficient use of computers will be left behind as were the farmers who clung too long to outmoded farming technologies.[44]

41. Cited by Otis Lipstreu and Kenneth A. Reed, *Transition to Automation* (Boulder: University of Colorado Studies, Series in Business no. 1, January 1964), p. 12.
42. *Business Week* (19 February, 1966).
43. Diebold, *Man and the Computer*, p. 10.
44. Cf. John Diebold, *Business Decisions and Technological Change* (New York: Frederick A. Praeger, 1970), pp. 94–96.

Even though there is evidence that automation of various types is being adopted by many business firms and government agencies, it cannot be assumed that all types of work will be done by such machines in the near future.

The National Commission on Technology, Automation, and Economic Progress has taken a rather conservative position:

"Past trends and current prospects suggest that the present is, and the near future will be, a time or rapid technological progress. The combination of increased expenditure on research and development, extended and deepened education, continued urbanization, and improved communications has led to spectacular accomplishments in science and engineering. But this is as far as we are prepared to go. It is beyond our knowledge to know whether the computer, nuclear power, and molecular biology are quantitatively or qualitatively more 'revolutionary' than the telephone, electric power, and bacteriology." [45]

THE INFLUENCE OF AUTOMATION ON OCCUPATIONAL REQUIREMENTS OF WORK ORGANIZATIONS

It is not possible to specify in detail the changes in occupational requirements that will accompany advanced types of automation, since these will vary by industry and type of installation.

There is some evidence that dial watchers and other automatic machine tenders can be trained to perform these specific operations quickly. Yet, at the same time, responsibility for decisions with far-reaching consequences for other operations tends to increase,[46] so that emphasis on "good" judgments may be anticipated. This will probably lead to higher educational requirements.

The evidence concerning supervision is not clear. Some writers have predicted a decline in supervisory personnel because a computer can be programmed to make certain decisions better than an intelligent and educated man in the

45. *Technology and the American Economy*, p. 1.
46. Lipstreu and Reed, *Transition to Automation*, pp. 70–71.

sense that it can process information, make comparisons, and arrive at judgments more quickly and more accurately.[47] Thus, some middle-management men, who make essentially routine decisions, may find the computer doing their work. Already there are programs for playing checkers that can regularly beat all but the masters.

Experience in an automated bakery suggests, however, that the need for supervisors and auxiliary personnel may be underestimated if based on the assumption of trouble-free operations. Otis Lipstreu and Kenneth A. Reed state the need as follows:

"It appears that what may be considered by management as excessive staffing will be typical for open loop automation processes. After the debugging operation, additional personnel will not be required except occasionally. When required, however, their absence can result in rather fantastic materials and machine damage. Moreover, the added tensions of operators who envision production irregularities which they cannot handle alone may produce indirectly man-caused machine malfunctions." [48]

THE INFLUENCE OF AUTOMATION ON EMPLOYMENT

Herbert Simon says automation is merely the latest stage of the Industrial Revolution. He and many economists believe that it will prove beneficial in much the same way as earlier stages and confidently expect that past experience will enable us to solve its problems, including technological unemployment.[49]

47. See Thomas O'Toole, "White Collar Automation," *The Reporter* (5 December, 1963); Diebold, *Business Decisions and Technological Change*, pp. 44–45; Herbert Simon, "The Corporation: Will It Be Managed by Machines?" in Simon Marcson, ed., *Automation, Alienation and Anomie* (New York: Harper & Row, Publishers, 1970), pp. 212–19.
48. Lipstreu and Reed, p. 67.
49. "The Corporation: Will it be Managed by Machines?" in Phillipson, *Automation, Implications for the Future*, p. 230. See also Richard A. Beaumont and Roy B. Helfgott, *Management, Automation, and People* (New York: Industrial Relations Counselors, 1964).

There is considerable evidence, however, that automation may reduce the need for workers in some occupations. In testimony before a congressional committee in 1963, the president of a New England firm that manufactures automation equipment estimated that automation was then eliminating approximately 40,000 jobs per week or over 2 million a year. Senator Jennings Randolph of West Virginia, after listening to testimony, estimated that 4 million jobs a year were being eliminated.[50] The Bureau of Labor Statistics (BLS) of the U.S. Department of Labor has acknowledged that the impact of automation on employment is likely to be substantial but not catastrophic. The BLS advised the Commission on Technology, Automation, and Economic Progress that even though there is a rising demand for scientific and technical personnel the total demand for less-skilled workers is likely to remain at 1964 levels until 1975, although the *proportion* employed in unskilled nonfarm work will probably decline from 5.2 to 4.2 per cent.[51]

There is no doubt that substantial numbers of workers have been displaced by technological developments including automation. It appears, however, that, as of 1973, the great majority of them have found other work, as Herbert Simon predicted. The characteristics of unemployment will be discussed in chapter 6.

AUTOMATION AND ORGANIZATIONAL CHANGE

John Diebold suggests that the integrated nature of automated systems conflicts with the industrial system of dividing work into relatively simple specialties developed to utilize unskilled blue-collar workers, which he identifies as the legacy of the first industrial revolution. He points out that a major shift from the factory to the office occurred throughout industry during the 1950s and 1960s, and then argues that these

50. John I. Snyder, Jr., chairman of U.S. Industries, Inc.; cited by A. H. Raskin, "Mr. Meany's Curse," *The Reporter* (5 December, 1963), p. 22.
51. *Technology and The American Economy*, pp. 30–31.

occupational changes, involving greater intellectual preparation and performance, require fundamental changes in organizational structure and labor-management relations which run counter to existing traditions.[52]

Studies by several industrial sociologists lend support to Diebold's conclusions concerning the need for organizational changes adapted to the new technology.[53]

THE INFLUENCE OF AUTOMATION ON WORKERS

It is reasonably clear that the economic implications of automation may be very considerable, particularly for those unable to find work that provides a "good" income. For example, persons who cannot realistically be expected to attain employment in skilled, technical, or professional occupations or in managerial posts that provide high incomes, cannot be expected to obtain through work at their occupations the level of income that is essential in contemporary America to maintain what is thought of as a decent level of living. For such persons, the solution obviously does not rest with the individual alone. Work organizations and probably government will have to intervene if the current objective of banishing poverty is to be attained.

The prospect of acceleration of technological developments, including automation, and the accompanying decline in the availability of certain types of occupations, especially unskilled occupations that can be performed by those who have relatively little formal education, have generated concern about the extent to which income gained through work will continue to be the primary mechanism for the distribution of the products of industry and agriculture in the future. The *Ad Hoc* Committee on the Triple Revolution has suggested

52. Diebold, *Man and the Computer*, pp. 138–139.
53. *See* the following articles reprinted in Simon Marcson, *Automation, Alienation and Anomie*: William A. Faunce, "Automation in the Automobile Industry: Some Consequences for In-Plant Social Structure"; Floyd C. Mann and L. K. Williams, "Organization Impact of Automation in White-Collar Industrial Units"; and Frank J. Jasinski, "Adapting Organization to New Technology."

that, in the economy of the future, productive activities can be handled by machines and that, with the subsequent decline and perhaps even the eventual disappearance of human labor from production processes, opportunities for gainful employment in most productive occupations will disappear. The committee has advanced the suggestion that if and when this occurs every member of society should be given a generous supply of goods and services simply because he is a human being and a member of society. The committee holds the view that individuals should not be penalized for inability to participate directly in productive occupations.[54]

The National Commission on Technology, Automation, and Economic Progress recommended a number of changes in government programs to facilitate adjustment to technological change. Among these were proposals that the government (1) provide more adequate education for all, with emphasis on expanded educational opportunities for the poor and for those who need occupational training or retraining; (2) provide work on useful community enterprises for the "hard-core" unemployed; (3) guarantee economic security by a "floor under family income"; (4) establish a computerized nationwide federal employment service to match men and jobs; and (5) make permanent a current experimental program to assist in relocating workers and their families who are stranded in declining areas.[55]

These suggestions are directed primarily to the maintenance of economic support of individuals and families. The possible psychological and sociological consequences of widespread adoption of automation do not appear to have been given much consideration by the commission.

Automation has many effects on work, including an increase in the intellectual requirements of many tasks and new roles involving supervision of the machines and maintenance and repair activities. Many of these operations, however, particularly routine ones, apparently are not viewed by the workers

54. The *Ad Hoc* Committee on the Triple Revolution, *The Triple Revolution* (Santa Barbara, Calif., 22 March, 1964).
55. *Technology and The American Economy*, pp. 109–113.

who have been transferred to automatic operations as intellectually stimulating.[56] Communication with a machine is, in many respects, an unsatisfactory substitute for communication with other workers. Consequently, some question may be raised as to whether claims are true that the automated machinery will make work intrinsically more interesting. Greater interest may actually be realized only by those who have nonroutine relationships with computers and the machines which they control. These are the engineers who design the machines, the mathematicians who direct computing centers, those who teach computing developments, and research workers who perform nonroutine operations.

It is not clear what would take the place of work as a stabilizing force in personality and in social relationships when the time comes, if it ever does, when a very substantial portion of our labor force finds itself without work and without the opportunity of obtaining useful work because of automation.

To consider this question, we need to remember that the satisfactions and the rewards associated with work for pay or profit are very substantial in our society. This is not necessarily true everywhere. As noted earlier, the ancient Greeks and Romans regarded work as a curse. Even today there are societies in which work is not regarded as a desirable activity. With us it is different; research shows that even high school students report that they think of work as an activity valuable in its own right, not merely a means to an end.[57]

There may be some question, as we said earlier, concerning the extent to which the Puritan ethic has permeated the unskilled labor force. For example, do unskilled manual laborers or assembly-line operators necessarily share this view? Nevertheless, even people who do not feel this way about work find that participation in the labor force provides discipline and

56. Ida Rusakoff Hoos, "When the Computer Takes Over the Office," *Harvard Business Review* (July-August 1960), pp. 102–112.
57. Walter L. Slocum, *Occupational and Educational Plans of High School Seniors from Farm and Nonfarm Homes* (Pullman, Wash.: WAES Bulletin 564, February 1956).

tangible rewards. As noted earlier, it seems reasonably clear that for most men in our society, the occupational role is the key role around which other roles are organized. Thus, we may express serious concern about what will take the place of the work role if it is not available to a substantial portion of our labor force.

It is clear that the impact of automation will not fall equally on everyone. Some will be unemployed, others will have leisure, some will be overworked. Donald Michael has directed attention to what he calls the transitional stage, between now and some time in the future when we will have passed through the unsettling period occasioned by the rapid rate of technological change. During this transition period, he says, there will be four different leisure classes: (1) the unemployed; (2) low-salary employees working short hours; (3) the adequately paid to high-salary group working short hours; and (4) those who will have no more leisure than they now have.

In discussing the leisure activities of these classes of people, he confesses that he is baffled about what might be done for the unemployed and the low-salaried people working short hours. He suggests that perhaps some of these people may turn to aggressive activities.[58] In this connection, Ralph McGill, former editor of the Atlanta *Constitution*, pointed out in his syndicated column that the "Bully Boys" of Hitler were what we now call the drop-outs. They were the uneducated, the ignorant, who sought status through identification with the Nazis.[59]

Widespread adoption of automation would also create problems for families and communities. Since automated industries operate around the clock, some of those whose work is related to automated machines must work at other hours than eight to five. The computer runs through the noon hour, and it takes no coffee break.

Thus, in communities where a substantial automated indus-

58. "Cybernation: The Silent Conquest," in Phillipson, *Automation, Implications for the Future.*
59. *Lewiston Tribune* (21 November, 1963).

try or office operation exists, a portion of the labor force will not be able to follow the normal rhythm of an eight-to-five work day around which other activities are planned. This will create numerous problems for family life and for participation by the affected workers in organizations or community activities.

IMPLICATIONS OF AUTOMATION FOR CAREER PLANNING

The implications of automation and related developments in science and technology for occupational career planning are not entirely clear. Obviously, however, these developments cannot be ignored or overlooked. The prospects of accelerated occupational change that confront adolescents today will require greater emphasis on general education and less upon so-called vocational skills. What is needed, in my opinion, is a broad education that will facilitate flexibility in adjusting to unforeseen change with a minimum of personal and social disturbance. Great changes will occur, but we cannot foresee exactly what these changes are going to be. As a consequence, we cannot anticipate them in detail. Occupational retraining probably will be commonplace and will occur more than once during the work life of most young Americans. The problem will not be restricted to those who occupy blue-collar or clerical jobs, but will probably also affect those who pursue professional and managerial careers.

Selected References

Barber, Bernard. *Science and The Social Order.* New York: Collier Books, rev. ed., 1962. A broad-gauged discussion of the social implications of science.

Phillipson, Morris. *Automation, Implications for the Future.* New York: Vintage Books, 1962. This collection of papers deals with various facets of automation including implications for industry, labor, government, the social sciences, education, and leisure.

Technology and the American Economy. Report of the National Commission on Technology, Automation and Economic Progress. Washington, D.C.: U.S. Government Printing Office, 29 January, 1966. The report of a one-year study by a national commission of outstanding businessmen, labor leaders, and others appointed by President Johnson and approved by the Senate pursuant to Public Law 88-444 approved in August 1964.

Ellul, Jacques. *The Technological Society.* New York: Alfred A. Knopf and Random House, Vintage Books, 1964. Ellul's main thesis is that technology requires men to accommodate themselves to its standardized requirements with a resultant dehumanization of life. He thinks that this unhappy result is due to the natural laws of development of technique.

Diebold, John. *Man and The Computer.* New York: Frederick A. Praeger, 1969. A collection of essays on the impact of science and technology on education and business by a highly successful entrepreneur in the application of computer technology.

Marcson, Simon, ed. *Automation, Alienation and Anomie.* New York: Harper & Row, Publishers, 1970. A collection of essays dealing with the impact of technology on organizations, occupations and individuals.

4. Occupational Career Lines in Work Organizations

Knowledge of the occupational requirements of corporations, government agencies, and other work organizations is important to a clear understanding of the nature of occupational career opportunities.

As we said earlier, approximately 90 per cent of American workers are employees. In spite of the persistence of the ideological emphasis in our society on the independent entrepreneur, we live in an employee society.[1] Even the executives of most of the major business firms that operate on a national scope are employees. This means that work organizations are of great significance to nearly all workers. Their importance is likely to increase because the long-term trend in modern American industrial society is clearly toward greater dominance by organizations—large ones rather than small.

Almost all attractive career opportunities are found in business establishments, government agencies, educational institutions, and other work organizations. Even the majority of professional workers, including lawyers, clergymen, and scientists, now work in an organizational setting. This is especially significant for the person entering the world of work, who finds information about the occupational requirements and expectations of business establishments, government agencies, and other organizations indispensable for career planning.

The meaning of an occupation is not the same from the point of view of the managers of a work organization as it is from the point of view of the person pursuing the occupation.

1. *See* Peter F. Drucker, "The Employee Society," *American Journal of Sociology*, vol. 58 (1953), pp. 358–63.

The latter finds the significant aspects to be the occupational duties and skills, the social relationships with others in the work situation, and the money and other rewards derived from performance of the requirements of the occupation. Individuals tend to make an emotional commitment (in the case of the professions a deep commitment) to an occupation. A work organization, on other hand, is largely devoid of sentiment.

In this chapter we will first note some of the structural aspects of work organizations that have significance for careers; then we will examine some general features of the occupational requirements of farms, family retail businesses, corporations, agencies of the federal government, educational organizations, and the armed forces.

Structural Aspects of Work Systems

It may be useful at this point to present a generalized conceptual model of the structural aspects of a work system. Details vary from one concrete system to another, but the basic elements are the same as for any other social system.[2] The purpose of a work system, however, is different from that of others, say, a family, a school, or a social club. There have been many attempts to construct conceptual models of organizational structure. For our present purposes, the most useful model appears to be one which views these positions: (1) as linked horizontally through occupational or functional interdependence into divisions, departments, or other groups, (2) as arranged vertically in pyramidal patterns of rank which provides career lines and supervisory relationships, and (3) according to degree of centrality as reflected by tenure or "insider" status.[3] Other major structural aspects of concern to

2. See Charles P. Loomis, *Social Systems* (Princeton, N.J.: Van Nostrand, 1960).

3. Cf. Edgar H. Shein, "The Individual, the Organization and the Career: A Conceptual Scheme," *Journal of Applied Behavioral Science*, vol. 7, no. 4 (July-August 1971), pp. 401–426.

career seekers include the existence of a network of relationships among position encumbents, boundaries, organizational subculture as expressed in goals, values, behavior norms and roles, and linkages with other systems. The aspects of greatest concern are:

1. ORGANIZATIONAL RELATIONSHIPS

The existence of a network of regular and predictable relationships among members is the basic sociological characteristic of a social system.

Large work organizations such as those found in modern industry, business, and government are characterized from an organizational point of view by what sociologists and other social scientists have called bureaucracy that is, a rational as distinguished from a personal method of organizing work. In its most highly developed forms, it emphasizes recruitment, retention, and promotion of personnel on the basis of achievement or merit and rationalistic decision making based upon systematically collected and analyzed information. It also coordinates and integrates the activities of many diverse occupational specialties. Bureaucracy is a distinctive social invention, and, while it has defects, it represents a tremendous advance over the previously existing forms of organization, with many changes in organizational structures and procedures taking place at present, partly as a result of research by psychologists, sociologists, economists, and anthropologists.

Of special importance from a sociological point of view are the role-sets or subsystems, both formal and informal, that develop as the system operates.

2. POSITIONS

Every work system, viewed structurally, consists of positions or status-roles. These may be identified and given explicit names in a concrete work system such as a small newspaper: publisher, editor, reporter, copy boy, proofreader, linotype operator, pressman. Performance of the roles involved in each position consists of more or less faithful compliance with a set of expectations concerning the behavior of the incumbent with respect to his relationships with others in the system and with respect to technical functions assigned to the position. Thus, the linotype operator sets into type the copy brought by the copy boy from the editor, and he is not permitted to do any editing. Every member of the system, like every member of a football team, has to learn what is expected of him and what may be expected of others with whom he interacts. Furthermore, while some individual variations in performance may be tolerated, behavior outside the expectations is not. Thus, every editor must edit; as an editor he is not a pressman, though in a small plant a person may perform more than one occupational role.

3. CAREER LINES

To attract people with the necessary occupational skills and to retain them after they have been found, work organizations find it necessary to provide incentives. Where the essential operations require relatively little skill or education, these incentives may emphasize immediate wages rather than long-term considerations. With a rise in the level of skill and a concomitant increase in the educational requirements, greater incentives tend to appear. Annual salaries, rather than hourly, daily, or weekly wages, are provided; tenure, which provides protection from capricious dismissal, may be offered; and career lines probably will be established. As we said earlier, a career line consists of a graded series of related positions leading from the entry position to the pinnacle followed by retirement on a pension. There is a tendency for career lines with greater differences in rewards between the bottom and the top to be established for professional occupations rather than for those which are considered to be nonprofessional. There are also distinctions in rank between occupations and between varions positions within an occupational career line.

Policy level positions tend to be the upper steps of a long sequence of managerial positions. Those near the operating level, where the actual work of the organization such as manufacturing, relationships with customers, and similar operations are performed, may generally be considered "short" career lines; in these, the top positions are reached relatively soon after entry, and there may be little, if any, difference in salary or esteem between the new worker and the one who has been on the job for a substantial period of time.

In large complex organizations managerial positions are linked vertically into opportunity structures. Thus, resignation, retirement, dismissal, or death of a corporation president creates a vacancy that becomes an opportunity for a vice-president; and, likewise, a vice-presidential vacancy creates an opportunity for a department head and perhaps additional opportunities further down the hierarchical chain of command.[4] Of course, organizations do not always fill high-level vacancies by promotion. Frequently top executives are brought into the organization from outside.

In contemporary America there are substantial differentials in the salaries paid beginners and those paid experienced persons in the elite occupations. Charts 1 and 2 illustrate this dramatically for engineers, chemists, attorneys, and a few other specialists that were employed in business firms with 250 or more employees during February and March 1965.

The charts reveal much greater disparity between the salaries of those in entry positions and those in top positions in elite occupations than in white-collar occupations of less status. It is also evident that in the lower-status occupations there are fewer steps and the income differences between steps are relatively small. The data actually understate the case, the charts show data for only the middle 80 per cent of employees. This is probably not of great significance insofar as typists, file clerks, and key-punch operators are concerned, but among attorneys the upper limit of the monthly salary range might be $5,000 or more per month for the principal legal officers of a few great corporations.

4. For a study of such moves in the Episcopal Church, *see* Harrison C. White, *Chains of Opportunity: System Models of Mobility in Organizations* (Cambridge, Mass.: Harvard University Press, 1970).

CHART 1. Salaries in Professional and Technical Occupations, February-March 1965

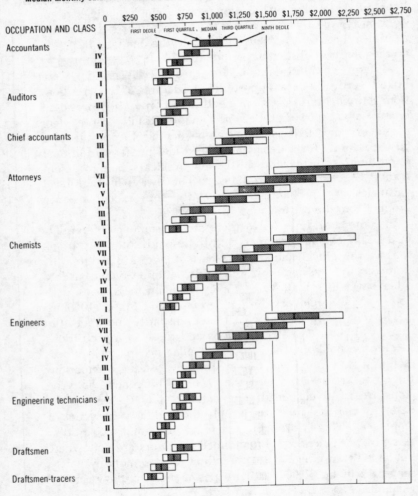

Median Monthly Salaries and Ranges Within Which Fell 50 Percent and 80 Percent of Employees

SOURCE: *National Survey of Professional, Administrative, Technical and Clerical Pay*, February-March 1965, Bulletin 1469, U.S. Department of Labor, Washington, D.C.

CHART 2. Salaries in Administrative and Clerical Occupations, February-March 1965

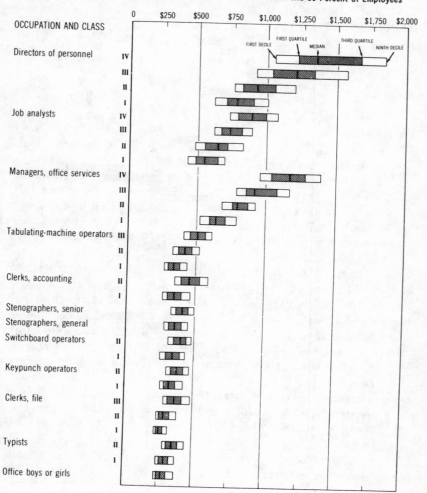

Median Monthly Salaries and Ranges Within Which Fell 50 Percent and 80 Percent of Employees

SOURCE: *National Survey of Professional, Administrative, Technical and Clerical Pay*, February-March 1965, Bulletin 1469, U.S. Department of Labor, Washington D.C.

81

Salaries have increased dramatically since 1965. Annual salaries of white-collar workers in private industry increased at a greater rate each year, from 1966 to June 1971; then there was a decrease in 1972.[5]

Year	Per cent increase
1966 to 1967	4.5
1967 to 1968	5.4
1968 to 1969	5.7
1969 to 1970	6.2
1970 to 1971	6.6
June 1971 to March 1972	4.4

This means that a monthly salary of $1,000 in 1966 would have increased to $1,378 by March 1972.

Comparable differentials exist in government agencies. In clerical occupations (GS2-7), the spread as of December 1972 in the salaries paid to workers in the first step in the grade was from $5,828 for GS3 to $9,053 for GS9. Among professionals and executives (Grades GS11-18) the spread was from $13,309 to $26,693.

In the armed forces, the differentials were even greater. As of March 1972, the monthly base pay for army enlisted personnel ranged from $307 for a beginner to $1,115 for a master sargeant with twenty-six or more years of service, plus meals, lodging, and uniforms. For commissioned officers, monthly base salaries ranged from $566 for a second lieutenant to $3,000 for a four-star general, in addition to his liberal fringe benefits.

Annual salaries for elementary and secondary teachers averaged $9,570 during the 1970-71 school year 1.5 per cent received less than $5,500 while 14.5 per cent received, $11,500 or more.[6]

Among college and university professors, salaries are much higher at some institutions than others, with a peak of

5. Richard L. Keller, "White Collar Pay in Private Industry, *Monthly Labour Review* (December 1972), p. 39.

6. U.S. Department of Health, Education, and Welfare, *Digest of Educational Statistics 1971*, p. 42.

$100,000 at the State University of New York. During 1971–72, average academic-year salaries and fringe benefits ranged from $8,970 for instructors in lower ranking four-year colleges to $27,190 for full professors at top universities.[7]

The number of steps in a career line and the level of salaries paid reflect the concern of a work organization with attracting and retaining competent occupational specialists. High salaries and attractive fringe benefits, together with high prestige and power for those who succeed in reaching the top positions, are believed to provide incentives not only for competent performance and loyalty but also for able young men to choose the occupation and make necessary educational preparation.

4. BOUNDARIES

Like other social systems, work organizations have boundaries. The physical boundaries of a factory, for example, enclose a certain amount of local space within which the facilities necessary for the fabrication of materials into the finished products are located. Large corporations, agencies of the federal government, and other organizations conduct activities throughout the United States and even in foreign countries, and thus have more territory within their boundaries. Physical boundaries are primarily relevant in the present context in relation to the location of the work to be done.

The fact that membership in most work organizations can be gained only by invitation can be viewed as evidence of the existence of social boundaries. Recruitment of new employees is, of course, essential for organizational maintenance and growth, and the criteria used for screening applicants determine the characteristics of those who are allowed to cross these boundaries. Since it is impossible to pursue a career in an organization unless one is a member, this is obviously an important matter for career seekers. In addition to the social

7. American Association of University Professors, *Bulletin* (June 1972), p. 197.

boundaries which separate organizational members from outsiders, there are also functional boundaries between departments, divisions, and other organizational units, as well as
informal boundaries between cliques or informal groups that
exist in all organizations. There are also hierarchical boundaries which separate various levels of positions.

Boundary maintenance is a vital process for organizational
survival and growth, Insofar as career seekers are concerned,
it is reflected in the criteria used by organizations for screening candidates for entry, tenure, and promotion—the major
boundary crossing operations, which will be discussed later.

5. THE ORGANIZATIONAL SUBCULTURE

Every legitimate work system has some legal sanction. In
the case of corporations, the state issues a charter that permits
the corporation to do certain things subject to applicable laws
and regulations.

Every business firm, government agency, school system, and
other work organization also has its own distinctive historical
experiences. In time, these experiences are codified into rules
and value positions that may be called the organizational subculture. This subculture provides guides covering the behavior
of position encumbents in relation to each other, in relation
to clients or customers, and in relation to others.

It has been found that people who work together over a
period of time tend to develop common orientations toward
work, toward politics, or toward other matters. One may observe, for example, a negative attitude toward government
power among employees of private utilities. In the Veterans
Administration in the late forties, I found a restrictive attitude
toward benefits, a pervasive feeling among administrators that
veterans might get more than they were entitled to and hence
that the Veterans Administration had to protect the public
treasury from possible "chiselers."

Goals. All work organizations have goals. These are frequently complex rather than simple, but for present purposes the goal of producing things, ideas, or services is of paramount importance because the nature of the product determines what occupations are required for organizational survival and growth. Thus, to provide medical care a hospital needs doctors, nurses and medical technicians, whereas an automobile agency needs salesmen, mechanics, and clean-up men—and both need bookkeepers and/or computer specialists.

Formal rules. In large organizations, many of the rules governing performance of work, including allocation of specific responsibilities to specific positions or occupational specialists, are specified in writing. These may be thought of as internal laws. Like the laws enacted by legislatures, some are more important than others; violations of rules that are regarded as important carry heavier penalties and compliance brings greater rewards.

Successful career employees soon learn, usually from other employees, which rules must be obeyed faithfully and which ones can be ignored with impunity. There is probably no way that these subtle distinctions can be identified by outsiders since the enforcement standards and procedures vary greatly between organizations and often within a particular organization at different periods.

Informal behavior norms. The unwritten norms governing behavior in organizations, including those of formal subsystems such as departments and those of informal groups, may be fully as important as the written rules. These norms may cover such matters as dress, personal care and grooming, acceptable ethnic and cultural backgrounds, which persons must be "paid" deference, and who is entitled to specific privileges.

Compliance with these informal norms is especially important for a person who joins a well-established organization. In some cases, the informal norms even extend to persons who interact with members. An interesting example of the latter was encountered by Erwin O. Smigel in his interviews with Wall Street lawyers. He reports that he considered it necessary to adopt the style of clothing worn by the lawyers he was interviewing rather than wearing the casual clothing customary on a university campus.[8]

The subculture of a specific work organization can be learned only as a member of the organization. This may create difficult problems for a new member who joins a work organization characterized by pronounced ideological views or rigid behavior norms; he may alienate powerful members of the system by an inadvertent act or comment.

Perhaps the most effective way for a new member to learn the unwritten behavior norms and values is to have a sponsor who is sufficiently interested in his success to give him the necessary information and to convince him of the importance of compliance.

6. LINKAGES WITH OTHER SOCIAL SYSTEMS

Work organizations are never isolated. They may have active relationships with other work organizations such as suppliers, advertisers, or buyers of their products, as well as with banks, governmental agencies, labor unions, and local communities. In large organizations, establishment and maintenance of these relationships frequently leads to the creation of specialized career lines. For example, a primary responsibility of a corporation legal department is to interpret relevant laws and government regulations. The legal department must also defend the interests of the corporation through court actions if necessary (boundary maintenance). Recognition of the importance of favorable public opinion has led corporations to emphasize service on community chest drives and similar "community building" activities.

Employees who are involved in interorganizational relationships, frequently receive, consider, and sometimes accept, invitations to join other organizations as managers or occupational specialists. Thus, these relationships can be viewed as

8. Erwin O. Smigel, *The Wall Street Lawyer* (New York: Free Press, 1964), p. 22.

a major source of interorganizational mobility of certain types of employees. Studies of interorganizational transfers indicate that both push and pull factors may be involved. An organization that seeks to hire an executive of another organization frequently offers higher pay, greater fringe benefits, a more attractive career ladder, or other inducements. Organizations that have decided that an employee is unlikely to fit its long-term needs may find a position for the employee in another organization. Erwin O. Smigel reports that Wall Street law firms frequently place recruits, who are judged unlikely to become partners, in the legal departments of corporations that they serve.[9]

Personnel Processes

To survive, work organizations must recruit new employees to replace those who die, retire, or leave for other reasons. In addition, other new employees must be recruited if the organization expands or assumes new functions that require different types of occupational specialists. These recruits must be socialized into the organizational subculture and the organization must supervise the performance of occupational roles by its members.

1. RECRUITMENT

Recruitment of new employees is considered of such importance to survival and growth that most organizations devote a great deal of time and effort to attempts to insure that those who cross its boundaries and become employees conform reasonably well to the organizational image of a good employee. Most employees are recruited for lower level positions. Organizations ordinarily prefer recruits near the begin-

9. Erwin O. Smigel, *The Wall Street Lawyer* (New York: Free Press, 1964), pp. 80–85.

ning of their careers because such persons are believed to be easier to train and indoctrinate. Personnel psychologists have constructed attitude profiles of desirable employees and, using a presumably "non-fakeable" technique involving "forced choice" questions, identify and reject applicants who do not conform to the profile.

Large organizations establish separate personnel departments staffed by personnel specialists, most of whom have university training relevant to this occupation. The federal government, most state governments, and many local governments also have civil service commissions or boards which conduct examinations and otherwise screen candidates for a wide range of occupations. In addition, "outside" candidates for high-level positions are frequently "screened" by selection committees appointed by chief executive officers or boards of directors; however, final decisions on such recruitment usually are made by the incumbent of the next higher position. Thus, candidates for a presidency may be screened by a committee and appointed by the board of directors.

The federal government recruits, insofar as possible, on a competitive basis, for positions other than elective offices, the judiciary, and policy-level positions in the executive branch. Except in times of great expansions, such as during the New Deal period and during World War II, most professional and administrative personnel are recruited at the lower ranks. At present, university graduates at the bachelors level generally enter the competitive service at grades GS-5 and GS-7. The salary offered an inexperienced person is at the bottom of the salary range for the specified grade. Persons with work experience in the field for which they are applying are hired at higher grades.

Recent college graduates and applicants for clerical positions are rated on the basis of written examinations, supplemented in many cases by interviews. Experienced professional men are recruited generally through an announcement of the need for persons with certain qualifications at certain grades. Those who are interested and think they qualify submit detailed applications that are evaluated by civil service examiners and graded prior to actual employment; interviews are usually also held.

As in the civilian branches of the federal government, the armed forces prefer to recruit young men to be officers. However, the tremendous expansion that occurred during World War II made it necessary to recruit many mature professionals and executives for officer positions, particularly occupational specialists. This was done by awarding direct commissions to those considered qualified and giving them a concentrated period of military indoctrination.

The personnel departments of corporations send recruiters to university campuses to interview engineers, scientists, and some liberal arts majors who may be considered as suitable management trainees. Professional employees of corporations also maintain contacts with university professors in their field of specialization. Candidates for professional positions are frequently invited to visit the corporation laboratories or head-quarters. While there, the candidate may meet selected members of the scientific staff or engineers or management officials who explore his interests and make some evaluation of his capabilities.[10]

A small number of large Wall Street law firms handle the legal business of many of the nation's giant corporations, and as a result, their influence is worldwide. Young men from Harvard, Yale, Columbia, and a few other elite law schools, who have outstanding academic records, good social backgrounds, pleasing personalities, and good physical appearance,[11] are recruited by these firms

Recruitment for university positions is seldom accomplished through open competitive procedures. Rather, the department with a vacancy obtains a list of names from professors, preferably in graduate schools of high caliber. Candidates who

10. Simon Marcson, *The Scientist in American Industry* (Princeton, N.J.: Department of Economics, Princeton University, 1960), pp. 52–58; and William H. Whyte, Jr., *The Organization Man* (Garden City, N.Y.: Doubleday & Co., 1956), pp. 121–42.

11. Erwin O. Smigel, *The Wall Street Lawyer* (New York: Free Press of Glencoe, 1964), chapter 3, "The Recruitment of Wall Street Lawyers."

indicate their interest in the position by submitting formal applications are ranked on the basis of academic record, recommendations from references whose names they supply, and sometimes by others who know of their achievements. After the field has been narrowed and priorities established, the top candidates may be invited to visit the campus for individual interviews. The candidate may be asked to present his ideas at a seminar. After this has been done, the staff of the department may vote, or the matter may be left entirely up to the personnel committee or to the chairman.[12]

A 1970 study of 150 graduate departments of sociology in the United States and Canada indicates that personal contacts are still used widely by American universities for recruiting new faculty; Canadian universities are more likely to send announcements of vacancies to other graduate departments.[13] The study also showed that new Ph.D.s from high productivity departments are most eagerly sought by other departments. Department chairmen who provided information overwhelmingly rated possession of the Ph.D. degree as the single most important criterion for judging candidates, followed by good recommendations (sponsorship), and departmental needs for specialists. Only half to three-quarters of those employed as assistant professors are expected to gain tenure. This expectation emphasizes the fact that a new member of a department is not immediately accepted as a permanent member of the "inner circle."

2. TRAINING FOR NEW EMPLOYEES

Although specific individuals and sometimes groups within an organization may sometimes be hostile toward new em-

12. Theodore Caplow and Reece J. McGee, *The Academic Marketplace* (Garden City, N.Y.: Doubleday & Co., 1965), chapter 6, Procedures of Recruitment."
13. Walter L. Slocum and Melvin DeFleur, "On Making it in Academe: The Successful Professor in the Graduate Department," *Research Studies*, Washington State University, vol. 40, no. 1 (March 1970), pp. 56–80.

ployees, the organization itself ordinarily seeks to assist such persons to perform their new roles effectively. Organizations seek loyalty and commitment.

Many organizations conduct formal indoctrination sessions, organizational manuals are often made available, and supervisors are expected to instruct new workers concerning their work and other responsibilities. Few civilian organizations are as thorough as the armed forces, which provide group indoctrination extending over periods of several weeks for enlisted personnel and for officers who receive direct commissions.

Although these formal efforts are probably helpful in most cases, it appears that informal socialization into organizational and work-group culture is usually more important. The new employee learns from his co-workers what is and what is not acceptable behavior. Studies by industrial psychologists and sociologists show that work-group norms such as restriction of output are learned rapidly and effectively by factory workers.[14]

W. H. Whyte, Jr. reported in *The Organization Man* that junior and middle managers in large corporations appeared to have learned from each other what he called the "social ethic" whereas top managers pursued the Puritan work ethic.[15]

3. MANAGEMENT OF CAREER REWARDS

Rewards and penalties administered by supervisors undoubtedly have some affect on learning of and degree of compliance with organizational values and norms as well as upon the quality of performance of occupational roles.[16]

As we said earlier, organizations establish hierarchical career lines and tenure at least partly to provide incentives for

14. Cf. W. F. Whyte, *Men at Work* (Homewood, Ill.: Dorsey Press and Richard D. Irwin, 1961), pp. 179–97.

15. W. H. Whyte, Jr., *The Organization Man* (Garden City, N.Y.; Doubleday & Co., 1956), pp. 69–166.

16. *See* Amitai Etzioni, *A Comparative Analysis of Complex Organizations* (New York: Free Press, 1961), pp. 23–67, for a discussion of compliance of workers with organizational rules.

employees to make long-term commitments. Naturally, it does not follow that all who enter a career line eventually gain tenure or reach the top step. The pyramid-like structure of management positions in modern corporations and other bureaucracies makes it virtually certain that all but a few of any group of entering management trainees will at some point find their further upward progress blocked. The competition is keen and the organizational decision as to which of several well-qualified candidates to promote may sometimes rest on very slender grounds.

Promotion and Demotion. Except in companies dominated by private owners, where the top positions may be filled by relatives, an effort is made to identify and promote executives who will be qualified to advance the goals of the organization. In other words, there is a tendency to promote on the basis of merit. In a bureaucracy, one of the standards for evaluation of managers is competence in performing the duties of the position; another is loyalty to the organization; and a third is satisfactory relationships with colleagues and especially with supervisors.

As we said, in most large-scale organizations in industrialized countries the declared objective is to promote the best qualified candidates. We also said that formal standards for evaluation of merit for promotion frequently exist in large organizations for achieving this goal. Nevertheless, the system is managed by human beings rather than by impersonal computers; therefore, patrimonial influences such as favoritism based on sponsorship by a prestigious organizational figure or personal "politicking" by a candidate may also be involved, especially for high-level positions.

Annual salary increases are now common in many organizations. In some cases such increases are allocated on a proportionate basis while in others they are given disproportionately on the basis of merit and thus involve decisions similar to those encountered in promotions.

In some organizations employees are expected to become dissatisfied and leave if they fail to receive periodic salary increases or promotions. Some employees, usually those who are judged by their supervisors to be incompetent, are demoted or discharged. Demotion is common in some business firms but relatively uncommon in government civil service and universities. Fred H. Goldner notes that demotions are sometimes obscured by assignments which may sometimes lead to promotion.[17] The ambiguous nature of some demotions has also been noted by Douglas M. More who has identified eleven separate forms of demotion.[18]

Others have also noted a tendency on the part of organizations to deal gently rather than severely with members whose performances fall below desired standards. The tendency for high officials of bureacratic organizations to be retained in such positions even when they do not perform their organizational roles satisfactorily was discussed by Lawrence J. Peter in the January 1967 issue of *Esquire*. His charge, which he calls the "Peter Principle," is that managers who are perceived by organizations to be competent are promoted until they reach what he calls their "level of incompetence," where they stay until retirement. Consequently, according to Peter, the top levels of organizations are staffed by incompetent people. Personal experience and observation, together with a review of the literature, leads me to question the sweeping claims made for the widespread applicability of the "Peter Principle," but there is little doubt that it is sometimes valid. One must bear in mind, however, that there are few, if any, generally accepted criteria for judging the overall performance of roles by presidents, board chairmen, supreme court justices, or incumbents in other high level positions. Consequently, judgments about their competence are frequently, if not always, colored by the vested interests and other biases of those who judge their performance.

William J. Goode, in a prize-winning essay, has suggested

17. Fred H. Goldner, "Demotion in Industrial Management," *American Sociological Review*, vol. 30, no. 5 (October 1965), pp. 714–24; reprinted in part in Barney G. Glaser, ed., *Organizational Careers* (Chicago: Aldine Publishing Co., 1968), pp. 267–279.

18. Douglas M. More, "Demotion," *Social Problems*, vol. 9, no. 3 (Winter 1962), pp. 213–21; reprinted in part in Glaser, *Organizational Careers*, pp. 287–299.

that ". . . both the able and the inept may move into high position." [19] He argues further that organizations therefore adopt arrangements that protect the organization from the inept and the inept from the ruthless weeding out that would be expected if achievement norms (the demand for efficiency and competence) were applied. He argues that once people are accepted as members of a work organization they are unlikely to be fired even though they may be incompetent. He suggests that one consequence of this practice is a tendency to set standards of education and other qualifications for recruits that are far above the actual requirements for adequate performance of the job.[20]

Tenure. Educational institutions, governmental civil service systems, and some other work organizations provide tenure (usually until retirement) after a probationary period. Tenure means essentially that an employee cannot be fired except for cause and then only after a hearing.

Employees of Japanese business firms customarily have lifetime tenure; if they are not competent they are assigned some harmless work.[21] In the American economy, tenure is seldom found in corporations, except among unionized workers. In the federal government, tenure, or permanent status, as it is called, is customarily awarded to nearly all employees of permanent agencies after a probationary period; policy-making officials at the top may be excepted. Cabinet officers and some others are appointed by the president of the United States with the advice and consent of the Senate. The president is able to fill only about 3,500 positions on a patronage basis, a small but important segment of the more than two million civilian employees of the federal government.

In the armed forces, tenure, as such, does not exist for officers and enlisted personnel.

19. W. J. Goode, "The Protection of the Inept" (1965 McIver Award Lecture), *American Sociological Review*, vol. 32, no. 1 (February 1967), p. 6.
20. Goode, "The Protection of the Inept."
21. Cf. James C. Abegglen, *The Japanese Factory* (New York: Free Press of Glencoe, 1960, pp. 86–90); reprinted in Glaser, *Organizational Careers*, pp. 300–302.

In universities, presidents, vice-presidents, and deans do not ordinarily have tenure in these positions, although they may have tenure as professors. Most associate professors and practically all full professors have tenure. The decision to grant or to withhold tenure is seldom automatic. In universities it is usually regarded as a crucial decision. Frequently, all members with tenure vote formally on whether or not to grant tenure.

Retirement. Most large work organizations provide pensions and other retirement benefits for employees who serve specified periods of time and reach retirement age. Consistent with the hierarchical principles of organizations, which provide more pay and greater fringe benefits to employees in elite occupations and/or higher level positions, retirement benefits are substantially greater for corporation presidents and other high-level managers than for assembly line workers and others who perform lower ranked occupational duties. Many of the latter are dependent primarily upon Social Security benefits after retirement.

Since pensions are regarded as incentives for long-term service by most organizations, managers, and workers alike, many forfeit pensions if they leave before reaching retirement age. Furthermore, since the formula for computing a retirement annuity usually provides larger payments for longer service, there is frequently a penalty for changing employers. Interorganizational mobility is not penalized by Social Security rules which provide full credit for all covered employment. In addition, transfers from one agency of the federal government to another are not penalized if both agencies are covered by the Civil Service Retirement. Universities and other nonprofit organizations that are members of Teachers Insurance and Annuity Association (TIAA-CREF) constitute another situs for interorganizational mobility without retirement penalties, as do teachers retirement associations which cover teachers in all public schools in specific states.

Early retirement incentives are provided by the armed forces, by civilian agencies of the federal government, and some other work organizations. These policies are designed to open up positions for younger, presumably better qualified, and sometimes lower-paid employees, and thus to increase responsiveness of the organization to change, improve efficiency, and, hopefully, to reduce costs.

Occupational Requirements of Selected Types of Work Organizations

Although it is not possible to consider the occupational requirements of all of the major types of work organizations found in contemporary American society, it may be useful to discuss a few selected types in some detail.

1. FARMS [22]

Probably no industry in America has experienced greater changes during the past half century than commercial farming. Dating from approximately the beginning of World War I, farming practices have been virtually revolutionized by the application of scientific knowledge and the adoption of improved technology and farm practices. Some relatively inefficient farms may still be found, but the farms that produce food and fiber for the market are so efficient that great surpluses of cotton, wheat, corn, and other commodities have piled up. This has not occurred without changes in the occupation of farming, which may perhaps be best illustrated by contrasting the occupation requirements on the traditional self-sufficing family farm with those found on a highly efficient commercial farm producing any one of the major agricultural commodities.

Self-sufficing Family Farms. The traditional self-sufficing family farm of American folklore represents a polar type of

22. Walter L. Slocum, *Agricultural Sociology* (New York: Harper and Bros., 1962).

work organization in which occupational roles and nonwork roles are intermingled. Although this simple undifferentiated organizational structure is not well adapted to modern agriculture, it is important because this type of farm is still found in many parts of the country, and historically such farmers were once very numerous. Furthermore, many attitudes that urban residents have toward work, leisure, and the fine arts stem from their rural farm antecedents, even though in most cases these are now a generation or two removed.

James S. Brown has described the essential features of the self-sufficing farm as it existed in an isolated Kentucky mountain neighborhood a quarter of a century ago:

"Beech Creek families differ greatly in their daily activities and the activities of every family vary with the season. Perhaps the best way of conveying some notion of the daily pattern which most families on the Beech Creek follow is to describe the activities of one more or less representative family on a single day.

"September is a busy time for Beech Creek people and the day began early for the family, usually before daylight. About five o'clock, the husband-father got up and built a fire in the cookstove, and then his wife arose, dressed, and started her first task of the day—getting breakfast. This was not a light, easily prepared meal such as urban people eat, but was a real job, preparation for which had begun the night before when kindling and wood were brought in and stacked by the stove and butter was churned. "Light bread" as bakery bread is known on Beech Creek is not easily available, and besides the Beech Creekers prefer homemade bread for a steady diet, and so the wife began the routine to which she had become so accustomed that she automatically measured and mixed the ingredients for hot biscuits. On this morning, breakfast consisted of hot biscuits, fried sweet potatoes left over from supper the previous night, fat meat served in deep fat, huckleberry jam, apple jelly, boiled coffee, and sweet milk. While the wife bustled around the warm kitchen cooking, her husband watched the fire and they talked together about what happened yesterday and what was to go on today. Together they planned the day's work. About 5:45 the four children still at home got up and came to the table, sat in their usual places, and ate. Conversation at breakfast was, as usual, not very lively.

"After the meal, the members of the family scattered to do their usual early morning tasks; the father and mother went to the barn and while she milked, he took care of the new calves. The older son who was nineteen, also went to the barn to feed the mule and the horse, and his younger brother, who was fourteen, vacillated between going to school or staying home to work with the family. Meanwhile the two girls, who were twenty-three and seventeen, washed dishes, cleaned up the kitchen, and made the first of many trips during the day to the well in the yard, this time to get water to fill the reservoir of the stove. The mother or the daughters fed the chickens scraps left from the meal supplemented by some corn which they shelled off by hand. By the time all of these chores were finished and the family had sat around talking for a while, it was seven o'clock or later, and the main work of the day was about to begin. The younger son finally decided to stay home from school (a not unusual decision), and the father, two sons and two daughters started up the branch to the cornfield to pull fodder, leaving only the mother behind to do the housework. (In younger families it is at this time that children go down the creek to school, leaving their mother alone at the house with the youngest children.)

"It wasn't far to the fields, but even in such a short distance everybody was wet to the knees from brushing against the dewy weeds which bordered the narrow path. Like most Beech Creek cornfields the family's fields lay on steep hillsides, and it was a long, hard climb to the highest part, just below the crest of the ridge. Because the fields were so steep and it was all but impossible to place the whole cornstocks into shocks or to haul them out of the field, they 'pulled fodder,' that is, they pulled the blades off, leaving the stalk with the ears of corn still standing. The blades were then tied into bundles and stacked, to be hauled to the barn later. A division of labor was worked out, with some pulling the blades, others tying and stacking the bundles. . . . Dinner was ready to put on the table when the family returned from the cornfield at noon, and after washing their hands and faces, they sat down at the table again and ate.

"It was a very hot day, and there was no great rush back to the field later after dinner. In fact the girls decided they wouldn't go back at all. But after sitting on the porch for a while, the men went back to foddering. The girls washed dishes and swept the kitchen and then rested a while. Then they went out on the porch and began to string beans for drying. The mother fed the chickens again, and then joined her daughters on the porch. Later, the girls walked the mile or so to the 'office' (post office) in the hope of getting a letter from their soldier-brother in Iceland; they returned without a letter but with news of the neighborhood gathered as they stopped and visited along the way.

"The men worked hard in the field and by 5 o'clock were glad to leave the heat, dust, 'pack-saddles,' and cutting blades. It was nearly 5:30 by the time they had climbed down the hill and walked home. Again barn-chores occupied the family. The younger son went up the branch to drive the cows home; the father and mother then went to the barn, the father to look after the calves, the mother to milk. The sons fed the horse and mule and threw some corn into the hog pen near the barn. Then they all went back to the house, and while the mother strained the milk and got part of it ready to hand down the well to keep cool, the boys and father drew water and washed on the porch. The girls were busy in the hot kitchen getting supper on the table. There were sweet potatoes, green beans, and cornbread left from dinner; and to these they added fried corn, fried Irish potatoes, sliced tomatoes, coffee, milk, butter, and as a special treat a cake, for a cousin from Flat Rock had come over to help them the next day and something extra was called for. Tonight the men and the mother sat down at the table together and the girls stood around and served. Conversation was free and lively at this meal as news about Flat Rock and Beech Creek was exchanged. Somehow attention was turned to the exploits of a woman in the neighborhood, and the mother and father rivalled each other in telling funny stories about her. By the time the meal was finished, everybody was roaring with laughter. The mother and the men went out to sit on the porch, and the older son went up and saddled his horse and rode down the creek while the younger son brought in kindling and wood to the kitchen and went up the branch to listen to the radio at his brother's house. The girls ate and again washed dishes, and they too brought chairs out to the porch and talked. The boys came back, and about 8:30 everybody went to bed.

"The work on the farm outside of the house was much more

variable, changing with the seasons, reaching peaks at certain times of the year, and ebbing to relative inactivity at other periods." [23]

Commercial Family Farms. A modern commercial farm operated by a farmer with some help from his family, and perhaps seasonal help during peak periods, may be regarded as a family farm. It is operated to produce commodities for sale, and most of the goods and services consumed by commercial farm families are purchased in the market just as non-farm families purchase their supplies. Very few commodities are produced for home use, although a few farms may still have gardens, cows, and chickens for this purpose.

Frequently commercial farms are specialized. In some cases, commodities such as poultry, sugar beets, and vegetables are produced on a contract basis for a price specified in advance. Very substantial expenses may be involved, including production credit, fertilizer, feed, seed, insecticides, herbicides, and pesticides.

As a work organization, a family farm can be described as a system of multiple occupational roles performed chiefly by members of the family. The leadership position is almost always occupied by the farm operator who usually is the husband-father. The area of responsibility covered by his position includes most of the farm management decisions, although wives frequently discuss such decisions and may share in the responsibility for the decisions. He is also the major source of labor and performs most of the varied occupational skills involved in the farming operations.

As I have observed elsewhere:

"In the traditional farm family, the operator allocated daily tasks to his children, usually at the breakfast table. He instructed them in the technical aspects of their work, provided

23. James S. Brown, *The Farm Family in a Kentucky Mountain Neighborhood* (Lexington: Kentucky Agricultural Experiment Station Bulletin, 587, 1952).

leadership for work done in groups, supervised the operation of various farm tasks, reprimanded or otherwise punished them when he considered that their work was improperly done, and managed the reward system for proper performance of the various roles involved in the operation of the farm.

"The wife on a traditional family farm performed the roles of mother and homemaker, taking responsibility for the work of maintaining the house, feeding and clothing the family, and supervising the household tasks. She also frequently had the duty of keeping the home garden and preserving and process-ing the home-produced food. In pioneer times the homemaker had the tasks of spinning, weaving, and making cloth into garments. On some farms, particularly those of immigrants, the farmer's wife and her adolescent daughters were also expected to help with field work and other hard physical labor. This, however, is generally not defined at present as a proper activity for women; their work activities are usually confined to the house, gardening, the care of poultry, and perhaps minor farm chores." [24]

On a modern commercial farm, some services may be pro-vided on a contract or fee basis by specialists. These include the treatment of sick animals by veterinarians, farm record-keeping services, milk pickup, harvesting of specialized crops, farm management advice, crop dusting by airplanes, applica-tion of fertilizer, and comparable services.

The traditional career line in agriculture is known as the agricultural ladder.

"In the ideal case, the farm boy who aspired to become a farm owner began his apprenticeship in agriculture as an un-paid farm laborer on the home farm. At 19 or 20 he obtained a job on the neighboring farm where he worked for cash wages. Since board and lodging was provided, he was able to save most of his wages, with which he purchased a team of horses and some equipment. This enabled him to rent a piece of land which he operated himself. If he was frugal his earnings even-

24. Slocum, *Agricultural Sociology*, pp. 294–95.

tually permitted him to accumulate a down payment and buy a farm of his own, the balance being secured by a mortgage." [25]

This method of becoming a farm owner is no longer practicable for most people. The capital required to operate a commercial farm is now so great that it is almost impossible for a young person to rise from a job as an agricultural laborer to the position of a farm tenant. It is even difficult for a tenant to become an owner. In fact, there is evidence that the majority of corn-belt farms are inherited.[26]

Nearly all farmers are sons of farmers, but the declining opportunities for employment in agriculture, due to the adoption of improved technology in farm practices, requires most farmers' sons to find other occupations.

Large Farms. Modern large-scale machinery has made it possible for a farm operator and his family, with some incidental help from others at peak seasons, to operate large holdings, and there is no clear-cut or generally agreed-upon boundary in terms of size. Whenever the farm operations are large enough to require the supplementation or replacement of unpaid family labor by a regular hired labor force, the differences may be considered to be sociologically significant. Some farm operations are of very great magnitude; the census reports 1,200 farm units, that had each sold more than a half million dollars worth of farm commodities in 1959.

The southern plantation, which was the dominant form of farm organization in commercial agriculture in the South from colonial times until the widespread adoption of the mechanical cotton picker, has been studied in detail by T. J. Woofter.[27] Although no longer prevalent, a description of the social structure will indicate the occupational and organizational complexity that was involved:

25. Ibid., p. 353.
26. *See* E. M. Rogers and George M. Beal, *Reference Group Influences in the Adoption of Agricultural Technology* (Ames, Iowa State College, 1958), p. 53.
27. T. J. Woofter, Jr., et al., *Landlord and Tenant on the Cotton Plantation* (Washington, D.C.: WPA Research Monograph V, 1936).

"The system of labor organization on the traditional cotton plantation included the following roles: the owner who established major policies and made basic decisions on the overall operations of the enterprise . . . ; a bookkeeper, a farm manager, an overseer of farm laborers, and an overseer of croppers; and, of course, wage hands and croppers. On a large plantation, there would also be assistant overseers or riders to supervise from 20 to 30 wage hands or croppers. Business relationships involving the operation of the plantation such as purchasing, marketing, and credit would normally be carried on by the owner or manager. A plantation may also employ artisans such as blacksmiths, mechanics, tractor operators, truck drivers, and other agricultural specialists. . . . The organization of work on a plantation involves domination by owners and supervisors with subordination of those at the bottom who take orders and carry them out as directed by overseers who in turn work under managers. . . .

"During the period of slavery when the southern plantations were established and took shape as a form of farm organization, the domination of the master was reinforced by the fact that his slaves were actually property. They could be bought, sold, and punished at will." [28]

Although comprehensive statistics on farm incorporation are not available, it is known that there are a fairly large number, most of which are believed to be of substantial size.

The social structure of the corporation farm includes the members of the corporation, generally a hired manager, and, depending on the size and complexity of the operations involved, a variable number of other regular employees who perform specific functions. In addition, if the farm has high seasonal labor requirements, such as fruit, vegetables, nuts, or other specialty crops, seasonal laborers will ordinarily be employed during peak periods. In many high labor requirement areas, the negotiations between farm operators and seasonal laborers are maintained through crew bosses who maintain contractual relationships with the farm managers on

28. Ibid.

the one hand and with laborers on the other. In fact, the crew leader may not only supervise the workers, but actually collect their wages and then pay them what they have earned less his commission, transportation expenses, etc.[29]

The position of farm manager on a large farm now usually requires substantial formal education in agricultural economics and other agricultural subjects as well as some practical experience as a county agricultural agent or assistant farm manager. Although the position is not hierarchically graded to any appreciable extent, differences in salary and bonuses do effectively establish prestige levels, which are probably closely related to the magnitude of the farm operation. There is considerable effort on the part of farm managers to establish recognition of their occupational specialty as a profession.

Occupational roles on large farms other than those of the seasonal work force also tend to be highly specialied and to require a substantial amount of skill, particularly in the operation and maintenance of large-scale machinery, and, on some specialty farms, agronomic or horticultural knowledge.

2. FAMILY-OPERATED RETAIL BUSINESS

The number of retail businesses in the United States is very large, but most are relatively small-scale operations, consisting of the proprietor, some members of his family, and perhaps a few others. Even though outnumbered, the large chain stores, department stores, and retail mail-order houses take the "lions share" of the business volume and employ most of the paid workers in retail business.

As in the case of a family farm, a family retail store is a small enterprise—a grocery, a delicatessen, a hardware store, a shoe shop, or other enterprise—in which most of the necessary work is done by the proprietor and other members of his immediate family. The social structure of this work organization is much like that of a family farm and characterized by multiple occupational roles performed at different times by

29. Slocum, *Agricultural Sociology*, pp. 84–86.

the same person. The proprietor is the traditional "jack-of-all-trades": he carries out such diversified occupational tasks as bookkeeping, cleaning, inventorying, buying, stocking the shelves, and, of course, selling. These may be thought of as part-time rather than full-time occupational roles; the most crucial role for the survival of the organization is that involving relationships with the customers. Unless these relationships are successful over a period of time, the small store cannot survive. With low sales volume, it cannot hope to meet the prices or to provide the variety of products available in a large chain store or department store. Consequently, personal relationships and, in some cases, credit are of great importance.

The family retail business may be thought of as a closed system that ordinarily can be entered only by birth or by marriage to one of the members of the family. However, the career ladder is short, with few desirable positions other than that of the proprietor. Consequently, this closure is not a matter of great public concern. Most of the desirable employment opportunities for young people, including the children of the proprietor, lie elsewhere. The major avenue of entry into this field is establishing a new business, which requires capital and some experience if the business is to be successful. Many such establishments fail; others keep going chiefly because the proprietor and members of his family work long hours at low rates of pay.

3. CORPORATIONS

Most manufacturing establishments, many retail businesses, most banks, most transportation companies, and even some farms are corporations. It is probably correct to say that nearly all American profit-making organizations, except family-operated businesses and farms, are corporations. Corporations are characterized by written regulations—that is, internal laws—and by a formal social system that consists of definite positions connected by an explicit network of communication channels arranged in accordance with the authority patterns and work requirements of the organization. Informal interpersonal relationships exist among those who fill the positions, and there is a body of unwritten rules and customs that may be fully as important as the written ones.

The corporation is a true social invention that has largely replaced the individual capitalist in the American economy,[30] although a few of these rugged individualists are still found on the scene; a fairly large number of millionaires have made their fortunes on the stock market, in real estate, in oil, or in other speculative ventures. Nevertheless, nearly all the largest business enterprises in the United States are corporations, and a very large, although unknown, proportion of the labor force is employed by corporations. Many of the more attractive occupational career lines exist within corporations.

Bureaucracy. Large corporations are characterized by what is called *bureaucracy,*[31] which is used in sociology to describe the rational organization of modern work systems. However, the term has a derogatory connotation in common parlance, and consequently Wilbert E. Moore uses the term *administrative organization* instead.[32] Although this usage may have merit when communicating with nonsociologists, *bureaucracy* seems preferable in discussion of the sociology of occupations, since it is less cumbersome term that can be defined precisely. In the present context it is used without value connotations.

The initial use of this concept in sociology has been traced to the German sociologist, Max Weber, who presented a theoretical analysis of the characteristics of formal organizations. Robert Presthus has summarized Weber's presentation of the characteristics of bureaucracy. He says that bureaucracies have:

30. W. Lloyd Warner and Norman H. Martin, eds., *Industrial Man* (New York: Harper and Bros., 1959).

31. Robert Presthus, *The Organizational Society* (New York: Alfred A. Knopf and Random House, Vintage Books, 1965), p. 5.

32. *The Conduct of the Corporation* (New York: Random House, 1962).

"1. Fixed and official jurisdiction areas, which are regularly ordered by rules, that is, by laws or administrative regulations.
2. Principles of hierarchy and levels of graded authority that ensure a firmly ordered system of super- and sub-ordination in which higher offices supervise lower ones.
3. Administration based upon written documents; the body of officials engaged in handling these documents and files, along with other material apparatus, make up a 'bureau' or 'office.'
4. Administration by full-time officials who are thoroughly and expertly trained.
5. Administration by general rules which are quite stable and comprehensive." [33]

Peter Blau and William Scott observe that Max Weber's model of bureaucracy was not derived from empirical analysis but was an attempt to present a model of "a perfectly bureaucratized organization." [34] "A careful reading of Weber indicates that he tends to view elements as 'bureaucratic' to the extent that they contribute to administrative efficiency. This contribution to efficiency appears to be the criterion of 'perfect' embodied in his ideal type." [35] This indicates that bureaucracy was actually used by Max Weber as a superlative rather than a derogatory term.

Blau and Scott propose that the hypotheses involved in Weber's concept of bureaucracy be tested empirically as a basis for moving beyond his insights. This is a reasonable suggestion, since Weber's views were based to some extent upon his own experience with the German state bureaucracy, which has always tended to be highly sensitive to relationships between superiors and subordinates.

Alvin Gouldner, although recognizing the contribution of

33. Presthus, *The Organizational Society*, p. 5.
34. Peter Blau and William Scott, *Formal Organizations* (San Francisco: Chandler Publishing Co., 1962), p. 33.
35. Ibid., p. 34.

Weber's theory of bureaucracy, has criticized its ambiguity regarding the source of bureaucratic discipline or obedience to authority; he says Weber emphasized obedience as an end in itself. Gouldner suggests that two types of bureaucracies may be involved, one of which he calls the "representative" form, which tends to emphasize participation by members of the bureaucratic organization in the establishment of rules on a consent basis, as distinguished from what he calls the "punishment-centered" type, which is characterized by expectations of obedience to orders from superiors.[36]

Weber's model has also been criticized by Philip Selznick[37] because Weber tended to emphasize only the formal social structure, the role aspects, overlooking the important fact that members of an organization interact as persons as well as incumbents in formal positions. Many empirical studies have established clearly that the formal arrangements emphasized by organization charts and official rules are supplemented and modified by informal cliques and relationships that emphasize informal rather than formal channels.[38] Fred Bates takes the view that "informal" interpersonal relationships should be considered part of the actual structure of an organization rather than unanticipated because the official organization chart does not specify them.[39]

Formal work organizations such as corporations may be analyzed from other points of view. Herbert Simon, for example, has analyzed administrative organizations primarily from the point of view of decision making.[40] He noted that formal organizations promote rationality in decision making by defining responsibilities and establishing mechanisms including information channels, training programs, and formal

36. *Patterns of Industrial Bureaucracy* (Glencoe, Ill.: Free Press, 1954), pp. 22–24.

37. Philip Selznick, "Foundations of the Theory of Organizations," *American Sociological Review*, vol. 13 (1948), pp. 25–35.

38. Robert Dubin, *The World of Work* (Englewood Cliffs, N.J.: Prentice-Hall, 1958), chapter 9.

39. Personal conversation, March 1964.

40. *Administrative Behavior* (New York: Macmillan Co., 2d ed., 1957).

rules that serve to facilitate decision making by limiting the range of alternatives to be considered. This is a useful way of conceptualizing formal organizations if the focus is on the actual functioning of the organization. For our purposes the bureaucratic model suggested by Max Weber, as modified by Gouldner and others, seems more useful.

Although it would be incorrect to regard the interpersonal relationships among position incumbents in a bureaucracy, such as a corporation, as mechanistic and entirely impersonal, it is correct to say that one of the most important character- istics that distinguishes a corporate bureaucracy from earlier types of business organization is the application of rational principles to its design and operation.

Especially in manufacturing corporations, the effort to ar- rive at rationality was directed initially by engineers, many of whom thought of employees as simply another and cheaper kind of machine. They disregarded almost completely many psychological and sociological imperatives. The result was that the followers of early industrial management experts such as Frederick W. Taylor, Frank Gilbreth, and their colleagues, who developed time study and work simplification and per- fected the assembly line, largely removed the satisfactions which artisans had previously obtained from their work.

This extreme emphasis on efficiency by engineers and time- study men provoked a counteraction known as the "human re- lations" emphasis which in turn has been pursued to extreme lengths by some of its adherents.[41] As in many other aspects of American life, management style seems to be characterized by a pendulum-like cycle. The human relations approach tends to be a manipulative approach used by management to attain its goals. As first applied, it was based on half-truths about the importance of nonrational aspects of human person-

---

41. This emphasis stemmed initially from studies made by Elton N. Mayo and his colleagues at the Hawthorne Plant of Western Electric. *See* Fritz J. Roethlisberger and William J. Dickson, *Management and the Worker* (Cambridge, Mass.: Harvard University Press, 1950), and William Foote Whyte, "Human Relations Reconsidered," in Warner and Martin, *Industrial Man*, pp. 307–22.

ality. The fact that workers, in response to questionnaires and projective tests, frequently placed noneconomic aspects of work above money was interpreted to mean that workers were more interested in recognition and prestige than in income, but this particular idea did not have much success. In our culture, economic incentives are a very powerful means of motivating people to work, although other incentives are unquestionably important. Nearly all employees want both money and favorable recognition from supervisors and peers.

Reaction against the extreme specialization of assembly-line operations has resulted in "job enlargement" to restore meaning to occupational roles by permitting a worker to perform a number of operations that are clearly related to the accomplishment of an important task.

Occupational Requirements of Corporations. The occupational requirements of corporations are not simple. However, it is possible to distinguish two major levels: (1) the technical level, and (2) the managerial level.[42]

Fifty years ago occupational requirements at the technical level were primarily the specialized skills required to perform basic production or basic service to customers or clients. Typical occupations were engineer, sales clerk, assembly-line worker, and bank teller. The establishment of laboratories and planning departments by large corporations to conduct research and development activities has greatly enlarged the range of occupations required. In addition, the changed technology based on research and development activities continues to create new occupational needs while older occupational roles become obsolete.

Under current conditions of rapid technological change, substantial changes in occupational requirements, and consequently in career lines, may be anticipated. Under these con-

---

42. *See* Talcott Parsons, *Structure and Process in Modern Societies* (Glencoe, Ill.: Free Press, 1960), pp. 16–96. Parsons identifies a third level, but since this consists mainly of board members, it can be disregarded for present purposes. *See* Simon Marcson, *The Scientist in American Industry* (Princeton, N.J.: Department of Economics, 1960), for a discussion of the nature of and demand for colleague control.

ditions, a corporation may not require occupational stability, but rather demand flexibility to meet the requirements of a rapidly changing technology. Consequently, both the corporation and its workers face the problem of how best to meet changing conditions. From the standpoint of the corporation, several choices may be open: some workers may be retired early, others may be retrained, and still others may be discharged at the same time that new personnel with more appropriate education and training are hired.

To attract and retain competent scientific and professional personnel, such as chemists, chemical engineers, physicists, and economists, corporations have had to establish career lines that provide adequate opportunities for upward career mobility. These career lines are characterized by much larger salary differentials between the top and the bottom than those found in the older technical operations, thus altering the pyramidal nature of corporate structures. In the earlier stages of the transition, tensions tended to develop between scientists, who preferred to have considerable autonomy (colleague control), and managers, who considered that scientists should conform closely to the directives of management (hierarchical control).

Corporations require capable and loyal managers at all decision-making levels. The primary task of managerial personnel is to make the decisions required to meet the problems that arise as the corporation carries on its functions and attempts to make a successful adjustment to changing conditions in its industry and in the society in general. Thus, the content of supervisory and administrative tasks does not remain constant. Furthermore, expectations with respect to initiative, knowledge of technical procedures, and human relations skills also change with the prevailing patterns of the times and with changing technology; they also change (at an increasing rate) because of the impact of new knowledge from the social and behavioral sciences.

Corporations are administered from the top of a pyramidal authoritative structure. Policies, procedures, and major operating decisions are made by board chairmen, presidents, and other high-ranking executives. These officers also establish and administer punishments and rewards for performance, and they establish and monitor the major outlines of the social structure. Really major decisions may be ratified by the board of directors, but operating decisions, some of tremendous magnitude, are made by the principal officers and carried out by subordinates. Although conformity with some of the forms of democracy (for example, participation in minor decisions) seems slowly to be gaining ground in corporations, it appears that, for the most part, lower-ranking officers and workers are expected to obey directives and comply with the rules established by high-ranking supervisors and other officials.[43] Ordinarily, obedience is exacted subtly and rude coercive tactics are seldom employed; this is to a considerable extent a result of the human relations emphasis to which we have already alluded. But even though subordinates are frequently encouraged to call their supervisors by their first names, major decisions, in most cases, are still in the hands of top management rather than in the hands of workers or middle management. In fact, there is evidence that democratic forms are used for manipulative purposes. As Blau and Scott have argued, real democracy would permit workers to veto management decisions and, except when exacted through strikes or threats of strikes, this seldom occurs.[44]

Some available evidence indicates, particularly in the case of corporations employing professionals, that an approach that gives professionals the sense of participating in decisions affecting their activities leads to better morale and possibly to higher productivity.[45]

The bureaucratic hierarchically arranged form of organization, as might be anticipated, has the effect of focusing the attention of the employees and officials of corporations upward, especially the attention of those who aspire to administrative careers themselves. It is also true that many studies of

43. James C. Worthy, *Big Business and Free Men* (New York: Harper and Bros., 1959), p. 56.
44. Blau and Scott, *Formal Organizations*, p. 186.
45. Presthus, *The Organizational Society*, chapter IX, "The Social Dysfunctions of Organizations."

the structure and operation of corporations have focused on the higher levels of administration, especially on the use of authority. Again this is to be expected because of the central importance of the higher-ranking positions to the conduct of the affairs of a corporation.

As we said, the structure of management positions in most corporations is shaped like a pyramid, with many first-line supervisors and only one president. Thus, the generalized model of the managerial career line leads from the lowest level of management through successive stages to the office of president. As a practical matter, however, the foreman very seldom has an opportunity for promotion to higher administrative levels. Members of higher management are now generally college graduates, frequently recruited as management trainees, who have been promoted through the several successive steps in the hierarchical career line.

In view of the pyramidal shape of management structures, only a few of any particular cohort of young men who start together as management trainees, if any, will eventually succeed in reaching the higher positions in the corporation. From the corporation's standpoint, this weeding-out process is one way to build efficient managerial staffs and to keep staff members alert. From the standpoint of the person who has great expectations, but who is unsuccessful, grave personal and social adjustments may be involved. In some cases, those failing to win advancement to the next position simply remain at the lower position; in other cases, they are discharged or resign and seek other employment. As in the case of technical workers, early retirement is one device sometimes used to meet the problem of what to do with managerial personnel who do not keep up with the timetable for advancement to the highest positions.

Norman H. Martin and Anselm H. Strauss have described the operation of managerial career lines in specific but unnamed industrial firms. They report that lower levels of management in a firm with complex technology were staffed by technical specialists whose promotion opportunities were confined to specific occupations, whereas in another firm with simpler technology, junior managers were shifted from one type of work to another to provide them with experience in different types of supervision. In both cases, the patterns were considered to be due to the perceptions of organizational requirements by top managers.[46]

Martin and Strauss also report that the industrial organizations they studied had well-established time tables or age ranges for various positions; thus, a person might fail to be promoted because he was too young but if he had not been promoted by a certain age he was unlikely ever to be promoted. They note that managers who reach high executive positions are promoted rapidly, frequently being promoted ahead of nominal superiors.[47] In an automobile parts company with several plants, the principal career line leading to top management was located in the largest plant, and most top executives had worked there.[48] Commenting further about managerial career lines in this company, Martin and Strauss observed that managers who were not able to compete for positions on the central career line had alternative, though less attractive, career opportunities in middle management, including smaller plants.[49]

It appears that industrial corporations move managers through various levels of their career lines in accordance with perceived organizational needs.

4. AGENCIES OF FEDERAL GOVERNMENT

The federal government, with hundreds of agencies and field installations in the United States and abroad, now provides many career opportunities. A very large number of different occupations are required, most of them professional,

46. Norman H. Martin and Anselm H. Strauss, "Patterns of Mobility within Industrial Organizations," *Journal of Business*, vol. 29, no. 2 (April 1956), pp. 101–10. Reprinted in part in Glaser, *Organizational Careers*, pp. 203–10.
47. Ibid, p. 204.
48. Ibid., p. 206–7.
49. Martin and Strauss, "Patterns of Mobility," p. 207.

managerial, and other white-collar occupations rather than blue-collar occupations.

In the executive branch of the federal government, only the president and the vice-president are elected. Most other employees, except policy-level officials, are occupational specialists.

Nearly all civilian agencies are organized and operated in accordance with bureaucratic principles, although modifications have been made to accommodate the career needs of scientists and professional personnel. Little, if any, corruption is found, and a high level of performance is maintained by most agencies. This outstanding record of accomplishment is due in large measure to high standards of recruitment, rewards for competent occupational performance, protection from capricious dismissal, and other career incentives.

Professional career lines, especially in research and development agencies, provide opportunities for promotion comparable to those found in major universities.

5. EDUCATIONAL ORGANIZATIONS

The growing emphasis on education at all levels provides, and will continue to provide, attractive career opportunities in educational organizations for many men and women.

Even though the demand for teachers is no longer as great as it was during the 1960s, educational organizations will continue to provide attractive career opportunities for both men and women. In 1970 the number of teachers in elementary and secondary schools totaled 2,540,000, of whom 743,000 were men and 1,797,000 were women. Institutions of higher learning reported 933,000 positions for teachers and administrators in 1971–72.

Professional employment in educational systems is restricted to those who successfully complete the educational requirements specified. These requirements differ for the different levels of education with increasing subject-matter specialization at the higher levels. Many occupational specialties are required and diverse career lines have been established, including lines for subject matter specialists of all types, counselors, research workers, and supervisors and administrators.

Education is already "big business," and it is certain to get bigger. With growing recognition of the essential nature of the contribution of intellectual activity to national growth and survival, the prestige of educational occupations will doubtless improve still further in the future.[50]

Elementary Schools.[51] It appears that elementary education at public expense was initially designed in large measure to assist in the process of "Americanizing" or assimilating the children of immigrants. It was not until 1850 that the principle of the use of property taxation as a basis for the support of elementary education had been established in the northern states. Free public education at the elementary level did not become available generally in the South until 1870.

Most of the early public elementary schools were rural schools, because the great bulk of the population of the United States in the early nineteenth century lived on farms. These early rural schools were mostly one-teacher, one-room schools located in the open country serving principally the children of farmers. They were not very good schools by modern standards, but they did provide basic literacy training, usually during a term of three to five months during the winter. Uniform textbooks and graded courses of study did not appear much before 1880.

With the growth of industry and the concomitant concentration of population in cities, elementary schools were enlarged and their offerings extended, largely at public expense. In the northeastern part of the United States, however, private schools are still of considerable importance, as well as parochial schools operated by the Catholic church and some other religious orders in many sections of the country.

The "founding fathers" did not consider education of suffi-

50. Gilbert Burck, "Knowledge: The Biggest Growth Industry of Them All," *Fortune* (November 1964), pp. 128–31.

51. *See* Elwood P. Cubberly, *Rural Life and Education* (New York: Houghton Mifflin Co., 1914), for a discussion of the development of early elementary schools.

cient public importance to be given specific treatment in the Constitution because education, at the time, was largely restricted to sons of gentlemen. Accordingly, its support and control were left to the several states. The states, in turn, delegated responsibility for many aspects of elementary and secondary school operations to counties and local school districts.

In most instances, members of local school boards are elected. Their defined responsibilities include approval of budgets, employment of teachers, determination of certain aspects of curriculum, and, in some cases, selection of school books, although the major outlines of curriculum are ordinarily prescribed by the chief state school officer and his assistants. This has been true from the beginning of free public elementary education in America, and this tradition of local control is one reason why the elementary schools are generally regarded primarily as agencies for the transmission of the existing culture rather than as systems for the development of new ideas and values.

Most elementary schoolteachers are women. The teacher and her pupils can be regarded as a social system, and the school is a formal organization rather than an informal group. The teacher is appointed by outside authority and pupils are required to attend, if able-bodied and mentally competent, until they have completed a certain grade or reached a certain age. The teacher provides leadership for both educational work and extracurricular activities. In a one-room rural school, the several roles are intermingled. In the city schools and in consolidated rural schools, specialization of roles tends to develop, although until junior high school, students generally are in contact with a single teacher, whose role, since most elementary schoolteachers are women, has been characterized by some social psychologists as that of a substitute mother.

Secondary Schools.[52] The expectation that all adolescents should obtain a high school education is a unique American

52. H. G. Good, *A History of American Education* (New York: Macmillan Co., 2d ed., 1962), pp. 233–61.

development of the twentieth century that has occurred in response to public demand.

Many more men teach in secondary than in elementary schools, and secondary teachers tend to be specialists in specific subject areas, particularly in the larger urban schools. In addition to teachers, vocational counselors and other occupational specialists are required. Changes in curriculum and course contents due to scientific and technological progress make it necessary for many teachers to update their knowledge in order to perform adequately. This is usually accomplished through summer school courses.

As in the case of elementary schools, the control of secondary education resides to a major extent in the hands of local school boards, and many of the observations concerning elementary education also apply to secondary education.

Institutions of Higher Learning. There are a number of different types of institutions of higher learning, including small liberal arts colleges, institutions devoted mainly to the preparation of teachers (formerly called normal schools, later teachers colleges, and now state colleges), public universities, and private universities.

The Land-Grant colleges and universities played a very important part in the development of higher education in this country as it exists today.[53] Prior to the establishment of these institutions under the Morrill Act of 1862, American universities emphasized classical learning and preparation for the professions of medicine, law, and the ministry. In contrast, the Land-Grant colleges and universities emphasized science, especially its practical applications in agriculture and engineering. At present, the Land-Grant institutions do not differ materially from other large institutions of higher learning, and nearly all state colleges of agriculture and mechanical arts have now adopted the name of universities. Most of them are universities in the sense that they are large and complex organizations consisting of many subsidiary colleges or schools,

53. Slocum, *Agricultural Sociology*, pp. 432–41.

each with subsidiary departments usually organized on the basis of one or at the most two academic disciplines.

Modern universities conduct a substantial amount of research. In terms of the employment opportunities and the occupational specialties that are involved, the major distinctions today are not between public and private universities but between universities that carry out research and liberal arts colleges, teacher-training institutions, and junior colleges that do relatively little research.

Various aspects of the career line of the university professor have been discussed in some detail by sociologists.[54] The occupation of professor is not a single professional field but many professions; all professors must "profess" something. Most of them are professors of an established academic discipline, such as chemistry, physics, sociology, or English, but occasionally their titles show that they are authorities in some extremely specialized branch of knowledge. The University of Nebraska, for example, has a Professor of Sweet Clover.[55]

The four standard academic ranks in the professional career line in most American institutions of higher learning are: instructor, assistant professor, associate professor, and professor. In addition, a few universities have endowed chairs in particular fields. In large universities a fairly large number of professional employees do not teach but carry on research, conduct adult education activities, or perform duties other than classroom teaching. These positions occasionally have professorial titles, but some universities give "equivalent" titles such as artist in residence, soils scientist, or agricultural extension specialist.

Administrative career lines exist, but there is a tendency in academic circles to regard administration as an occupation that "seeks the man" rather than vice versa. Furthermore,

54. *See* Logan Wilson, *The Academic Man* (London: Oxford University Press, 1942), and Theodore Caplow and Reece McGee, *The Academic Marketplace* (New York: Basic Books, 1958).
55. *USDA Directory of Experiment Station Workers* (Washington, D.C.: U.S. Department of Agriculture, 1971).

many faculty members have ambivalent feelings about administration because they prefer an alternative that has been called "colleague control," a system where final authority is vested in the faculty rather than in the administrator.[56] Adherence to this model is strongest in universities of the highest prestige. In some institutions of higher learning, the faculty has little voice in policy decisions.

The administrative career line in a university is often entered "through the back door." In many institutions, a professor is not supposed to seek to become a department head or a dean, nor a dean to become a president, and it is not unusual for a person who does make overt efforts to shift to the administrative career line to be passed over because he has sought the appointment.

6. THE MILITARY

The armed forces can be regarded as work organizations, although their basic mission is much different from the missions of other work organizations. From colonial times until World War I, the American military establishment was small and enjoyed relatively little prestige. Even in 1973, when approximately 2.2 million men were in uniform, and much of the federal budget was allocated for defense activities, many people thought of the military organization as temporary. Some people still hold the traditional pre-World War II view that the United States can meet peacetime national defense needs with volunteers and meet potential wartime emergencies with hastily trained civilian manpower as in the past. Contrary to such views, the defense needs of the nation appear to require permanent large-scale armed forces. The fact is that military services offer meaningful occupational career lines for commissioned officers, noncommissioned officers, and various technical occupations.

The social structure of the military service is characterized by marked differences in social status between enlisted men and officers; in addition, there are specific ranks within the

56. Marcson, *Scientist in American Industry.*

officer corps and specific grades among enlisted personnel. Traditionally, seniority (even down to date of rank) has been very important in determining duty assignments and housing and other perquisites. Seniority is still important, but promotion by merit rather than chiefly by seniority is now customary. To insure rational consideration of merit, selection boards periodically review the records of officers above the lowest three ranks and recommend retention, promotion, or retirement. Because of the emphasis on physical fitness, early retirement is prevalent, and second careers are possible for many early retirees.

The impact of science on military technology has greatly changed the required occupational skills. In contrast to the relatively simple skills of the medieval archer, cavalryman, or swordsman, great complexity now characterizes occupations of combat forces and supporting personnel. Further changes may be anticipated, since still further complexity will characterize the weapons systems of the future.

As the technology of the military services has changed, so have the occupational assignments of military personnel. Chemists, physicists, psychologists, and sociologists have occupational knowledge and skills now used by the armed forces. Many professional roles used by the military are the same in all essential respects as those performed by their civilian counterparts. Unskilled personnel now constitute a minority, rather than a majority, of military personnel. This is a recent development, because even as late as World War II the majority were not technicians.

This emphasis on skill and knowledge requires a higher level of educational attainment than in the past. The military services could not function successfully if staffed by school drop-outs, delinquents, or other unskilled or undesirable elements of society. To fulfill their mission, the armed services must have at least a proportionate share of the best-qualified, best-educated, and most competent personnel. To obtain and retain such personnel, attractive career lines have been established, salaries increased, and efforts made to improve the image of the military.

The U.S. Department of Defense also employs a large

number of civilian workers, most of these employed under the provisions of the classified civil service. Some are hourly rated employees who work in navy yards, arsenals, and similar military factories, even though most arms, ammunition, equipment, and supplies used by the armed forces are manufactured by civilian corporations.

Thus, it appears that the occupational requirements of the armed services resemble, in many important respects, those found in the civilian sector of the economy, although the specialized training and indoctrination in the combat mission of the armed services are unique.

Conclusion

The information reviewed in this chapter indicates that there are many similarities in the general occupational requirements of different types of modern work organizations. For example, all except family farms and small family businesses need occupational specialists and managers. There are many differences in detail, since we know that the specific occupational specialties required by a particular firm, agency, or other work organization are governed by the nature of the services or products involved. Furthermore, the technical requirements, folkways, and ideological orientations of members of a particular work organization may create rather unique role expectations for occupational specialists. Thus, it may be necessary for an economist, for instance, to reorient his occupational skills as well as to gain acceptance as a person when he moves from a government agency to a business firm. Although details of this kind cannot be covered adequately in a general treatment of occupational careers, they obviously have great importance to individuals. Reading company regulations and job descriptions, questioning prospective employers and colleagues, and observation of the behavior of others within a specific work organization appear to be the most useful methods of gathering relevant information.

Selected References

Presthus, Robert. *The Organizational Society*. New York: Alfred A. Knopf and Random House, Vintage Books, 1965. A provocative discussion of how individuals cope with organizational realities.

Warner, W. Lloyd, and Martin, Norman H., eds. *Industrial Man*. New York: Harper and Bros., 1959. A collection of articles on various facets of life in modern industrial organizations. See especially chapter 3, "The Career Line . . ." and chapter 5, "Industrial Hierarchies: The Social Structure of Business Enterprise."

Glaser, Barney G., ed. *Organizational Careers: A Sourcebook for Theory*. Chicago: Aldine Publishing Co., 1968. A compilation of articles from monographs and professional journals.

5. Occupational Status Levels

Social inequalities are found in every human society. This conclusion is based on evidence from history, from archeological studies of prehistoric man, and from anthropological studies of primitive contemporary societies as well as from sociological studies in modern industrialized countries. Research has also revealed that substantial differences exist in the social ranks assigned to members of all types of social systems within a society, including informal groups, business firms, government agencies, voluntary social organizations and communities. In contemporary America, the type of work a man does, together with the reputation he establishes at work, must be regarded as among the principal determinants of his social rank. In fact, occupation is such an important factor that it is frequently used by sociologists as the principal indicator of social class.

Our interest in this chapter is in the classification of occupations according to status level. This matter must be discussed at this point because many of the other concepts to be presented and much of the empirical data available to us from the census and from sociological studies can be interpreted satisfactorily only by reference to the concept of occupational status level. Our concern is not the social rank of a particular doctor or a particular carpenter or a particular farmer but rather the relative ranks that may be assigned to these and other occupations. This does not mean that differences in social rank do not exist among practitioners of a particular profession or other occupation. Such differences obviously do exist; the esteem with which a particular doctor (or an occupant of another occupational role) is held is extremely important in determining *his* personal social rank. Furthermore, the reputation that an individual establishes in performing his occupational roles is one of the principal factors in determining the nature of his career in the occupation; discussion of this aspect of the subject, however, must be deferred until later.

The status level of an occupation may be regarded as an aspect of culture. This becomes evident when we note that the status level of a given occupation at any particular time is based upon collective judgments, particularly those made earlier and thus regarded as customary.

Over long periods of time changes of very substantial magnitude occur in the status levels of various occupations. For example, in the United States the status level of scientific occupations appears to be rising, primarily because of the recognition by others of the contributions of scientists to the development of modern industrialized society; at the same time, the prestige of manual workers, although never really high, has obviously declined and is likely to decline further.

A principal component of occupational status level is the prestige of the occupation. Other important dimensions are money, power, and the nature of the work involved in the occupation. Another dimension involves the amount of education or other prerequisites for entry into the occupation. All other elements are reflected in prestige, except for illegitimate occupations such as those of the underworld.

A number of thorny problems are involved in the determination of occupational status levels. It is not difficult to determine that status differences exist between king and commoner, between corporation president and assembly-line worker, between master and slave, or between professional and unskilled manual worker. Nevertheless, how to assign status levels to occupations that fall between the high and the low extremes has not been answered in a completely satisfactory way; it may indeed be unanswerable. Another difficulty is attributable to the proliferation of occupational roles in modern industrialized society. Many modern occupational roles are unknown outside the specific factory, research laboratory, or other work organization in which they are found. The general public is unable to rank such occupations, although rankings are undoubtedly established within the specific work system where they are found. The relationship of the specific new technological role to a general occupational category must be considered in order to ascertain its probable status level in relation to other occupations.

It is not possible in this book to consider in detail the complex problems involved in the development of an adequate system of classification affecting occupational stratification or to review the voluminous literature that already exists on the subject.[1] As suggested above, there are many unsolved problems. Nevertheless, the concept of occupational status level is essential to a discussion of occupational mobility and also to a consideration of the sociological aspects of occupational careers. Consequently, in the next few pages we shall present information concerning the systems of classification that have been employed in most recent studies.

The U.S. Census Classification of Occupational Status

The occupational status scale most widely used in the United States is the occupational status classification adopted by the U.S. Bureau of the Census for the 1940 census. The basic developmental work on this scale was done by Alba M. Edwards, a former member of the Census Bureau staff.[2] With

1. For additional information, *see* Reinhard Bendix and Seymour M. Lipset, eds., *Class, Status and Power*, A Reader in Social Stratification (Glencoe, Ill.: Free Press, 1963), and A. J. Reiss, Jr., *Occupations and Social Status* (Glencoe, Ill.: Free Press, 1961), for material prior to 1963. For publications in the last few years, *see* the *American Sociological Review*, the *American Journal of Sociology*, and other sociological journals.

2. Alba M. Edwards, *Comparative Occupational Statistics for the United States, 1870–1940* (Washington, D.C.: U.S. Government Printing Office, 1943).

some modifications, this scale has been used in classifying individual census returns since 1940.

As initially proposed, the major categories of the occupational classification scheme as proposed by Edwards are[3]:

> "1. Professional persons
> 2. Proprietors, managers and officials:
>   2-a. Farmers (owners and tenants)
>   2-b. Wholesale and retail dealers
>   2-c. Other proprietors, managers, and officials
> 3. Clerks and kindred workers
> 4. Skilled workers and foremen
> 5. Semi-skilled workers
> 6. Unskilled workers
>   6-a. Farm laborers
>   6-b. Laborers, except farm
>   6-c. Servant classes"

This system of classification is based primarily upon occupational duties.[4] The occupational composition of the six categories is reasonably clear except for the placement of technicians and sales workers. However, the Census Bureau has since made a number of modifications. The classification, used in the 1970 census, included the following categories: Professional, technical and kindred workers; farmers and farm managers; managers, officials and proprietors, except farm; clerical and kindred workers; sales workers; craftsmen, foremen and kindred workers; private household workers; service workers, except private household; farm laborers; laborers, except farm and mine; and operatives (unskilled).

Trends in these major occupational categories for the United States as a whole are presented and discussed in the next chapter.

Edwards regarded his occupational classification as a scale

3. Ibid., p. 176.
4. P. K. Hatt, "Occupations and Social Stratification," in Reiss, *Occupations and Social Status*, p. 245.

reflecting real and significant differences in the duties and life-styles of members of the labor force classified into the major categories or "social-economic groups." In his words:

> "The social-economic groups are something more than large subdivisions of the nation's labor force; and they are something more than mere summary groups constructed to facilitate the discussion of the broader aspects of the labor force. Each of them represent a distinctive part of the labor force—a part with its own peculiar characteristics and having its own peculiar significance. . . . In some measure, also, each group has characteristic interests and convictions as to numerous public questions—social, economic, and political. Each of them is thus a really distinct and highly significant social-economic group." [5]

Edwards asked if these categories fulfilled the need for an occupational status scale. "We need a scale for measuring the *social-economic status* of large segments of a labor force. . . . Do the social-economic groups . . . constitute such a scale?" [6] He answered his question affirmatively, pointing out that 1939 median incomes and years of school completed by workers as of 1940 were consistent with this interpretation.

In spite of its use by the Census Bureau, other government agencies, and many researchers, however, the census occupational classification is not without its critics. In response to early criticism, Edwards acknowledged that six categories are too few for more than approximate measurement.

> "When over 52,000,000 workers are grouped into only 6 groups . . . the groups will . . . be somewhat general, with some overlapping of groups, and with a considerable range in the social-economic status of the workers included in each group." [7]

5. Ibid., p. 179.
6. Ibid., p. 181.
7. Ibid., p. 182.

Paul K. Hatt criticized the census scale for overlapping between categories and because he was not convinced that the categories reflected differences in prestige recognized by the public.[8]

The NORC Scale of Occupational Prestige

The sociological importance of occupational prestige has led a number of sociologists to ask respondents representing various populations to rank selected occupations. Experience has demonstrated that people are able to make judgments about the relative prestige of many occupations. Furthermore, there is a substantial amount of agreement about the ranking of certain well known occupations, especially those usually classified as either high or low. Not only is this true in the United States, but, as Alex Inkeles and Peter Rossi have shown, it appears to be true among the industrialized nations of the Western world.[9] This suggests that the values that underlie occupational prestige in such countries are associated with and affected by scientific and technological developments.

The prestige scale most widely used is the NORC scale which was developed by Paul K. Hatt and Cecil North. In 1946, these sociologists made an exploratory study of the "social standing" of occupations in Columbus and Hamilton, Ohio.[10] Responses to their list of 79 occupations led them to propose to the National Opinion Research Center at the University of Chicago (NORC) that their approach be utilized in a nationwide sample. The proposal was accepted and the list of occupations was enlarged to ninety.

8. Ibid., p. 245.
9. "National Comparisons of Occupational Prestige," *American Journal of Sociology* (January 1956), pp. 329–39.
10. National Opinion Research Center, "Jobs and Occupations: A Popular Evaluation," reprinted in Bendix and Lipset, *Class, Status and Power.*

Ratings of the prestige of these occupations was obtained by personal interview from 2,920 respondents in a nationwide study conducted by NORC in 1947. The respondents were asked to rate each of the ninety occupations in accordance with the following instructions:

"For each job mentioned, please pick out the statement which best gives *your own personal opinion* of the *general standing* that such a job has: 1. *excellent* standing. 2. *good* standing. 3. *average* standing. 4. *somewhat below* average standing. 5. *poor* standing. x. I don't know where to place that one."

Eighty-three per cent of the respondents rated the position of United States Supreme Court Justice as excellent; out of a maximum of a possible 100 points, the average score for the supreme court justice was 96. The nine occupations with the next highest scores were: physician, 93; state governor, 93; cabinet member in the federal government, 92; diplomat in the United States foreign service, 92; mayor of a large city, 90; college professor, 89; scientist, 89; United States representative in Congress, 89; and banker, 88,

The ten lowest ranking occupations, of which only three received rankings of excellent from more than 1 per cent of the respondents, were: dock worker, 47; night watchman, 47; clothes presser in a laundry, 46; soda fountain clerk, 45; bartender, 44; janitor, 44; sharecropper, 40; garbage collector, 35; street sweeper, 34; and shoeshiner, 33.

The comparative rankings of general categories of occupations as reported by North and Hatt are listed in the table on page 131.

Specific occupations have been placed in categories which correspond rather closely to those developed by Edwards and used by the United States Census Bureau.

In an attempt to ascertain what factors people believe to be responsible for the high prestige of occupations that they rate as excellent, the following question was included in the 1947 survey: "When you say that certain jobs have 'excellent standing,' what do you think is the one *main* thing about such

Classification of Occupation[11]	Number of Occupations	Average Score
Government officials	8	90.8
Professional & semiprofessional workers	30	80.6
Proprietors, managers and officials (except farm)	11	74.9
Clerical, sales and kindred workers	6	68.2
Craftsmen, foremen, and kindred workers	7	68.0
Farmers and farm managers	3	61.3
Protective service workers	3	58.0
Operatives and kindred workers	8	52.8
Farm laborers	1	50.0
Service workers (except domestic and protective)	7	46.7
Laborers (except farm)	6	45.8

jobs that gives this standing?" The pattern of response revealed relatively little agreement. The most frequent response, which emphasized a good income, was given by only 18 per cent. This pattern of response suggests that in 1947 not many people had given previous thought to this question. In all probability this is still the case. In appraising the evaluation of the relative prestige of an occupation by members of the general public, it should be borne in mind that, while some people are very sensitive to social rank, including occupational status level, others probably give matters of this kind little, if any, attention.

A. J. Reiss, Jr., has observed that "few empirical studies have achieved a place in the scientific literature of sociology comparable to that of the NORC–North-Hatt investigation."[12] P. K. Hatt claimed that the scale could be used to identify exactly or estimate accurately the prestige ratings of two-thirds to three-fourths of gainfully employed persons.[13] The scale has been used in this manner by a number of investigators.[14]

11. Adapted from ibid., p. 414.
12. Ibid., p. 7.
13. Ibid. p. 250.
14. Reiss has listed seven studies illustrating the use of the NORC scale as a "skeletal prestige structure, within which the prestige standing of unrated occupations may be guessed," *Occupations and Social Status.*

Duncan's Socioeconomic Status Index

Using data from the 1950 census and the NORC study, Otis Dudley Duncan constructed a socioeconomic status index that makes it possible to assign socioeconomic status scores to the census categories. The categories thus apparently reflect more accurately the prestige evaluations of the public and may presumably be used with greater confidence in studies of occupational stratification or occupational mobility.[15] In developing the scale, Duncan utilized census information on income and education for workers of various age groups and prestige information from the NORC study.[16]

The scores on the socioeconomic index of the major occupational categories of the census as computed by Duncan for 1950 are as follows[17]:

Major Occupation Group	Score
All occupations	30
Professional, technical and kindred workers	75
Managers, officials, and proprietors except farm	57
Sales workers	49
Clerical and kindred workers	45
Craftsmen, foremen, and kindred workers	18
Operatives and kindred workers	18
Service workers, excluding private household	17
Farmers and farm managers	14
Farm laborers and foremen	9
Private-household workers	8
Laborers except farm and mine	7

It will be noted that sales workers rate slightly above clerical workers and that farmers rate far below other proprietors. Duncan has suggested that it is doubtful if farmers should be placed in the same status category with other proprietors and

15. O. D. Duncan, chapter VI, "A Socio-Economic Index for All Occupations," in Reiss, *Occupations and Social Status*.
16. Ibid., pp. 114–28.
17. Ibid., p. 155.

managers, as Edwards proposed, although he has acknowledged that some farmers operate larger farms and hence, by implication, may deserve higher ranks than indicated by the average score. Duncan presents evidence that the average scores for most categories (but not for farmers) hide sizable variations in the rankings of specific occupations.[18]

Occupational Differences in Income

The emphasis given by sociologists to prestige fails to give adequate weight to the fact that for most people achievement of life-styles characterized by high levels of consumption of goods and services depends mainly upon earned income. Compensation levels are obviously an important determinant of occupational status.

Differences between major occupational categories are substantial but differences between male and female workers can only be described as tremendous (table 1). On the average, among year-round full-time workers, men earned almost twice as much as women in 1971, and in some major occupational categories the differentials were even greater.

The differences between specific occupations in earnings are obscured by the broad categories of the modified Edwards scale used by the U.S. Census Bureau. This is made clear by information from table 1 which shows that two-thirds of self-employed and 42 per cent of salaried male physicians and surgeons earned $25,000 or more in 1971, an income level earned by only 8.3 per cent of all male (and only 0.2 per cent of all female) professional, technical, and kindred workers.

Even the statistics for physicians and surgeons presented in table 1 do not show the large differences that undoubtedly exist between specialists and between beginners and well established practitioners.

18. Ibid., pp. 156–59, and table VII-5.

TABLE 1. Total Earnings of Year-Round Full-time Civilian Workers 14 Years Old and Over in 1971

Occupation	Number of Workers (Thousands)		Average Earnings		Per cent $25,000 and over	
	Male	Female	Male	Female	Male	Female
Professional, technical and kindred	5,733	2,920	$13,960	8,436	8.3	0.4
Physicians and surgeons						
Self-employed	111	4	31,604	(B)	67.3	(B)
Salaried	116	23	25,100	(B)	42.0	(B)
Engineers	980	7	15,177	(B)	6.1	(B)
Teachers, elementary and secondary	770	1,356	10,526	8,299	0.7	0.1
Farmers and farm managers	1,280	34	5,194	(B)	1.7	(B)
Business proprietors	1,079	195	11,090	4,695	7.2	0.7
Retail trade	590	143	9,401	4,087	3.8	0
Managers, salaried	4,642	797	14,948	7,959	10.8	0.5
Clerical work	2,597	6,273	9,232	5,791	0.8	0.5
Sales work	2,287	682	12,000	4,951	6.1	0.2
Retail trade	681	531	8,860	4,326	2.1	0.3
Craftsmen and kindred	7,889	235	9,772	6,129	0.3	0.6
Foremen	1,197	84	11,081	7,550	1.0	3.5
Craftsmen	6,691	151	9,537	5,335	0.2	0
Operatives	6,514	2,260	8,081	4,873	0.2	0.1
Service work	2,554	2,139	7,499	4,214	0.1	0.1
Farm labor	399	50	4,062	(B)	–	(B)
Laborers, nonfarm	1,839	107	6,958	4,447	0.4	0
Domestic servants	9	309	(B)	2,180	–	0
All workers	36,819	16,002	10,395	5,900	3.5	0.2

(B) Base less than 75,000.
(Z) Less than 0.05 per cent.
SOURCE: U.S. Census Bureau, *Money Income in 1971 of Families and Persons in the United States*, series P-60, no. 85 (Washington, D.C.: USGPO, 1972), pp. 128–129.

Change and Stability in Occupational Stratification

Occupational status level is used not only as a measure of the relative ranks of various occupations but also in judging the career achievements of individuals and in evaluating their social ranks. Consequently, it is important to us to know whether occupational stratification is relatively stable or whether it is subject to rapid and drastic change.

The best available evidence indicates that the American occupational status structure has been quite stable for at least forty years. Robert W. Hodge, Paul M. Siegel, and Peter H. Rossi of NORC, in a small-scale replication in 1963 of the 1947 NORC study, found that only small changes had occurred in the prestige ratings of major occupational categories. On the other hand, there was evidence of change in the prestige ratings of specific occupations. For example, all of the scientific occupations, except economists, had higher prestige ratings in 1963.[19] The same authors compared their findings with those of earlier investigators and concluded that ". . . *there have been no substantial changes in occupational prestige in the United States since 1925*"[20] (emphasis in the original).

It is interesting to learn that the major features of occupational stratification have been relatively stable during the past forty years, but we should not assume that this means that the same kind of stability will persist indefinitely. It seems reasonable to expect continuation of the current pattern for the next ten years or so, but it is my opinion that it would be quite hazardous to project these trends very far into the future in view of the sweeping changes in occupations that rapid scientific and technological development may cause.

Another attempt to measure changes in occupational status was made by Charles B. Nam and Mary G. Powers who compared the 1960 and 1950 status scores of nearly 500 occupations using the Duncan Index for 1950 and a similar scoring scheme for 1960.[21] They found ninety-two occupations for which the scores differed by ten points or more; of these, only four had higher scores while eighty-eight had lower scores. Those with higher scores were professional athletes, hucksters and peddlers, laborers employed by manufacturers of photographic equipment and supplies, and pattern and model

19. Robert W. Hodge, Paul M. Siegel, and Peter H. Rossi, "Occupational Prestige in the United States, 1925-1963," *The American Journal of Sociology* (November 1964), pp. 286–302.

20. Ibid., p. 296.

21. Charles B. Nam and Mary G. Powers, "Changes in the Relative Status Levels of Workers in the United States, 1950-60," *Social Forces*, 47 (December 1968), pp. 167–70.

makers. The higher status of professional athletes was attributed to higher incomes; pattern and model makers had more education and higher incomes; and the other two occupations both had sharp increases in educational levels of workers.

The occupations with declining status were classified into four categories according to major characteristics of workers. All of these occupations experienced relatively smaller increases in educational levels and income during the decade. The first category, with increasing numbers and a rising age level, included such occupations as bus drivers, proprietors of restaurants and bars, messengers and office boys, operatives in business and repair services, housekeepers, and stewards and farm foremen. The second category, with increasing numbers and a declining age level, included such occupations as cashiers, bank tellers, recreation and group workers, guards, watchmen and doorkeepers, and gardeners. The third category, with decreasing numbers and an increasing age level, included such occupations as bakers, bookbinders, loomfixers, tailors, upholsterers, and operatives and laborers in many industries—occupations thought to be declining in importance or in which workers are being replaced by technology. The fourth category, with decreasing numbers and age levels, included apprentices, railroad inspectors, and some operatives.[22]

A review of the changes identified by Nam and Powers makes it clear that the conclusion of Hodge, Siegel, and Rossi that there have not been any *substantial* recent changes in occupational *prestige* can also be extended to other aspects of occupational *status*.

Selected References

Edwards, Alba M. *Comparative Occupational Statistics for the United States 1870–1940*. Washington, D.C.: U.S. Census

---

22. Nam and Powers, "Changes in the Relative Status Levels of Workers in the United States," pp. 163–65.

Bureau, U.S. Government Printing Office, 1943. This publication describes the occupational classification scale proposed by Edwards and presents comparative occupational data for the period covered.

National Opinion Research Center. "Jobs and Occupations: A Popular Evaluation," in Reinhard Bendix and S. M. Lipset, eds., *Class, Status and Power*. Glencoe, Ill.: Free Press, 1953. This description of the 1947 NORC study of occupational prestige is reprinted from the September 1947 issue of *Opinion News*, vol. IX.

Nam, Charles B., and Powers, Mary G., "Changes in the Relative Status Levels of Workers in the United States 1950–60," *Social Forces* 47 (December 1968). This article presents a comparison of the status scores of nearly 500 occupations, reflecting changes during the decade of the 1950s.

Reiss, Albert J., Jr., with Duncan, Otis Dudley, Hatt, Paul K. and North, Cecil C. *Occupations and Social Status*. Glencoe, Ill.: Free Press, 1961. This book presents a critical review by Reiss of the methodological problems of the NORC scale and the procedure and rationale for Duncan's socioeconomic index as well as papers written by Hatt and North concerning the scale.

6. Labor Force, Employment and Unemployment Trends

Many people neither work nor seek gainful employment. Some are too young, some are retired or mentally or physically ill, others devote themselves exclusively to homemaking, or abstain from paid work for other reasons. A substantial number of people work on a part-time basis, and at the other extreme, some hold two or more jobs. We are concerned primarily with those who work for pay or profit, but it is impossible to disregard entirely those who are not working at any given time, because many people work on an intermittent basis. During their lifetime, nearly all able-bodied men and the great majority of women will be employed. All who work or seek work are considered members of the labor force.[1]

Nearly all American men participate continuously in the world of work after their first entry until retirement. The majority of women also participate in paid employment but, if they are married, generally on an intermittent basis as contrasted with men. Single women tend to participate in employment on substantially the same basis as men.

Before considering employment trends, we should note briefly some of the factors affecting the supply of workers and hence occupational competition.

Changes in Length of Working Life

Until the beginning of the twentieth century, relatively few women worked outside the home, the average expectation of

1. See U.S. Census of Population, 1960, for an operational definition of the labor force concept.

life was relatively short, and most men died while still employed. Great changes have occurred since 1900. The life expectancy for males at birth has increased from 48.2 years to 67.1, an increase of more than eighteen years; women have entered paid employment outside the home in increasing numbers; and retirement has become commonplace.

"Many older workers now withdraw from the labor force before they die. Fifty years ago death and disability accounted for practically all labor force separations. Only a small proportion of the population survived to the age which is now considered conventional for retirement. Moreover, in an agrarian economy, where self-employment predominated, those who reached an older age were often in a position to continue to do some work. Today, most important among the reasons for men fifty-five and over leaving the labor force are: age restrictions in hiring practices, compulsory retirement ages in private pension plans, widespread availability of social security for older persons, and inability to go on working (which tends to rise with age)." [2]

Another major change that has occurred since 1900 is the tendency for both males and females to enter full-time employment much later; the proportion of males aged fourteen to nineteen in the labor force dropped from 62.1 per cent in 1900 to 32 per cent in 1960 (Labor force statistics are no longer reported for persons under sixteen.) This change reflects the influences of legislation governing the conditions of employment of young people and especially of the rising educational requirements for participation in many occupations.

In spite of the increase in the age of average entry into and termination by retirement of full-time work, the work life expectancy of men has increased from thirty-two years in 1900 to forty-two years in 1955.[3] During the same period,

2. Stuart Garfinkle, "Changes in Working Life of Men, 1900–2000," *Monthly Labor Review* (March 1955), p. 299.

3. Seymour F. Wolfbein, "Labor Trends, Manpower, and Automation," in Henry Borow, ed., *Man in a World at Work* (Boston: Houghton Mifflin Co., 1964), pp. 156–57.

twelve additional years were added to the work life of women.[4] Seymour F. Wolfbein has commented on the significance of these changes:

"The sheer manpower potential from a given number of people has increased enormously. A group of 100,000 boys born in 1900 would produce about 3,200,000 man-years of work during their lifetimes; a similar number of boys born in 1960 will yield about 4,200,000 man-years of work during their lifetimes. A comparable group of girls today will produce close to 2,000,000 years of work during their lifetimes—triple the performance of their 1900 counterparts." [5]

Apart from the benefits to individuals from longer life, including a longer work life, substantial benefits have accrued to society because most of the young people educated at public expense now live long enough to make a substantial contribution as gainful workers. However, the increase in the number and proportion of older workers has also created some problems, because many employers prefer younger workers. This is particularly true of unskilled and semiskilled men, but it is also true of others including professionals. Unemployment rates are higher than average for young workers and for those over age forty.[6] Because many employers prefer younger men, those who lose their jobs after age forty find it difficult to obtain satisfactory employment even after retraining.

Increase in New Workers

Perhaps the most important population development since 1940 was the tremendous increase in births that followed the

4. Ibid.
5. Ibid., p. 157.
6. John F. Kennedy, *Manpower Report of the President* (Washington, D.C.: U.S. Government Printing Office, 1963), p. 40. *See* also Richard M. Nixon, *Manpower Report of the President*, 1970, p. 31.

end of World War II. The impact of this postwar "baby boom" has already been felt by the elementary and secondary schools and by many types of industrial and business establishments. In the middle 1960s, the first of these post-war babies reached maturity. As a consequence, college enrollments are increasing at phenomenal rates, and many hundreds of thousands are entering the job market. Additional increases will occur each year until the peak of 4.1 million is reached in 1975. The impact of the postwar increase in births will continue to be felt as young people compete with each other and with older persons for employment.

There will be very keen competition for many types of occupational positions in the future, particularly those with relatively low educational and skill requirements. It is not unlikely that pressure will mount before the end of the seventies for early retirement of older workers in order to create work opportunities for younger people. A further increase in the already great demand for education to prepare young people for occupations may be anticipated.

Employment of Women

The tremendous increase in the employment of women, especially middle-aged women, that has occurred in recent years has offset the removal of children from the labor force so that approximately the same percentage of the population was employed in 1960 as in 1900; the proportion of all persons fourteen years of age or over in the labor force was 53.7 per cent in 1900 and 55.5 per cent in 1970.[7]

Large numbers of women worked during World War II. This was thought at the time to be a temporary phenomenon that would disappear with the return of peace, but women have continued to work outside their homes in increasing numbers. Although only about one-third of employed workers

7. Wolfbein, "Labor Trends, Manpower, and Automation," p. 157.

in the United States in 1960 were women, about three-fifths of the increase in the labor force during the period of 1947–62 consisted of women; during this period the number of women workers age forty-five and over doubled.[8]

This pattern continued through the 1960s. In 1970, 39.2 per cent of employed workers were women, and the number of women forty-five and over in the labor force increased 45 per cent from 1960 to 1970. Seymour Wolfbein has characterized the contemporary pattern of work by women as follows:

> "The teen-age girl has a relatively low (and declining) worker rate since more girls remain in school, coming into the labor force in significant proportions in the early 20's. The rate falls as they marry and have children. It begins to rise after age 35, reaching its peak at age 45–54 but remaining quite high up to age 65, as children grow up, go to school, and become adults. An impressive fact is that about half of all women in the country between the ages of 25 and 54 are workers, more than triple the proportion in 1900. One-third of all of the women 55–64 are workers, too—again, triple the proportion at the turn of the 20th Century." [9]

The proportion of women who work part time is relatively high. This is due primarily to the fact that most women workers also have household duties and the demands of their family roles tend to take priority.

Part-time Workers

In December 1972, 68,373,000 members of the civilian labor force were employed full time and 14,508,000 were employed part time. Women were much more likely to be working part

---

8. Kennedy, *Manpower Report of the President*, p. 11.
9. Wolfbein, op. cit., p. 159.

time than men. In fact, only 10.4 per cent of employed men compared to 40.4 per cent of employed women worked part time. More than 87.6 per cent of the women who worked on a part-time bases did so voluntarily.[10] By the standards of the late nineteenth century, when a large percentage of employed men worked a sixty-hour week, a large percentage of today's workers would be classified as employed part time.[11]

Part-time work also tends to be more characteristic of non-whites than of whites, and it is more prevalent among young beginning workers than among older experienced workers. Some people work part time because they prefer to do so; others are only able to obtain part-time employment. The data show that those of both sexes who work part time tend to be those who are very young and those who are very old.[12] Nearly three-fourths of the employed males sixteen to twenty-one and about half of the employed females of this age in December 1972 were part-time workers.

In addition to the fact that many workers are employed for short weeks, a very substantial number work for less than a full year. Some of these are new workers; others are older persons who retired before the end of the year. Others work in seasonal types of occupations such as harvesting farm crops or working in the woods as loggers. Still others substitute for regular workers while they are on vacation or help with peak loads such as the pre-Christmas sales in stores or the postal service. Thus the number of people who have done some work during any given twelve months period is substantially greater than the number at work on any particular date.[13] Those who worked on an intermittent and irregular basis were mostly very young workers, very old workers, or women.[14]

10. U.S. Bureau of Labor Statistics, *Employment and Earnings*, vol. 19, no. 7 (January 1973), p. 31.
11. Donald J. Bogue, *The Population of the United States* (Glencoe, Ill.: Free Press, 1959), p. 449.
12. U.S. Bureau of the Census, *Annual Report on the Labor Force*, 1956, series P-50, no. 72, 1957, table 18.
13. Bogue, *Population of the United States*, p. 453.
14. Ibid., p. 554.

Multiple Job Holders

More than four million workers in May 1971 held more than one job. Thus, multiple job holding affected a little less than 5 per cent. This has been a fairly stable percentage for a number of years.[15] Most multiple job holders (69 per cent) worked at their main jobs on a full-time basis and worked part time on the second job. Most of the rest were employed part time on both jobs. A few (6 per cent) reported that they worked full time, that is, thirty-five hours or more on two jobs. Those who worked on more than one job worked an average of fifty-two hours in May 1962, compared to around forty hours for those who had only one job.[16]

Studies of the characteristics of workers who hold other jobs in addition to their primary position indicate that there is quite a wide occupational distribution of multiple job-holding among men, with the heaviest concentration found among teachers in elementary and secondary schools, firemen, policemen, and guards. Medical workers and other professional personnel have a high rate of multiple-job-holding. Other occupational categories with rates above the average are farmers and farm managers, farm laborers, and clerical workers. Contrary to what many people believe, blue-collar workers had lower rates than the occupational categories cited.[17]

Trends in Employment and Unemployment

In December 1972, 82,881,000 were employed in civilian occupations and 4.1 million or 4.7 per cent were unemployed.

15. *Statistical Abstract of the United States* (1972), p. 24.

16. Ibid., for the hours of multiple job holders; *see Manpower Report of the President* for 1964, p. 230, for hours of others.

17. J. Schiffman, "Multiple Job Holders in May 1962," *Monthly Labor Review* (May 1963).

TABLE 2. Employment Status of the Civilian Labor Force (annual averages in thousands)

Date	Total	Employed Number	Unemployed Number	Unemployed Per cent
1929	49,180	47,630	1,550	3.2
1933	51,590	38,760	12,830	24.9
1940	55,640	47,520	8,120	14.6
1944	54,630	53,960	670	1.2
1947	60,168	57,812	2,356	3.9
1950	62,208	58,920	3,288	5.3
1960	69,628	65,778	3,852	5.5
1966	75,770	72,895	2,875	3.8
1967	77,347	74,372	2,975	3.8
1968	78,737	75,920	2,817	3.6
1969	80,734	77,902	2,832	3.5
1970	82,715	78,627	4,088	4.9
1971	84,113	79,120	4,993	5.9
1972	86,542	81,702	4,840	5.6

SOURCE: Bureau of Labor Statistics, U.S. Department of Labor, *Employment and Earnings*, vol. 19 no. 7 (January 1973), p. 24.

Table 2 shows the trends in civilian employment and in unemployment since 1929.

Many people without work are not counted among the unemployed because the definition of unemployment used in collecting statistics on the subject includes only those who are both out of work and looking for work. Students while in school, many housewives, retired persons, and those who are ill are, therefore, not counted as unemployed, although they may be without gainful employment.

But the specter of unemployment, the fear of being without gainful work, is a definite element in the employment picture. There are probably few people who manage to go throughout the full length of their working lives without being unemployed, at least for brief periods. During the depth of the great depression of the 1930s, approximately 25 per cent of the adult male labor force was unemployed. During the early 1960s, the rate of unemployment has been between 4 and 6 per cent most of the time. The lowest recorded figure for the United State was 1.2 per cent during World War II when millions of men were in the armed forces and labor needs were very great.

The rates of unemployment are highest among workers in rural areas, among nonwhites, among the very young and the very old, and among unskilled manual workers, especially those who have low educational attainments.[18]

There are also substantial differences in rates of unemployment among major occupational categories. The *Manpower Report of the President* for 1964 shows that unemployment rates are highest among unskilled laborers and lowest among professional, technical, and kindred workers, managers, officials and proprietors, and farmers. This was still true at the end of 1965 with 8.3 per cent of nonfarm laborers unemployed. Furthermore, the outlook for employment of unskilled manual workers is not encouraging. New machines and automated production techniques are rapidly displacing such workers, and the remaining jobs require more education and greater skill than displaced workers have.

The impact of technological changes falls most heavily on the uneducated, who tend to be found in particular geographic areas, especially the southeast. Older workers have been affected by technological unemployment to a greater extent than younger workers; higher proportions of the older workers have relatively low formal education, and in many cases their skills have been made obsolete or obsolescent by the onward sweep of technological developments. Furthermore, prevailing employment practices, a traditional aspect of industrial culture, tend to discriminate against older men. The problem for the older worker is not so much that there is a high rate of unemployment, but that once he loses his job he may have great difficulty finding a new one, and if he does find a new one, he may have to accept lower wages. These conditions discourage some older men from attempting to find new work, and substantial numbers of them evidently withdraw completely from the labor force.[19]

The Negro rates of unemployment are more than twice as high as those of whites, and the rates for American Indians

18. Lyndon B. Johnson, *Manpower Report of the President*, 1964 (Washington, D.C.: U.S. Government Printing Office), pp. 8–10.

19. Lyndon B. Johnson, *Manpower Report of the President*, 1965 (Washington, D.C.: U.S. Government Printing Office).

TABLE 3. Unemployed Members of the Full-time Labor Force by Age, Sex, and Race, December 1972

| | Males | | Females | |
Age	White	Nonwhite	White	Nonwhite
16 and over	3.4	6.6	4.2	8.6
16 to 21	10.9	21.5	8.7	26.1
16 to 19	13.8	27.7	11.1	40.8
20 and over	3.0	5.3	3.7	6.7
20 to 24	7.1	10.7	5.5	13.2
25 to 54	2.4	4.2	3.6	5.8
55 and over	2.7	4.3	2.2	1.7

SOURCE: Bureau of Labor Statistics, U.S. Department of Labor, *Employment and Earnings*, vol. 19, no. 7 (January 1973), p. 31.

are still higher. The problem for the Negro is partly a matter of low educational attainments, but not entirely, for employment statistics reveal that many Negroes are employed at jobs below the level for which their educational attainments appear to qualify them.[20]

The high unemployment among teen-agers and young adults, as shown by table 3, does not represent a new development. Attempts to explain it generally assume that these young people would like to be employed but that their inexperience combined with the decline in unskilled occupations makes it impossible for most of them to find jobs. Considerable doubt has been raised concerning the validity of this assumption by a study made by Edwin Harwood in Houston, Texas. He undertook the study to find out why unemployment of boys in selected urban ghettos ranged from 25 to 36 per cent according to the Bureau of Labor Statistics surveys. He found that most of these unemployed boys lived at home and worked only when they needed money for "extras." Then such a boy would take a job at a gas station or some other place and work until he had enough money to meet his need for "spending money." Since he does not support a family he feels no great pressure to stay on a job.[21]

20. Ibid.
21. Edwin Harwood, "Poverty and Plenty: Young Americans at Work and Elsewhere," *Bell Telephone Magazine*, vol. 49, no. 3 (May-June 1970), p. 12.

Harwood suggests that the sharp drop in unemployment among young adults is due to greater need for income after marriage. In his words, "When today's young person establishes his own family, he finally makes the serious commitment to a full-time job." [22]

Selected References

Bogue, Donald J. *The Population of the United States.* Glencoe, Ill.: Free Press, 1959. Although written prior to the publication of the returns of the 1960 census, this scholarly work provides many useful insights into demographic factors which affect labor force participation and occupational trends. *See* especially chapter 16, "The Labor Force and Its Composition."

Manpower Report of the President and A Report on Manpower Requirements, Resources, Utilization, and Training. U.S. Department of Labor. Washington, D.C.: U.S. Government Printing Office. The first report was transmitted in March 1963. These reports provide timely information concerning changes in conditions which affect occupational employment as well as the results of special studies made by the Department of Labor and other government agencies.

Wolfbein, Seymour L. *Work in American Society.* Glenview, Ill.: Scott, Foresman and Co., 1971. This book is a discussion of changes in labor supply, occupations, and technology by a leading authority in the manpower field.

Taeuber, Irene B., and Taeuber, Conrad, *People of the United States in the 20th Century.* Washington, D.C.: U.S. Census Bureau, U.S. Government Printing Office, 1971. Including more than 1,000 pages of text and tables, this scholarly tome covers various aspects of American life from 1790 through 1960 as reflected in U.S. Census data.

22. Ibid.

7. Occupational Trends and Outlook

The demand for workers in various occupations is determined chiefly by the occupational employment needs of work organizations. These in turn are influenced by such matters as the general economic situation, scientific and technological developments, and defense needs. Desirable occupational careers, as the term is used in this book, depend upon the existence of sufficient number of new employment opportunities to provide jobs for new entrants to the world of work and for those displaced through technological developments. In addition, as we have already seen, an essential condition is the existence and maintenance in work organizations of occupational career lines that provide career opportunities.

Historically, most occupational changes have been evolutionary and gradual rather than revolutionary and radical in nature, occurring over time and with reference to already established patterns. However, we must not lose sight of the fact that the accelerated rate of adopting scientific and technological developments tends to shorten the period available for adjustment and to speed up greatly the tempo of changes in occupations. Predictions of the future of specific occupations are quite unreliable because of the unpredictable character of scientific and technological developments.

There are so many occupations that a book of this kind cannot present information about each. As a matter of fact, full details are not available. Even the U.S. Census Bureau's voluminous reports present data only for occupational categories rather than for specific occupational titles. But this is too extensive for present purposes. The Bureau of Labor Statistics of the U.S. Department of Labor prepares outlook material for the major occupational categories and for many specific occupations,[1] and this should be consulted for current details.

Occupations and Sex

Table 4 shows the distribution by major occupational categories of employed men and women, 1940, 1950, 1960, and 1970. It will be noted that although there are some women in each of the major occupational categories, the heaviest concentration in 1970 occurred in the following: clerical and kindred workers (73 per cent female); private household workers (97 per cent female), and service workers except private household (55 per cent female); sales workers (38 per cent female); and professional, technical, and kindred workers (40 per cent female).

An examination of the sex distribution of workers employed in various occupations reveals that a number might be classified as women's work, and others, because of the presence of a very small number of women, may be thought of as men's work. Typical women's occupations include: dieticians and nutritionists, librarians, nurses, social workers, elementary schoolteachers, stenographers, typists and secretaries, telephone operators, bookkeepers, cashiers, dressmakers and steamstresses, private household workers, hospital attendants, practical nurses, midwives, and waitresses.

Few women are found in occupations that are hazardous, strenuous, or highly technical. They are seldom high executives, scientists, engineers, or bankers, nor are many traveling salesmen, inspectors, or skilled craftsmen.[2]

The data for the thirty-year period 1940–70 (Table 4) shows a slight increase in the proportion of women employed

1. Bureau of Labor Statistics, U.S. Department of Labor, *Occupational Outlook Handbook* (Washington, D.C.: U.S. Government Printing Office, revised frequently).

2. Donald J. Bogue, *The Population of the United States* (Glencoe, Ill.: Free Press, 1959), p. 450.

TABLE 4. Employed Persons, by Sex and Major Occupation Group: 1940 to 1970 (In thousands of persons 14 years old and over. Beginning 1960, includes Alaska and Hawaii. Annual average except as indicated).

MAJOR OCCUPATION GROUP AND SEX	1940[a]	1950[a]	1960[a]	1970[b]
Total	*44,643*	*59,648*	*66,681*	*73,048*
Professional, technical and kindred workers	3,579	4,490	7,475	10,831
Farmers and farm managers	5,147	4,393	2,780	1,900
Managers, officials, and proprietors	3,633	6,429	7,067	6,140
Clerical and kindred workers	4,382	7,632	9,783	13,034
Sales workers	3,080	3,822	4,401	5,268
Craftsmen, foremen, and kindred workers	5,170	7,670	8,560	9,997
Operatives and kindred workers	8,079	12,146	11,986	12,583
Private household workers	2,091	1,883	2,216	1,093
Service workers, except private household	3,199	4,652	6,133	8,064
Farm laborers and foremen	3,141	3,015	2,615	924
Laborers, except farm and mine	3,142	3,520	3,665	3,214
Male	*33,641*	*42,156*	*44,485*	*45,295*
Professional, technical, and kindred workers	2,082	2,696	4,768	6,517
Farmers and farm managers	4,995	4,154	2,670	1,281
Managers, officials and proprietors	3,242	5,439	5,967	5,126
Clerical and kindred workers	2,020	3,035	3,154	3,452
Sales workers	2,266	2,379	2,707	3,268
Craftsmen, foremen, and kindred workers	5,048	7,482	8,338	9,502
Operatives and kindred workers	6,053	8,810	8,652	8,741
Private household workers	115	125	45	40
Service workers, except private hosehold	1,969	2,560	2,873	3,640
Farm laborers and foremen	2,816	2,042	1,728	783
Laborers, except farm and mine	3,035	3,435	3,583	2,945
Female	*11,002*	*17,492*	*22,196*	*27,753*
Professional, technical, and kindred workers	1,497	1,794	2,706	4,314
Farmers and farm managers	152	239	111	619
Managers, officials, and proprietors	391	990	1,099	1,014
Clerical and kindred workers	2,362	4,597	6,629	9,582
Sales workers	814	1,443	1,695	2,000
Craftsmen, foremen, and kindred workers	122	188	222	495
Operatives and kindred workers	2,026	3,336	3,333	3,542
Private household workers	1,976	1,758	2,171	1,053
Service workers, except private household	1,230	2,092	3,260	4,424
Farm laborers and foremen	335	973	887	141
Laborers, except farm and mine	107	84	82	269

SOURCES: [a] U.S. Census of Population, 1960, *General Social and Economic Characteristics*, U.S. Summary; [b] U.S. Census of Population, 1970.

in professional, technical, and kindred work (13.6 per cent and 15.5 per cent), a rather substantial increase among clerical and kindred workers (20.6 per cent and 34.5 per cent), and a very large decrease in private houeshold workers (18 per cent and 3.8 per cent). It seems clear from this and other evidence that the patterns of occupational participation by women are determined to a very large extent by the culture, specifically the expectations concerning the occupational roles of women, which are governed to an appreciable extent by tradition. Even though women are legally free to enter many occupations dominated by men, they do not generally do so.

This results in a loss of talent that is particularly detrimental in the professions (other than public schoolteaching) where the prevailing culture patterns effectively prevent most women (approximately half of all talented individuals) from developing effective occupational careers and making the contributions that might be expected of people of high ability.

There is little prospect that the existing patterns of men's and women's work will change materially within the foreseeable future. The outlook is that increasing numbers of women will participate in the world of work, but that they will continue to do so on an intermittent basis in relatively low-status occupations rather than making career commitments to professions and other high-level occupations.

Occupations and Age

The occupations young workers pursue when they first enter the world of work tend to differ in important respects from those held by experienced older workers. In many cases, the first jobs involve temporary part-time work such as delivering papers, baby-sitting, doing housework, or working at various tasks during the summer vacation. Poorly educated men expect to enter low-status occupations, but even university graduates are usually assigned to less responsible tasks than experienced older workers. However, these entry positions are frequently the initial step of an attractive occupational career line. Thus, the beginning worker who is a college graduate may have great career expectations.

Many young workers tend to enter new occupations created by technological change and to avoid occupations where technological obsolescence is evident. Here is what Donald J. Bogue had to say with respect to 1950 data:

"Younger workers are concentrated in:
    a. New and rapidly expanding occupations. Much occupational change is due to the fact that the younger generations enter new fields that are just opening up, and avoid fields that are declining in importance. . . .
    b. 'Junior' occupations which, in some firms, are prerequisites to better occupations. . . .
    c. Part-time and temporary jobs. Jobs that can be held during a summer vacation, or on Saturdays, evenings, and holidays while the worker is attending school.
    d. Jobs requiring unusual speed, physical exertion, stamina, or those involving intense heat, pressure, or other uncomfortable and hazardous conditions.
    e. Low-paying occupations which are wanted only by new and inexperienced workers, and which mature workers with families to support cannot afford to accept.

"In contrast, older workers are concentrated in:
    a. Occupations that are dying out or declining—blacksmiths, tailors, farmers.
    b. Occupations into which one is promoted or to which one is appointed after many years of service or experience.
    c. Occupations that require prolonged training and experience (and perhaps also investment capital).
    d. Jobs which, through custom, have tended to become 'old folks' occupations—guards, elevator operators in certain types of structures, charwomen, practical nurses, etc.
    e. Low-paying occupations that can supplement a small pension, or that will support one or two persons, but not a family." [3]

3. Ibid., pp. 501–02.

The foregoing lists show that some occupations follow a cycle of growth and decline. Those who pursue such an occupation reach the age for employment at the proper time to enter it, and they tend to stay with it until it reaches its peak; a few may continue with it throughout their work lives. On the other hand, certain occupations, such as scientific and professional occupations, require long and arduous preparation and provide adequate incentives for long occupational careers. In addition, some occupations, such as "professional" sports, depending on physical qualities that are characteristic of youth, will continue to have few, if any, older people.

Occupational Trends and Outlook[4]

The number of specific occupations is so great that it is not feasible to consider, in detail, even those that have large numbers of practitioners. In chapter 5, we discussed some of the classification systems that have been used by sociologists and others in studying occupational stratification and mobility. A review of these approaches suggests that it would be worthwhile to consider career opportunities within broad industrial and occupational fields as well as in specific occupational specialties.

The demand for some occupational specialists, such as aerospace engineers, manufacturers' salesmen, and science teachers, has changed so much in the recent past that it is virtually impossible to make valid long-range forecasts concerning employment and career prospects. The best available information is to be found in the *Occupational Outlook Handbook*, a publication of the U.S. Department of Labor, which is revised approximately every two years, and the *Occupational Outlook Quarterly*, also issued by the U.S. Department of Labor, which is designed to keep users of outlook information informed

4. Information in this section is chiefly from the *Occupational Outlook Handbook*, 1972-73 edition (Washington, D.C.: U.S. Government Printing Office).

about developments between editions of the *Handbook*. For each of the occupations covered, the *Handbook* presents information concerning: nature of work, places of employment, training and other qualifications, employment outlook, earnings and working conditions, sources of additional information.

1. MAJOR OCCUPATIONAL FIELDS

Before discussing specific occupations, the *Handbook* first presents an overview of the outlook in broad occupational fields.

Professional and Technical Workers. It is anticipated by the *Handbook* that occupations in this category will continue to expand greatly during the 1970s. This may be a valid projection, but there are indications of marked changes in outlook for specific occupations within the category. Recent decreases in the birthrate will probably be accelerated sharply by the January 1973 decision of the U.S. Supreme Court legalizing abortion in all fifty states. This will further curtail the demand for elementary schoolteachers and later for high school teachers.

Because a large proportion of attractive occupational careers are in the professions, the leveling off of professional employment after 1970 is of great concern. During the 1960s shortages of professionals stimulated large numbers of college students to undertake the long and arduous training required. Unfortunately for them, the decline in demand occurred just as sharply increased numbers of newly-trained professionals entered the job market. Not only was there a shortage of positions for new professionals, but a record number of engineers, scientists, and teachers became unemployed between 1969 and 1971.

This turnaround was due not only to an increased supply of professionals but perhaps even more to declining demand due to a number of developments. Teacher demand has declined because the school-age population has leveled off, taxpayer revolts in many communities have curtailed local funds, and federal grants to schools are now lower.

Curtailment of the rapid rate of growth in federal support

for scientific research and development and aerospace activities resulted in considerable unemployment of certain types of scientists and engineers during 1970–72. Although it does not appear that scientific research and development will be curtailed greatly, it does not seem probable that the growth rates of the 1960s will be resumed. The production of Ph.D.s, already reduced somewhat from peak levels, will probably be further restricted by present and prospective reductions in federal support for graduate students.[5] In many fields, persons with Ph.D.s who had expected to find employment in prestigious universities or research laboratories, may find themselves teaching in community colleges or doing other work not previously done by persons with such impressive credentials.

Expansion of federal support for health services appears probable, although it is not certain what form the support will take. In any case, the outlook for physicians and surgeons, nurses, and other health service professionals appears excellent.

Managers, Officials and Proprietors. For business proprietors the outlook is for continued decline; only 7 per cent of nonfarm workers were self-employed in 1970, as compared to 21 per cent in 1950. The *Handbook* projects continued increases in requirements for salaried managers during the 1970s, although the rate of increase is not expected to equal the 70 per cent growth experienced during the 1960s. In 1966, Donald Michael suggested that many middle-level managers would be displaced by computers;[6] if this has happened, it apparently had no discernible effect on the total number of managers as of 1970.

Clerical Workers. Computer operators, as well as secretaries, stenographers, typists, bookkeepers, and file clerks, are included in this category. Continued growth is expected in the number of clerical workers.

5. *See* Charles V. Kidd, "Shifts in Doctorate Output:, History and Outlook," *Science*, vol. 179, no. 4073 (9 February, 1973), pp. 538–43.
6. Donald Michael, *Technical Innovations in Society* (New York: Columbia University Press, 1966), pp. 118–54.

Sales Workers. Demand for some types of sales persons fluctuates in accord with the state of the economy; when business is good, demand is high and vice versa. Such jobs are marginal and relatively unattractive from a career point of view. Selling sophisticated technological products such as computers, on the other hand, may require a degree in engineering and offer career-type incentives. The *Handbook* projects continued strong demand for sales workers during the 1970s.

Craftsmen. The *Handbook* projects only moderate growth in opportunities for craftsmen because of the prospect that technological development will displace workers. In my opinion, this forecast underestimates the difficulties involved in changing building codes and other regulations which protect the building trades fully as much as they protect homeowners. It is more likely that growth will be restricted, as in the past, by union restrictions on entry and attainment of journeyman status.

Semi-skilled Workers (Operatives). The Handbook projects an 11 per cent increase in semi-skilled workers even though continued displacement of many such workers by technology is anticipated. It is expected that diversion of freight to motor trucks will continue, providing additional opportunities for truck drivers. It is also possible, in my opinion, that worsening of gasoline shortages may stimulate increased use of buses and trains, which would, of course, increase employment demands for many types of semi-skilled workers.

Unskilled Workers. Opportunities for unskilled workers of all types are expected to decline further in the 1970s, with the largest declines affecting farm workers. These prospects are due chiefly to the expectation that technological developments will continue to displace unskilled workers. Prospective increases in minimum-wage levels will provide additional incentives for employers to substitute machines for unskilled men and women.

Service Workers. Many writers have commented on the phenomenal growth of service industries and occupations since World War II. The *Handbook* expects this trend to continue and projects a 35 per cent increase in employment in service occupations during the 1970s.

2. OCCUPATIONS BY INDUSTRY

The last fourth of the *Handbook* contains an assessment of the prospects for employment of various occupational specialists in each of nine broad industrial groupings. These groupings serve to emphasize the interdependent nature of the occupations that are required to provide ideas, goods, and services.

Agriculture. Employment in agriculture has been declining since 1910. During the decade of the 1960s, there was a further decline of two-fifths to about 3.25 million in 1970. The *Handbook* predicts a further decline of 15 per cent during the 1970s. These decreases are attributable mainly to technology and not to decreases in farm production. Attractive career opportunities will continue for farm managers, agricultural scientists, and specialists. In addition, there will be need for many different types of occupations in farm supply firms, agricultural processing plants, marketing organizations, and other off-farm organizations performing activities essential to the production of food and fiber.

Mining. Although demand for minerals, oil, gas, and some other mining products is expected to increase, total employment (620,000 in 1970) is expected to decline slowly during the 1970s largely because of improved technology. Attractive career opportunities will continue to exist for occupational specialists such as geophysicists, petroleum geologists, petroleum engineers, and skilled workers of various types.

Construction. In 1970, about 3.3 million workers were employed by construction contracting organizations and an additional 1.4 million were either self-employed or employees of local or state governments. About 2.75 million persons, nearly all of them men, were employed in more than two-dozen skilled building trades. There were 830,000 carpenters in 1970, and it is expected that employment opportunities for carpenters will increase rapidly during the 1970s. Employment of electricians, the second largest building occupation with 415,000 in 1970, is also expected to increase rapidly in the 1970s. Other building trades with large numbers of workers that are expected to experience rapid increases in employment in the 1970s are painters and paperhangers (385,000), plumbers and pipefitters (350,000), construction machinery operators (310,000), bricklayers (175,00), structural metalworkers (85,000), cement masons (65,000), roofers (60,000), and plasterers (35,000).

The construction trades accounted for 51 per cent of employment in the construction industry. Other important occupations include managers, officials and proprietors (12 per cent); operatives, including truck drivers (10 per cent); laborers (17 per cent); professional (including engineers and architects), technical and kindred workers (5 per cent); and clerical workers (5 per cent).

Manufacturing. Manufacturing is the largest industry, with 19.4 million employees in 1970. The firms that produce most of our manufactured products are large and complex and many different occupations are required. An overview of the composition of manufacturing employees by occupational strata in 1970 follows:

Occupational Strata	Per cent
All	100
Professional, technical, and kindred	10
Managers, officials, and proprietors	7
Clerical and kindred workers	12
Sales workers	3
Craftsmen, foremen, and kindred workers	19
Operatives and kindred workers	43
Service workers	1
Laborers	5

There is a heavy concentration of skilled and semiskilled blue-collar workers, but large numbers of engineers, computer specialists, and members of other white-collar occupations are also employed.

Prospects for employment growth vary greatly by type of

product. The most rapid increases in employment are expected in rubber, plastics, and furniture, with above average gains in machinery, apparel, instruments, stone, clay, and glass. Employment is expected to decline in petroleum refining, tobacco, food, and textiles. In addition to technological developments, imports influence employment in manufacturing. This is a matter of grave concern to labor unions and others who fear that jobs will be lost, as in camera manufacturing, for example.

Wholesale and Retail trade. Wholesale companies assemble products in large quantities for sale to retail stores, manufacturers, and organizations that use large quantities such as schools and prisons. Retail stores are more familiar to most people since they sell goods directly to individual consumers. In 1970, nearly 15 million paid workers were employed in wholesale and retail trade. Many different types of occupations were involved as may be noted from the following tabulation:

Major occupational group	Per cent
All occupational groups	100
Professional, technical, and kindred workers	2
Managers, officials, and proprietors	21
Clerical and kindred workers	17
Sales workers	23
Craftsmen, foremen, and kindred workers	7
Operatives and kindred workers	11
Service workers	14
Laborers	5

It will be noted that, while white-collar occupations are predominant, relatively few professionals work in wholesale trade. Sales work, with nearly a fourth of the total employment, was the largest single occupation, followed by managers and proprietors. The large size of the latter category (21 per cent) reflects the continued presence of many small retail outlets in which the owner is a major source of labor. The growth of chain grocery stores since the end of World War II has virtually wiped out the small neighborhood grocery store in most parts of the country, and small retail establishments in other fields have encountered similar competition. A major development, not discussed in the *Handbook*, has been the growth of franchising as a form of retailing. Examples are Independent Grocers' Association (IGA), Trustworthy Hardware, Coast to Coast, Kentucky Fried Chicken, and McDonald's Hamburgers. The franchise system allows a local owner to join an organization that has a distinctive name and which provides advertising, goods, management advice, supervision, and other services. In return, the owner pays a percentage of his gross income and surrenders some of his autonomy.

Transportation, Communications, and Public Utilities. This grouping includes production of energy, movement of goods and people through the air, over highways, railroads, and water, and communication by radio, telegraph, telephone, and television. About 4.5 million workers were employed in 1970 by private firms and an additional half million by state and local governments. Blue-collar workers accounted for more than half of those employed. Most of the semiskilled workers (the operatives) were drivers of trucks, taxis, or buses, or were railroad brakemen and switchmen. The craftsmen and foremen category included mechanics, telephone linesmen, locomotive engineers, and stationary engineers. The white-collar workers (another 40 per cent) were mostly clerical workers such as secretaries and typists, bookkeepers, ticket agents, and telephone operators. Professional and technical workers, many of them in communications, included engineers, actors, entertainers, writers, cameramen, and electronics technicians.

New positions are expected to increase slowly during the 1970s, but many thousands of workers will be needed to replace those who retire, die, or leave their jobs for other reasons. The prospects for slow growth are due to anticipated technological developments rather than to slowing of the rate of demand for services. Computers and other advanced electronic devices are expected to take over additional functions now performed by workers.

Finance, Insurance, and Real Estate. In 1970, nearly 3.7 million workers were employed in finance, insurance, and real estate. More than half of these workers were women. Nearly half (48 per cent) of the total were in clerical occupations such as bank teller, check sorter, insurance claim adjuster, secretary, typist, and office machine operator. Sales workers, most of them insurance and real estate agents and brokers, accounted for 17 per cent of the work force. An exceptionally high proportion (23 per cent) were classified as managers, officials or proprietors. Professional and technical workers, mostly accountants, programmers, economists, and business analysts, accounted for only 5 per cent of total employment. Few blue-collar workers are employed in these occupations.

Employment growth is expected to be moderate in the 1970s, primarily because of the increasing use of computers. The occupational profile noted above suggests that persons seeking managerial careers will be in demand but that the outlook for professionals is not promising except perhaps for those whose occupational specialties are now utilized.

Services other than Government. In 1970, about 21.9 million workers were employed in service producing organizations, including schools and colleges, hospitals and clinics, law firms, hotels and motels, laundries and dry cleaning establishments, beauty and barber shops, business and repair services, private homes, and entertainment. About 60 per cent of the workers in services were women.

Due to the inclusion of privately financed education, medical and health and legal services, the representation of professional and technical workers (35 per cent) is higher than any other broad industrial group. Employment in service industries has increased much more rapidly than production industries in the past twenty years, and this trend is expected to continue.

Government Services. Since the end of World War II, there have been large increases in state and local government and some increase in civilian federal government employment. In 1970, these workers totaled 12.6 million civilians, about one out of every six workers. Some were employed on a temporary basis, but the majority are protected by tenure and have more employment security than the typical private employee. More than one-fifth of these workers were employed by the federal government, a small proportion of them in embassies, foreign aid activities, and other duties in foreign countries.

Because of the widespread use of public funds for the support of schools and colleges, about 40 per cent of all government workers were employed in educational occupations. Other large functional groupings include 1.2 million federal workers in national defense, another 1.2 million federal workers in hospitals and clinics, and 780,000 postal service employees. Most government employees in hospitals and health departments, highway work, and police and fire protection worked for state and local agencies.

Due to the revenue sharing already initiated by the federal government, coupled with the possibility of increased efficiency, it appears that federal civilian employment is more likely to decrease than to increase. State and local employment, however, is expected to increase rapidly during the 1970s in response to demands for government services.

Two-thirds of government employees are white-collar workers. The major occupations represented are teachers, administrators, postal clerks, and office workers such as secretaries, stenographers, clerks, and computer operators. Blue-collar occupations with large numbers include mechanics, policemen, firemen, truck drivers, skilled maintenance workers, custodial workers, and laborers.

Conclusion

Employment prospects, of course, are better in some types of occupations than in others. Those offering the most attractive career opportunities ordinarily require higher educational qualifications. As we will note later, many occupational requirements are likely to change materially in the coming decade. This suggests that continuation of education will be essential not only for upward career mobility but even for employment security.

For further details concerning the outlook for specific occupations consult the *Occupational Outlook Handbook*.

Selected References

Bogue, Donald J. *The Population of the United States.* New work: Free Press, 1959. This book provides insights into demographic factors which affect labor force participation and occupational trends. *See* especially chapter 17, "Occupational Composition and Occupational Trends."

The Occupational Outlook Handbook. U.S. Department of Labor. Washington, D.C.: U.S. Government Printing Office. This handbook presents information concerning current conditions and projections for employment in the future in the occupations that are numerically most important plus some with smaller employment numbers that are considered crucial for economic development or national survival. The handbook is revised frequently. The handbook is an indispensable reference work for vocational counselors and others who are concerned with the trends and outlook in various occupations.

8. Scientific and Professional Occupations

The professions are "where the action is" insofar as attractive occupational careers are concerned. They provide greater opportunities for upward career mobility and higher prestige than most other types of occupations. Furthermore, the professions are more accessible to most young men and women than the skilled trades because entry is through the educational system. Studies of occupational aspirations have shown that the great majority of high school students would prefer a professional occupation. Consequently, it seems appropriate to examine the nature of the professions in some detail.

The concept of *profession*, like many of the concepts of contemporary sociology, is a folk concept, used in everyday communication by millions of people. Consequently it has emotional content, a morally desirable connotation. To be a professional is good; to be a nonprofessional is to be something less than adequate.[1] To become a professional, with certain exceptions,[2] implies a lifetime career commitment. Acceptance into a profession is normally attained only after compliance with rigorous requirements concerning education and training followed by "rites of passage" including examina-

1. Everett C. Hughes, *Men and Their Work* (Glencoe, Ill.: Free Press, 1958), p. 44; Howard S. Becker, "The Nature of a Profession," in Nelson B. Henry, ed., *Education for the Professions* (Chicago: University of Chicago Press, 1962), p. 31.
2. Professional athletes and practitioners of the performing arts must be regarded as exceptions to many of the presumed professional attributes generally accepted by students of the professions, yet we cannot overlook the fact that expert performers of almost any art or craft are acclaimed as professionals by the general public.

tions, awarding of degrees, and, in some cases, licenses to practice.

A great deal has been written about the professions, particularly in the past ten or fifteen years. Discussions have dealt with the nature of the professions, including changes due to new knowledge and other circumstances, predictions concerning their coming dominance in the society of the future, and a few empirical studies of specific professions.[3] In addition, a large number of empirical papers have been based upon small-scale studies of specific aspects of professional life in particular occupations in specific localities. Clark Kerr has predicted that the "knowledge industry," primarily dominated by professional scientists, engineers, educators, and others, will occupy a key position in the structure of American economy in the future.[4]

The U.S. Census Bureau does not provide a separate category for professional occupations but presents data for these occupations under the same major category as technical and kindred workers. In 1970 there were more professional, technical, and kindred workers than farmers, and, as we have already noted in chapter 7, it is anticipated that employment in professional occupations will continue to grow.

Many attempts have been made to define the concept of profession for scientific use.[5] After considering the problems involved, Howard S. Becker has suggested that efforts to rec-

3. See, for example, Morris Janowitz, The Professional Soldier (Glencoe, Ill.: Free Press, 1960); Anselm Strauss, The Professional Scientist (Chicago: Aldine Publishing Co., 1962); Erwin Smigel, The Wall Street Lawyer (New York: Free Press of Glencoe, 1964); Jerome Carlin, Lawyers on Their Own (Brunswick, N.J.: Rutgers University Press, 1962); Stephen J. Miller, Prescription for Leadership; Training for the Medical Elite (Chicago: Aldine Publishing Co., 1970); and Fred David, ed., The Nursing Profession (New York: John Wiley & Sons, 1966).

4. Godkin Lectures, Harvard University, Spring 1963.

5. Abraham Flexner, "Is Social Work a Profession?" in Proceedings of the National Conference of Charities and Corrections (Chicago: Hildmann, 1915), pp. 576–90; Becker, "Nature of a Profession"; A. M. Carr-Saunders and T. A. Wilson, The Professions (Oxford: Clarendon Press, 1933); Ralph W. Tyler, "Distinctive Attributes of Education for the Professions," Social Work Journal (April 1952), pp. 52–62; Morris L.

oncile conventional usage and moral criteria to create a concept that is useful for scientific purposes are doomed to failure ". . . because popular usage changes and becomes uncertain under the impact of concerted efforts by occupational groups to win the honorific title of *profession* for themselves."

His solution to the dilemma is to

"take a radically sociological view, regarding professions simply as those occupations which have been fortunate enough in the politics of today's work world to gain and maintain possession of that honorific title. On this view, there is no such thing as the 'true' profession and no set of characteristics necessarily associated with the title. There are only those work groups which are commonly regarded as professions and those which are not.

"Such a definition takes as central the fact that "profession" is an honorific title, a term of approbation. It recognizes that profession is a collective symbol and one that is highly valued. It insists that 'profession' is not a neutral and scientific concept but, rather, . . . a *folk concept,* a part of the apparatus of the society we study, to be studied by knowing how it is used and what role it plays in the operations of that society." [6]

This proposal has much to commend it in view of the effort being made by those who follow those occupations that seek to become recognized as professions in order to share the benefits of autonomy, high prestige, and high economic rewards presumed to be associated with that designation. Perhaps we can salvage the concept for social scientific use if we

---

Cogan, "Toward a Definition of Profession," *Harvard Educational Review* (Winter 1953), pp. 33–50; Ernest Greenwood, "Attributes of a Profession" in S. Nosow and W. F. Form, *Man, Work, and Society* (New York: Basic Books, 1962), p. 207; Bernard Barber, "Some Problems in the Sociology of the Professions," *Daedalus* (Fall 1963), p. 672; Edward Gross, *Work and Society* (New York: Thomas Y. Crowell Co., 1958), pp. 77–80; and Harold L. Wilensky, "The Professionalization of Everyone?" *American Journal of Sociology* (September 1964).

6. Becker, "Nature of a Profession," p. 32.

modify it with suitable adjectives: "established," "helping," "scientific," and so forth.

Characteristics of a Professonal Occupation

What characteristics are most commonly regarded as attributes of occupations accorded the honorific title of profession? How can a profession be distinguished from a "garden-variety" occupation that is not a profession? These are reasonable questions, but unfortunately there is no adequate short answer. The distinction between an occupation generally regarded as a profession and certain other occupations seems to be a matter of degree rather than a matter of kind. Similar to the established and recognized professions are occupations characterized by Carr-Saunders as near-professions and would-be professions.[7]

Many occupations are becoming "professionalized" because of the tremendous growth of knowledge and the trend toward brain work and away from manual work in all types of endeavors in our society. However, Harold L. Wilensky has scoffed at the idea that all occupations are moving toward professional status, calling it "a bit of sociological romance." [8] Ernest Greenwood has suggested that it might be helpful to consider occupations as distributed along a continuum with the established professions at one end and the unskilled manual occupations at the other.[9] The occupations at the professional end of the continuum, in his opinion, are characterized by possession of a greater degree of the following five attributes:

1. A system of theoretical knowledge which serves as the basis for the professional skill.

7. A. M. Carr-Saunders, *The Human Metropolis in Modern Life.* (New York: Doubleday & Co., 1955), pp. 279–88.
    8. Wilensky, "Professionalization of Everyone?", p. 156.
    9. Greenwood, "Attributes of a Profession," p. 207.

2. Professional authority: the power to prescribe a course of action for a client because of superior knowledge, for example, doctor's orders.
3. Approval of authority claims by the community.
4. A code of ethics designed to protect the client, provide service to the community, and provide a basis of elimination of unethical practitioners.
5. Professional culture patterns consisting of values (for example, the conviction that the professional service is valuable to the community), norms which provide guides for behavior in professional practice, symbols of professional status such as the title "Doctor" and the concept of a professional career.[10]

Bernard Barber, like Greenwood, has acknowledged that absolute differences between professional and other kinds of occupational behavior do not exist. In his view the following four attributes characterize the professions:

"a high degree of generalized and systematic knowledge; primary orientation to the community interest rather than to individual self-interest; a high degree of self-control of behavior through codes of ethics internalized in the process of work specialization and through voluntary associations organized and operated by the work specialists themselves; and a system of rewards (monetary and honorary) that is primarily a set of symbols of work achievement and thus ends in themselves not means to some end of individual self interest." [11]

Barber suggests that information concerning the extent to which an occupation has these four attributes may be used to construct a scale for use in measuring the extent to which occupational behavior can be regarded as professional.[12]

Edward Gross has suggested six criteria of professionaliza-

10. Ibid., p. 207.
11. Barber, "Some Problems," p. 672.
12. Ibid.

tion: "the unstandardized product, degree of personality in-
volvement of the professional, wide knowledge of a specialized technique, sense of obligation, sense of group identity,
the significance of the occupational service to society." [13]
These criteria resemble those suggested by Greenwood and
Barber in most respects, although they are worded differently.

Let us consider these presumed professional attributes in
greater detail:

INTELLECTUAL BASE

Except for professional athletes, actors, and a few other
occupations, the professions possess an intellectual base. That
is, the services performed are based on a body of theory-
oriented and/or scientific knowledge rather than on a set of
customary practices such as in the skilled crafts. In the larger
sense, this knowledge may be regarded as part of the subculture of the profession. Acquiring this knowledge today
requires formal training in institutions of higher learning.

This emphasis on the intellectual basis for distinguishing a
profession from other occupations has been stressed by Alfred
North Whitehead and others. Carr-Saunders and Wilson, a
generation ago, said, "It is this characteristic, the possession
of an intellectual technique acquired by special training which
can be applied to some sphere of everyday life, that forms
the distinguishing mark of a professional." [14] These authors
also note that the professions have been closely concerned
with the universities since they first emerged in the Middle
Ages. [15] Everett C. Hughes, who has devoted much of his professional life as a sociologist to the study of professions, has
stated, "It is part of the professional complex and of the professional claim, that the practice should rest upon some branch
of knowledge to which the professional are privy by virtue of

13. Gross, "Work and Society," pp. 77–80.
14. See Carr-Saunders and Wilson, *Human Metropolis*, p. 200.
15. Ibid., p. 201.

long study and by initiation, an apprenticeship under masters already members of the profession." [16]

In our times, the body of theory that forms the core of professional knowledge is based, with few exceptions, on empirical information obtained through scientific investigations. The rapid increase in such information creates new professional specialties and changes old ones.

Although some professions, such as the performing arts and the ministry, do not rest upon scientific investigation and theory, the great bulk of the professions, particularly the newer scientific professions, depend heavily upon the results of scientific research and will undoubtedly be more dependent in the future than at present. Consequently, there will be continued interest in the solution of the communication problems to which we have referred.

For our purposes, scientific occupations are regarded as professional. Even though they may not conform in all respects to the model,[17] they rest on an intellectual base of theory to a greater extent than most others.

PROFESSIONAL VALUES AND BEHAVIOR NORMS

Other aspects of the professional subculture need to be taken into account. These include the professional values—for example, the central values of science for the science-dependent professions—and the behavior norms that prescribe the proper behavior of the professional toward his client and toward others. These norms include standards relative to the style of life. Greenwood has said with respect to the possession of a distinctive culture, "All occupations are characterized by formal and informal groupings; in this respect the professions are not unique. What is unique is the culture thus begotten. If one were to single out the attribute that most

16. Everett C. Hughes, "Professions," *Daedalus* (Fall 1963), p. 656.
17. Wilensky, "Professionalization of Everyone?", p. 141, points out some of the differences.

effectively differentiates professions from other occupations, this is it." [18]

Many writers on the professions have stressed service to clients and devotion to the welfare of the community as a distinguishing characteristic of the professions, contrasting this with the self-seeking approach alleged to be characteristic of the business ethic. Because only the trained professionals in a particular field are presumed to have knowledge sufficient to evaluate the merit of the services rendered, special steps are required to keep out the unscrupulous and to keep others on the "straight and narrow" path. This is the function of codes of ethics and licensing. The relevant code of ethics is administered exclusively by each professional association. Licensing, although legally a governmental function, is actually in the hands of professional colleagues who are members of the licensing boards.

It must be acknowledged that some professionals have "feet of clay" and do not attain perfection when compared with the professional model. C. Wright Mills,[19] in particular, has taken a cynical view of the motivations of doctors, lawyers, and university professors. He intimates that most of them are hypocritical, that they really are motivated by self-seeking and selfish considerations rather than by idealistic concern with the community welfare. This matter is extremely difficult to evaluate. Almost no empirical information is available on any systematic basis to provide a basis for testing the validity of this evaluation, although occasional cases involving violations of professional ethics do come to public notice. It may be noted, however, that these are occasional rather than frequent, which indicates either that breaches of professional ethics are infrequent or that the professional colleagues of an

18. Ibid., p. 214.
19. C. Wright Mills, *White Collar* (New York: Oxford University Press, 1951), pp. 119, 121, 122, 129–36.

offender "cover up" for him, closing ranks to prevent members of the general public from having access to knowledge about unethical practices. Doctors seldom will testify in court against another doctor on a charge of malpractice, although it has occasionally happened. In the final analysis, however, public trust and confidence are necessary for a profession to survive, and this provides strong incentive for elimination of the unscrupulous and the incompetent.

CLIENT RELATIONSHIPS

A fundamental difference between the so-called "free" professions and business is that the professionals deal with clients or patients who are presumed to have insufficient knowledge to evaluate either the need for particular types of treatment or the adequacy of the treatment provided. Consequently, clients and patients are expected to defer to the authority of the professional, for example, "follow the doctor's orders." Business serves customers. The ideology of business emphasizes that "the customer is always right" and consequently is to be approached in a subservient manner. As Howard S. Becker has pointed out, however, few professionals actually have a monopoly on the knowledge on which their professional claims are based.[20] This is due to the rising level of education and hence may be expected to be even more prevalent in the future.

Harold L. Wilensky has questioned whether all scientists should be classified as professionals, pointing out that:

"A science in contrast to a profession, has no clients except, in an ultimate sense, society; and bosses, if any, are often indeterminate. The main public for the scientist is fellow-scientists, who are in a position to judge competence; the main public for the professional is clients or employer-clients who cannot judge competence. The ambiguity arises from the fact that the scientist as teacher or employer may come to view his

20. Ibid.

students or other groups as clients, while the professional may have a high degree of sensitivity to his colleagues and reduce his openness to influence from clients or bosses." [21]

As we have already said, we regard the significance of the intellectual base as ample justification for classifying scientists as professionals. In line with our decision to use the term "profession" for occupations generally regarded as such, we may note that Anselm L. Strauss has used the term "The Professional Scientist" as the title of a recent study of chemists.[22]

PROFESSIONAL AUTONOMY

Although the professional ideology emphasizes the idea that the qualified professional is supposed to be an independent self-directing person, it seems clear that this goal has not been achieved in many cases, even by doctors and lawyers.

Although American professors have always worked in an organized setting in colleges and universities, working conditions frequently have been such as to minimize administrative control on the part of others. A full professor in a major university has virtually full autonomy insofar as the direction of his own research and teaching is concerned, the major requirement being that he continue to be productive in his research, teaching, and public service responsibilities. Thus, the ideology emphasized in graduate training has been comparable to that of the so-called free professions. Scientists trained in this social environment are taught that free and unhampered pursuit of knowledge for its own sake is a fundamental value. Subsequent employment of scientists by private business, which is hierarchically organized and interested primarily in profit-making ventures, apparently has led to ideological conflict in some cases.[23]

21. Ibid., p. 141.
22. Anselm L. Strauss, *The Professional Scientist* (Chicago: Aldine Publishing Co., 1962).
23. W. H. Whyte, Jr., *The Organization Man* (Garden City, N.Y.: Doubleday & Co., 1956), pp. 225–38.

A larger measure of faculty self-government is typical of English universities. Full professors in German universities also are subject to fewer administrative restraints than American professors, although some of the latter are very independent. Christian clergymen have always worked within organized churches where they have been subject to ecclesiastical authorities in the hierarchically organized churches and to lay supervision in the others. Engineers, except those who have achieved great eminence, are seldom free professionals. Consequently, except for medicine and law and, to a lesser extent, university professors and occasional consultants in other fields, the ideal of the free professional appears to be a polite fiction.

In medicine and law, the current situation is somewhat different from that of a generation or two ago. The most lucrative law business, the external legal affairs of large corporations, is handled by a relatively small number of large law firms. Most large corporations and government agencies have some legal officers on their own staffs. While a substantial number of lawyers are in individual practice or in small partnerships, they are far from the apex of their profession.[24] Lawyers who work for government and as employees in business bureaucracies and in government agencies are like any other employees in the sense that they are hired, promoted, directed, and sometimes fired.

C. Wright Mills alleged that 80 to 90 per cent of the doctors in the 1940s were independent fee-charging professionals.[25] However, doctors do not work in isolation; even a general practitioner has a receptionist-nurse. It is virtually impossible to build a successful practice without access to a hospital, and hospital connections can be established only if the aspirant is accepted by the organized doctors who already are affiliated with the hospitals. Discrimination against Negroes and other minority groups has made it difficult for members of such groups to establish successful medical practices.

24. *See* Smigel, *Wall Street Lawyer*, and Carlin, *Lawyers on Their Own*.
25. Mills, *White Collar*, pp. 80–90.

In the past, relatively few women, blacks, or members of other minority groups have managed to become M.D.s.[26] Those who have done so may have had autonomy, but until the recent turnabout in the status of such persons (precipitated by the civil rights movement), they were seldom accepted by other doctors as fully equal.

PROFESSIONAL ASSOCIATIONS

Professional associations are characteristic of all the professions, not the medical profession alone. All of the others, whether well established or emergent, have active associations incorporating many of the features of the medieval guilds,[27] which is not strange since the older professions actually evolved out of the guilds.[28]

The critical importance of professional associations has been noted by others. For example, Carr-Saunders and Wilson called attention to the importance of "group consciousness," saying, ". . . It is only under the stimulus of the latter that the practitioners associate together and become a profession in the full sense of the word." [29]

Professionals are occupational specialists who deal with phenomena from a particular point of view. Within each of the professions (for example, sociology as a distinct academic discipline), subspecialties such as the sociology of occupations appear, and these subspecialties eventually form the basis for subdivisions within the professional association. This process of proliferation of occupational associations is currently taking place in the field of sociology, with eight sections in the American Sociological Association recently recognized, includ-

26. Elliott A. Krause, *The Sociology of Occupations* (Boston: Little, Brown & Co., 1971), p. 125.
27. *See* Arthur Salz, "Occupations in Their Historical Perspectives," pp. 58–63, and A. M. Carr-Saunders and P. A. Wilson, "The Emergence of Professions," pp. 200–03, both in Nosow and Form, *Man, Work, and Society.*
28. Ibid., p. 201.
29. Ibid., p. 202.

ing the Section on Educational Sociology, the Section on Methodology, and the Section on Organizations and Occupations.

The consequences of low social visibility are well known to the members of many emerging professions. Consequently, programs of public relationships are undertaken by many professional associations in an effort to acquaint members of the community with the value of the services performed and thus to convince others of the essential merits of their claims to professional recognition and perquisites.

PROFESSIONAL CAREERS

The professions provide opportunities in the most highly developed occupational careers. In fact, some sociologists restrict the term career to the professions.[30] Professional careers may extend over the entire period of the work life. The rewards provided by a professional career include the esteem of others and personal satisfactions derived from interest in the work itself as well as financial rewards, usually substantially greater at the peak than at the beginning. We will discuss some of the characteristics of professional careers in chapter 12 .

What Occupations Are Professional

Following Greenwood's suggestion, if we think of occupations as a vertical continuum, the established professions of medicine, law, the clergy, and university teaching would be placed at the top and unskilled manual labor at the bottom. There is little difficulty in identifying the occupations at the two extremes of the continuum. The problems arise in differentiating among those that lie in the zone of transition. For

30. Ernest Greenwood, "Attributes of a Profession," in Nosow and Form, *Man, Work, and Society*, p. 215.

example, is business management a profession? What about nursing or social work? Leading practitioners in these and other occupations aspire to professional recognition. They maintain vigorous "professional" associations and possess many of the attributes of professions that are listed above. Yet, none are universally recognized as professions in the same sense as the "established professions" already named.

Everett C. Hughes has called attention to the efforts of occupations such as these to gain professional recognition:

> "Many occupations, some new, some old, are endeavoring so to change their manner of work, their relations to clients and public, and the image which they have of themselves and others have of them, that they will merit and be granted professional standing. The new ones may arise from the development of some scientific or technological discovery which may be applied to the affairs of others. The people who 'process' data for analysis by computers are a recent example." [31]

The systematic evaluation of the extent to which a particular occupation is professionalized is a complex task, but it could undoubtedly be accomplished. One approach would be to ask knowledgeable people to rate various occupations in relation to a set of professional criteria. At any given time, the knowledgeable members of any modern community could evaluate the extent to which specific occupations of which they know possess any or all of the attributes to which attention has been called in the foregoing discussion. One difficulty with this public opinion type of approach is that many modern occupational roles lack social visibility because they are practiced away from the public view and do not directly affect the lives of ordinary citizens, although their accomplishments may be very consequential because of their impact in changing the essential nature of the physical and social environment. Typical of these would be scientists who perform most of their professional work in laboratories and classrooms. This

31. Hughes, *Men and Their Work*, p. 44.

is a marked contrast to free professionals such as independent physicians in general practice or attorneys who offer their services to anyone for a fee.

In spite of the voluminous literature on the professions, there apparently are few lists of the occupations that are recognized as professions. The U.S. Census Bureau, which might appear to be the logical source of such a list, has evaded the issue by listing professional and technical occupations under the same major heading.

The *Dictionary of Occupational Titles* (1948 supplement) classifies a large number of occupational titles as professional in nature, and table 5 presents information from the 1970

TABLE 5. Estimated° Employment in Selected Professional Occupations, 1970 by sex (Numbers in thousands)

Profession	Total	Male	Female	Per cent Female
Accountant	704	521	183	26.0
Architect	56	54	2	3.6
Clergymen	217	211	6	2.8
Engineers	1,208	1,188	20	1.6
Foresters	40	38	2	5.0
Lawyers and judges	272	259	13	4.8
Lawyers	260	248	12	4.6
Librarians	122	22	100	18.0
Mathematicians, actuaries and statisticians	33	23	12	36.4
Life and physical scientists	203	176	27	13.3
Agricultural	13	12	1	8.3
Biological	29	19	10	34.5
Chemists	109	96	13	11.9
Geologists	20	19	1	5.3
Physicists	22	21	1	4.5
Physicians and related professions	539	493	46	8.5
Dentists	90	87	3	3.3
Pharmacists	110	97	13	11.8
Physicians	281	255	26	9.1
Veterinarians	19	18	1	5.6
Registered nurses	827	22	807	97.5
Social scientists	101	88	21	21.8
Teachers, college and university	486	348	138	28.5
Teachers, elementary and secondary	2,415	741	1,674	69.5

SOURCE: U.S. Bureau of the Census, Census of Population, 1970, *Occupation by Industry*, Final Report PC(2)7C, table 1.
° Estimates based on 5 per cent sample.

census concerning the number of men and women in the civilian labor force who were employed in the major professional occupations listed.

Although determining the extent to which various occupations possess professional qualifications and characteristics would not be an insurmountable task, it has yet to be accomplished. Because it is essentially a task for empirical research, it cannot be attempted here.

Continued technological development based upon new scientific discoveries will add further occupations to those now recognized or seeking to be recognized as professions. However, the process of obtaining recognition as a profession is slow, and full professional status does not come rapidly or easily except to occupations that are offspring of established professions and thus able to use the established status of the mother profession as a starting point.

Where Do Professionals Work?

During the decade of the 1960s there was a marked decline in the proportion of professional men who were self-employed; the proportions declined from 15.7 per cent in 1960 to 10.6 per cent in 1970. Self-employment was the norm only in dentistry (86.6 per cent), law (54.5 per cent), and medicine (54.0 per cent). Self-employment of professional women declined from 6.4 per cent in 1960 to 4.0 per cent in 1970.

Members of some professions such as accountants and lawyers are found in virtually all industries. Other professions tend to be concentrated in specific industries. Thus, engineers are concentrated in manufacturing and construction; chemists are found in certain types of manufacturing as well as in institutions of higher learning; and economists work in colleges, business organizations and government agencies. Readers interested in the industrial distribution of a specific profession are referred to census reports and to the appropriate professional association.

These census statistics do not tell the whole story insofar as sources of income are concerned. Some lawyers and doctors are employees but may also maintain private practices. Leading scientists and university professors frequently receive substantial fees for consulting services to business firms and government agencies.

In ancient Greece and Rome, lawyers, doctors, and others, such as accountants, architects, and engineers, were not independent fee-charging entrepreneurs. In Greece, a lawyer was a friend who spoke in behalf of the accused. In Rome, lawyers were also friends of the litigants. Roman physicians were generally slaves attached to the household of a rich man, and others who did work now thought of as professional usually worked for salaries.[32] Carr-Saunders and Wilson have traced the rise of professionalism in western Europe and England, noting that the emergence of professions coincided with the rise of universities in England in the sixteenth century. Surgeons, apothecaries, and lawyers in England were first organized into guilds, which eventually became professional associations.

Relationship of Universities to the Professions

Formal training for most occupations regarded as professions is obtained in universities, theological schools, and military academies. Special schools such as the Army War College and the Foreign Service Institute provide training for professional personnel rather than for candidates for the professions.

The function of university professional schools and comparable institutions is twofold: (1) to serve as a recruiting and training agency for the profession by screening out unsuitable candidates and providing the others with substantive knowl-

32. Carr-Saunders and Wilson, "The Emergence of Professions," pp. 199–200.

edge as well as what Robert K. Merton has called "anticipatory socialization" into the fundamental values and behavior norms of the particular profession; and (2) to create, principally through research, new and more comprehensive knowledge as a basis for the improvement of professional practice.[33]

For the better established and more prestigeful professions such as medicine, law, and university teaching, professional training in the university is a long and arduous matter.[34]

Selected References

Becker, Howard S. "The Nature of a Profession," in *Education for the Professions*, the 61st Yearbook of the National Society for the Study of Education. Chicago: University of Chicago Press, 1962. This article presents Becker's evaluation of the difficulties involved in development of an adequate definition of the concept profession and presents also his solutions to these problems.

Carr-Saunders, A. M., and Wilson, P. A. *The Professions*. Oxford: Clarendon Press, 1933. This book presents an historical account of the emergence of the professions in England and in western Europe. An excerpt from the book, "The Emergence of Professions," is persented in S. Nosow and W. F. Form. *Men, Work and Society*. New York: Basic Books, 1962.

Daedalus, Fall 1963, Issue on the Professions, Kenneth S. Lynn, ed. This is an important collection of essays on various aspects of professions and includes contributions by such authorities as Bernard Barber, Everett C. Hughes, and others.

33. *See* Barber, "Some Problems," pp. 673–76.
34. For recent studies of sociological aspects of medical training, *see* Howard S. Becker et al., *Boys in White* (Chicago: University of Chicago Press, 1961), and Robert K. Merton, Patricia Kendall, and George G. Reader, *The Student Physician* (Cambridge, Mass., Harvard University Press, 1957).

Hughes, Everett C., *Men and Their Work*. New York: Free Press, 1959. This is a collection of essays presenting many of Hughes's insights and comments gained through his long experience as one of the leading American students of the professions.

Pavalko, Ronald M., ed. *Sociological Perspectives on Occupations*. Itasca, Ill.: F. E. Peacock Publishers, 1972. This reader contains a number of articles concerning various aspects of professional careers.

Vollmer, Howard M., and Mills, Donald L. *Professionalization*. Englewood Cliffs, N.J.: Prentice-Hall, 1966. This book brings together fifty-seven readings on the process of professionalization in twenty-seven occupations.

Wilensky, Harold L. "The Professionalization of Everyone?" *American Journal of Sociology*, vol. LXX, no. 2, September 1964. This is a discussion of the nature of professions and of the prospects that all occupations will become like the professions.

9. Education and Occupation

Most Americans are aware, at least in a general way, that there is a close connection between education and occupational achievements, but, except for the learned professions, this is a comparatively recent development. The United States was long known as the land of the self-made man, a heroic figure who rose from rags to riches without the benefit of education or family connections. In the late nineteenth century, even members of the "established professions" (doctors, lawyers, and preachers) usually had only a high school education, if that much.[1] Even a generation ago, many top American business leaders were not college graduates.[2] The situation is different now. Whether it is justified or not, there is widespread confidence in America that education will provide the solution to all kinds of problems including those associated with occupations.

Robert E. L. Faris, in his presidential address in 1961 to the American Sociological Association, called attention to the increase in effective ability that the United States has attained through education. He said:

"Aware as we all are of the educational boom in the United States, we may still overlook its spectacular implications for

1. Earl J. McGrath, "The Ideal Education for the Professional Man" in Nelson B. Henry, ed., *Education for the Professions* (Chicago: University of Chicago Press, 1962), p. 283.
2. F. W. Taussig and C. S. Joslyn, *American Business Leaders* (New York: Macmillan Co., 1932), and W. Lloyd Warner and James C. Abegglen, *Big Business Leaders in America* (New York: Harper and Bros., 1955).

the future. What is happening at the present time is that the nation is quietly lifting itself by its bootstraps to an importantly higher level of general ability—an achievement which, though less dramatic than the space voyage to the moon and less measurable than the Gross National Product, may mean more to the national future than either." [3]

Peter F. Drucker, a management economist, has emphasized the need for educating people as a prerequisite for national survival.

"An abundant and increasing supply of highly educated people has become the absolute prerequisite of social and economic development in our world. It is rapidly becoming a condition of national survival. What matters is not that there are so many more individuals around who have been exposed to long years of formal schooling—though this is quite recent. The essential new fact is that a developed society and economy are less than fully effective if anyone is educated to less than the limit of his potential. The uneducated is fast becoming an economic liability and unproductive." [4]

Both Faris and Drucker imply that formal education makes it possible for workers to perform sophisticated occupational roles which are essential for the proper functioning of contemporary society.

Formal educational requirements for many occupations, both old and new, are high and rising. Such increases have been justified primarily on the basis that more formal education is necessary to insure competent performance of increasingly sophisticated occupational roles.[5]

3. Robert E. L. Faris, "The Ability Dimension in Human Society," *American Sociological Review* (December 1961), p. 839.

4. Peter F. Drucker, *Landmarks of Tomorrow* (New York: Harper and Bros., 1959), p. 114.

5. Cf. Burton K. Clark, *Educating The Expert Society* (San Francisco: Chandler Publishing Co., 1962) and Clark Kerr, John Dunlop, Frederick H. Harbison, and Charles A. Myers, *Industrialism and Industrial Man* (Cambridge, Mass.: Harvard University Press, 1960).

This favorable appraisal of the occupational utility of education has been challenged recently by a number of writers. Ivar Berg concluded on the basis of information from samples of workers in a wide range of occupations that better educated workers are not necessarily more productive.[6] Accepting Berg's conclusion as valid, Randall Collins argued that "the technical function theory of education . . . does not give an adequate account of the evidence,"[7] and offered an alternative explanation based on conflict theory. The crux of his theory is the notion that high educational requirements for employment are imposed because they protect the advantages enjoyed by those who are already privileged.

He argues that because educational requirements are most easily met by persons from privileged families, others are relegated to lower level jobs but are nevertheless socialized by the school system to respect elite values and styles and hence become docile employees.[8]

This is an interesting theory. If accepted, it would appear to justify (in the interests of equality or social justice) the attacks on the educational system by Ivan Illich. He argues that this system as now operated restricts the dissemination of technological knowledge to a few elite specialists educated at high cost, and thus denies to most people the great benefits made possible by science. He believes that it would be possible to break up what he sees as the monopolization of useful technological knowledge by elite members of privileged occupations by creating what he calls basic "kits of tools" that provide services or goods desired by many but available only to a few.[9] As an example, he describes a military medical kit incorporating sophisticated medical knowledge ordinarily restricted to a few specialists which permits enlisted personnel

6. Ivar Berg, *Education and Jobs; The Great Training Robbery* (New York: Frederick A. Praeger, 1970), pp. 85–104, 143–176.

7. Randall Collins, "Functional and Conflict Theories of Educational Stratification," *American Sociological Review*, vol. 36, no. 6 (December 1971), p. 1007.

8. Ibid., p. 1011.

9. Cf. Ivan Illich, "The Alternative to Schooling," *Saturday Review* (19 June, 1971), p. 59.

to provide services worthy of full-fledged M.D.s.[10] Illich proposes that schools as such should be "disestablished" in order to abolish what he sees as their dominant function of allocating people to various occupations and thus restricting the life chances of those who do not do well in school.

It is highly unlikely that radical proposals such as "disestablishment" of schools will ever be adopted. Nevertheless, attacks on the educational system by reformers may be expected to continue precisely because it is now one of the dominant institutions in industrialized countries. These attacks will inevitably result in changes, some of which may eventually reduce the centrality of formal education for occupational placement. At present, however, the trend appears to be in the opposite direction.

Educational Attainments of Workers

Data concerning the educational attainments of adult workers in 1970 show a heavy concentration of college graduates in professional, technical, and kindred occupations. Substantial numbers were also found among managers, officials, proprietors, clerical, and sales workers, and some college-trained personnel were found in all major occupational categories.

Great strides have been made, particularly in the last twenty-five years, in raising the educational level of the population of the United States. By 1962, 55 per cent of all workers eighteen to sixty-four years of age had completed four years of high school or more, compared with 45 per cent in 1952 and only 32 per cent in 1940. There was an especially rapid increase in the proportion of college graduates during the decade 1952–62; the proportion of workers with a baccalaureate degree rose from 8 per cent to 11 per cent during the period. Data for March 1972 show that for employed men twenty-five to sixty-four years of age, only 19.4 per cent were

10. Ibid.

not high school graduates while 17.6 per cent had completed four or more years of college.[11]

The increased valuation placed on education is indicated by the virtual disappearance, during the decade 1952–62, of the difference of about two years of school that favored women. The improvement in the educational attainments of men was especially pronounced among men 35 to 44 years of age in 1962. Approximately 10 million veterans of World War II and the Korean War had taken advantage of the educational provisions of the G.I. Bill by the end of 1962, approximately one-third in institutions of higher learning.

It is reasonable to suppose that the rather dramatic recent improvement in the educational attainments of younger men is attributable, in part, to the well-documented and widely publicized fact that there is a close positive correlation between years of formal education and income. In 1971 the average annual income of male college graduates was $15,133 and that of high school graduates was $9,566, while those who had not finished elementary school averaged $5,825.[12] In 1954, Paul C. Glick estimated that a college education would be worth approximately $100,000 more to a man than a high school education, assuming continuation of 1949 economic levels.[13] The gross economic return is indicated by the following estimates (made by the U.S. Census Bureau in 1968) of the lifetime incomes of men by years of school completed:[14]

Less than 8 years	$213,505
8 years	277,000
High school graduate	371,094
1–3 years college	424,280
4 years college	584,062
5 years or more college	636,119

11. U.S. Bureau of the Census, *Educational Attainment: March 1972*, series P-20, no. 243 (November 1972).

12. U.S. Census Bureau, *Money Income in 1971 of Families and Persons in the United States*, series P-60, no. 85 (December 1972), p. 113.

13. Paul C. Glick, "Educational Attainments and Occupational Advancement," *Transactions of the Second World Congress of Sociology*, vol. II (London, 1954), pp. 183–93.

14. Kenneth A. Simon and W. V. Grant, *Digest of Educational Statistics, 1971* (Washington, D.C.: U.S. Department of Health, Education and Welfare, 1972, p. 17).

These statistics should not be interpreted to mean that high educational attainments guarantee employment in a high-status occupation or a high income, even though the probability of such a favorable outcome is increased.[15]

Although the median educational level of nonwhite workers is still below that of whites, it has risen more rapidly than that of whites since the end of World War II, especially with respect to the proportions attending or finishing secondary school. In 1962, for example, there were almost twice as many high school graduates as in 1952. The educational accomplishments of the nonwhite labor force, however, were still not very high, less than one-third finishing high school or attending college compared to over half of the white workers. In 1970, 54 per cent of Negro males and 58 per cent of Negro females twenty-five to twenty-nine years old had completed four years of high school or more as compared to 36 per cent and 41 per cent respectively of those who were in this age group in 1960. The educational attainments of Negroes still lagged behind those of whites; in the twenty-five to twenty-nine year age group in 1970, 79 per cent of the males and 76 per cent of the females had completed four years of high school or more. In 1970, in the age group twenty-five to thirty-four years, only 6.1 per cent of Negroes compared to 16.6 per cent of whites had completed four years of college of more.[17] Evidence of continued discrimination against nonwhite workers is found in the fact that in 1962, among college graduates 70 per cent of the nonwhite men had positions in occupations classified as professional, technical, or managerial compared

15. Paul C. Glick aand Herman P. Miller, "Educational Level and Potential Income," *American Sociological Review*, vol. 21 (June 1956), pp. 307–12.

16. The following information concerning the comparative education levels of whites and nonwhites is from Lyndon B. Johnson, *Manpower Report of the President* (Washington, D.C.: U.S. Government Printing Office, 1964), pp. 97–102.

17. U.S. Census Bureau, *The Social and Economic Status of Negroes in the United States, 1970*, p. 23, no. 38 (July 1971), pp. 80–81.

to 80 per cent of the white men. A similar disadvantage was experienced by nonwhite high school graduates, a great majority of whom were unskilled or semiskilled workers or service workers, while most of the white male high school graduates were employed either as white-collar workers or craftsmen or foremen. Exactly comparable current information is not available, but in 1972, 86.9 per cent of Negro male college graduates and 93 per cent of white male college graduates were employed in white-collar occupations.[18]

Nonwhite women also tended to encounter problems in finding employment commensurate with their attained educational levels. In 1962, nearly 20 per cent of the nonwhite female high school graduates, including those with some college training, were working as domestic servants, and an additional 30 per cent were employed in service jobs outside private homes. The comparative figures for white women were 2 per cent and 12 per cent, respectively. On the other hand, among women who were college graduates, a higher proportion of nonwhites were employed in professional occupations than was true of whites; most of these persons were probably employed as teachers.

The Screening Function of Education

Early identification of talented individuals has become a function of schools and colleges. High scholarship is recognized in an effort to motivate gifted students to select and prepare for elite occupations, and these activities have met with general approval.

But there is a darker side to the picture. When the educational system acts as a screening device to identify and give special training to those who are perceived to have talent, it also screens out the others. They are the failures, the drop-

18. U.S. Census Bureau, Current Population Reports, series P-20, no. 243, "Educational Attainment: March 1972."

outs, those who do not make high grades. The same teachers who select and stimulate the talented discourage the less talented. This is seldom, if ever, done by means of personal criticism; neither is there normally any attempt by individual teachers to oust those who do not perform well. Instead, efforts are made to motivate students to perform their tasks more effectively. The principal screening mechanism is the grading system. Assignment of a low grade for substandard performance is supposed to motivate the student to work harder and improve his performance. Sometimes it does, but for some, the result is defeat and apathy.

It is widely believed that, in some elementary and secondary schools and even in some college, little effort is made to screen out the incompetents, and that high academic standards prevail in others. There is unquestionably a wide variation in grading standards just as there is a wide variation in the quality of teaching among various school systems. The American norm of local control over many aspects of elementary and secondary education makes community variation a certainty.

European school systems are generally controlled by the central government. Teachers are civil service employees, and finances come from general rather than local taxes. Curricula and academic standards are imposed by central authorities and local citizens have virtually no voice in school affairs. In England and France, the most important event in the life of a child has been the examination given when he is approximately eleven years old to determine academic ability.[19] Only those with high marks continue in the academic course that leads to the universities and thus into elite occupations. Those who fail may attend vocational schools, withdraw from school and enter the labor market, or, if their parents can afford it, attend a private college preparatory school.

The selection function of our educational system does not

19. Jean Floud and A. H. Halsey, "Social Class, Intelligence Tests, and Selection for Secondary Schools," in A. H. Halsey, Jean Floud, and C. Arnold Anderson, *Education, Economy, and Society* (New York: Free Press of Glencoe, 1961), pp. 209–15.

operate in this drastic manner, and in England, at least, the complaints of parents have finally resulted in some revisions in the direction of the American pattern.

At the same time, the attempt at early identification of talent, triggered by the 1957 Russian Sputnik, has led to some important American developments. In many school systems, gifted children are now identified in the elementary grades, segregated, and provided with a more sophisticated level of studies than the others. Slow learners are also segregated and presumably given special attention.

Although definitive information is not readily available, it seems likely that the gap between the gifted and the less talented widens rather than narrows as the students get older. Those who receive early recognition continue to receive it through the high school years. Students with outstanding high school records are eagerly sought by famous universities, and those who do well as undergraduates have little difficulty in entering prestigious graduate schools. Furthermore, outstanding graduate students may receive stipends from foundations or public agencies and thus establish connections that in effect give them preferred status as applicants for research grants when they achieve professional status.

This is how the educational system operates to establish what has been called the meritocracy. It has much to commend it. Nevertheless, it is not a perfect system for selection and training of talents.

Before educational attainments became so crucial for the allocation of elite occupations, the occupational selection function of the educational system was relatively unimportant. Even today many men in positions of power and influence are not college graduates. But they are fast disappearing from the scene, and there is almost no chance now for a person to rise to high position without a college education. In the near future, college graduates will be so plentiful that graduate training may be as essential as undergraduate training is today. Educational attainments have risen dramatically in the last thirty years. In March 1972, 58 per cent of persons twenty-five years old or over were high school **grad**uates and

12 per cent were college graduates, as compared to 24.5 per cent and 4.6 per cent respectively in 1940.[20]

In the automated economy of the future, most men without a high school education may be regarded as unskilled and incompetent. Today, a great many people do not finish high school. In March 1972, according to the U.S. Census Bureau, 39.7 per cent of white males and 64.2 per cent of Negro males twenty-five years of age or over had completed less than four years of high school. At that time, 5.7 per cent of white males and 25.9 per cent of Negro males who were forty-five years of age or older were functional illiterates—that is, they had less than five years of formal schooling.[21]

If those who fail their studies continue to accept personal responsibility for their failure, the results will resemble those obtained in the classical European class system where the lower classes were taught not to aspire above their "station in life." There is some chance that the greatly increased numbers of failures will lead to transfer of blame to the educational system. Educators are not unaware of the potential trouble this might create. Burton Clark has taken the position that one important function of the junior colleges is to provide a setting within which the less capable can rationalize and readjust their aspirations downward under less stressful circumstances than failure in a university with rigid academic standards.[22]

The competition for grades and academic recognition as steps on the ladder to elite occupations has been called "contest mobility." [23] It can be argued that this competition provides realistic preparation for occupational performance in our society. Whenever the ruling principle for promotion, sal-

20. U.S. Bureau of the Census, *Educational Attainment: March 1972*, series P-20, no. 243 (November 1972).

21. Ibid.

22. Burton R. Clark, "The 'Cooling-Out' Function in Higher Education," in Halsey, Floud, aand Anderson, *Education, Economy, and Society*, pp. 513–27.

23. Ralph H. Turner, "Modes of Social Ascent Through Education: Sponsored and Contest Mobility," in Halsey, Floud, and Anderson, *Education, Economy, and Society*, pp. 121–39.

ary increases, and other types of recognition is merit, however defined, newcomers may displace older workers at any time. This leads to insecurity and, if displacement actually occurs, may result in personality disorganization.

Educational Preparation for Occupational Roles

As we have noted, educational requirements for various occupations have risen dramatically and are continuing to rise. Except for scientific, professional, and technical occupations, however, the specific contribution of formal education to occupational competence has been chiefly a matter of faith. Seymour L. Wolfbein has suggested that the increasing complexity of occupational change over time, coupled with the marked shift in the occupational structure toward professional and technical occupations rather than those which utilize primarily unskilled manual labor, accounts for the rising educational requirements in the United States.[24]

Educational attainments are related to occupational placement. Scientific, professional, and technical occupations obviously require vocationally oriented training. For most other occupations, there is a widespread belief that employers tend to place more weight on the possession of diplomas and degrees than on the nature of the educational program, with a special bonus in terms of occupational placement and income for the graduate of elementary school, high school, or college.[25] Perhaps as a consequence of this view, high scholarship tends to be valued less at the high school level than athletic accomplishments or social skills.[26]

The increasing emphasis upon education as the primary

24. Seymour L. Wolfbein, "Labor Trends, Manpower, and Automation," in Henry Borow, ed., *Man in a World at Work* (Boston: Houghton Mifflin Co., 1964), pp. 164–65.

25. Glick and Miller, "Educational Level and Potential Income," p. 311.

26. James S. Coleman, *The Adolescent Society* (New York: Free Press of Glencoe, 1961).

means of preparing for occupations has led to a substantial increase in the period of time young people spend in school. The role of student is the key role for those who attend schools, colleges, or universities. Except for the fact that few, except graduate students, are paid, the role closely resembles occupations that require intellectual activities. Students generally regard study as work, and much school work is oriented toward occupations. Thus the role of student may reasonably be regarded as an occupational role in its own right. Successful performance of the role requires work to achieve scholastic performance in accordance with the standards established by the particular school.

Donald Michael has suggested that in the future occupational education may be characterized by increasing differentiation in the education for those who will be prospectively professionals, skilled technicians, and unskilled workers.

"The most accomplished of the professionals . . . will for the next two decades tend to work long hours, be time-oriented, require a deep and broad background in their fields, and need a lifelong ability to absorb fresh intellectual material. The youth aiming for such a career will begin to prepare for it early in life—certainly in high school, in most cases probably in primary school—if he is to compete successfully for access to the advanced education needed for professional success." [27]

Since the occupational roles of technicians will be less demanding than those of professionals, there may be a difference in preparation for technical occupations. Education for such occupations is likely to be more relaxed.[28]

The failures—the dropouts, the slow learners, and others who are uneducated—will be qualified to work at unskilled occupations, if they work at all. Because they lack occupational knowledge and skill, they will be poorly paid.[29]

27. Donald Michael, *The Next Generation* (New York: Random House, 1963), pp. 99–100.
28. Ibid., p. 101.
29. Ibid., pp. 101–102.

FORMAL EDUCATION FOR OCCUPATIONAL ROLES [30]

The Office of Manpower, Automation, and Training of the U.S. Department of Labor conducted a nationwide survey in April 1963 to find out how adult workers (ages twenty-two to sixty-four) had been trained for their occupational roles. The study was focused on the relationship of vocational training to formal education and showed that adult workers reported the following with respect to formal vocational training:

"Overall, some 54 per cent (about 32 million) had taken or were then taking formal training or had completed 3 or more years of college. About 3 per cent (1.4 million) of those with less than 3 years of college were taking training at the time.

28 per cent (16.9 million) had no more than an eighth grade education. Four-fifths of these had no formal job training either.

20 per cent (12.2 million) had some high school education but had not graduated. Over half of these had no job training.

30 per cent (18.1 million) were high school graduates who had not gone on to college. One-third of these had no job training.

8 per cent (4.6 million) had 1 or 2 years of college. One-fourth of these had no job training.

14 per cent (8.7 million) had 3 or more years of college, and were considered to have training for a professional occupation. . . . In this group were 7.2 million who had completed at least 4 years of college." [31]

The majority of the nation's workers with less than three years of college reported that they had not learned their occupational roles through formal education; 56 per cent had learned on the job, to some extent through company training courses, but mainly through experience supplemented by in-

30. The information in this section is drawn from Johnson, *Manpower Report of the President*, pp. 66–72.
31. Ibid., p. 66.

struction from supervisors, and by learning from a friend or relative.

Formal training for occupational roles was reported most frequently by workers in occupations classified as professional or technical. More than half of the clerical workers (53.6 per cent) reported formal occupational training. Only about 40 per cent of craftsmen employed in construction occupations reported that they had learned their occupational specialties through formal training including apprenticeship. Only one in ten semiskilled workers in factories had received formal job training.

In contrast to the experiences reported by workers who had received less than three years of college training, the college-trained workers overwhelmingly (more than 80 per cent) reported that they were employed in occupations which enabled them to use their major college subjects. However, the percentages ranged from over 85 per cent of those who had majored in health sciences, engineering, and business administration to a low of about 65 per cent of those with training in biological sciences, social sciences, humanities, and agriculture.

Nearly half of those not working in occupations directly related to their major field of college study reported that they were employed at other professional, technical, or managerial occupations.

SEMIPROFESSIONAL AND TECHNICAL EDUCATION

Systematic programs designed to prepare students for employment in technical and semiprofessional occupations are provided by institutions of higher learning as well as by other types of schools. In 1969–70, 124,327 students were awarded diplomas or other certificates for completion of such training; 102,119 of these awards were based on organized occupational curriculums of at least two (but less than four) years. Of the total, 28,959 had completed engineering-related curriculums, 3,907 science-related curriculums, 26,778 health service curriculums, 46,431 business and commerce-related curriculums, and 16,625 other types of studies.[32]

Information concerning enrollments in private schools, which are operated for profit, does not seem to be available on a national basis, but it is certain that many technicians are trained in such schools. In addition, technical schools operated by the armed forces, though operated primarily to produce military technicians, have contributed materially to the supply of civilian technicians in electronics and some other occupations. Nearly all military men are now occupational specialists, and many skills are useful in civilian as well as military occupations. Armed forces recruitment advertising emphasizes training as an incentive for enlistment.

LOCAL-STATE-FEDERAL VOCATIONAL TRAINING

Since 1917 the federal government has contributed funds for vocational education of high school students and adults. In 1969–70 enrollment in such courses was[33]:

Vocational Category	Enrollment
Agriculture	852,983
Distributive occupations	529,365
Homemaking	2,570,410
Trades and industry	1,906,133
Health occupations	198,044
Technician training	271,730
Office occupations	2,111,160

Greatly increased federal funds for vocational training are now available under the terms of the Vocational Education Act of 1963, which also provides substantial financial support for research and development activities.[34] This support lowers the financial barriers to the development of new approaches

32. Kenneth A. Simon and W. V. Grant, *Digest of Educational Statistics, 1971*, op cit., p. 96.
33. Ibid., p. 37.
34. *The Vocational Education Act of 1963*, U.S. Office of Education, OE80034 (Washington, D.C.: U.S. Government Printing Office, 1965); *see also School Life* (March-April 1964).

that will be needed to prepare people for the occupations of the future. Many problems exist that are not likely to be solved either readily or rapidly. From a sociological point of view, the main problem may be conceptualized as the difficulty of effecting changes in the accepted values and bevior norms of a well-established social system. Changes do occur, but it usually takes considerable time, and if the need for change is urgent, new organizations may have to be established.

SCIENTIFIC AND PROFESSIONAL EDUCATION

Education for most professional occupations is provided by the following types of professional schools and colleges[35]:

Agriculture
Business administration
Education
Engineering
Forestry
Home economics
Hospital administration
Library science
Medicine

Nursing (college and university only)
Optometry
Pharmacy
Physical therapy
Theology
    Jewish
    Protestant
    Roman Catholic

Most of these schools and colleges are units of universities, but a few of them are independent.

Colleges and universities provide basic training in subject matter required for performance of scientific and professional occupations. As a complementary function, these institutions identify and encourage promising candidates for such occupations and screen out others. Many of the latter obtain college degrees and subsequently perform a variety of occupational roles.

Educational preparation for careers in nearly all scientific occupations now involves graduate training. Almost without exception, those who receive recognition for scientific accom-

35. Lloyd Blauch, *Education for the Professions* (Washington, D.C.: Government Printing Office, 1954), p. 15.

plishments and reach the high organizational positions have earned a Ph.D. or its equivalent. Post-baccalaureate education is also involved in preparation for law, medicine, and many other professional occupations. In some professions, such as engineering, pharmacy, and public schoolteaching, it is possible for a person to enter employment without graduate work. However, there is increasing pressure for teachers and probably others to secure advanced degrees.

Advanced degrees awarded in selected science fields during 1969–70 were:[36]

	Masters	Doctors		Masters	Doctors
Agriculture	1,466	726	Mathematics and statistics	5,636	1,236
Anthropology	664	215	Physical sciences	5,935	4,312
Biological sciences	5,800	3,269	Chemistry	2,111	2,166
Economics	1,988	794	Physics	2,200	1,439
Forestry	327	97	Political science	1,663	525
Geography	637	145	Psychology	4,111	1,668
			Sociology	1,138	534

Graduate education will continue to grow in numbers, in areas covered, and in importance to the occupational careers of students and faculty, to government, industry, and other work organizations, and to society at large. The "information explosion" to which reference has already been made virtually assures the development of new specialties. Furthermore, as Bernard Berelson has pointed out, doctorates are in demand by "everyone." [37]

In a very real sense, selection of a scientific or professional occupation and recruitment into that occupation occurs in the university. The graduate school is of special importance. "The graduate school stands at the center of a vast screening mechanism that makes it one of society's major devices for selecting intellectual talent." [38]

36. Simon and Grant, *Digest of Educational Statistics*, pp. 91–92.
37. Bernard Berelson, *Graduate Education in the United States* (New York: McGraw-Hill Book Co., 1960), p. 219.
38. Ibid. p. 227.

The functions performed by the university include the development of a sense of occupational commitment and some anticipatory socialization in respect to occupational values and behavior norms.

Howard S. Becker and J. W. Carper have described socialization into an occupational role:

"One of the most compelling instances of personal change and development in adult life in our society is to be found in the typical growth of an 'occupational personality' in the young adult male who, as he matures, takes over an image of himself as the holder of a particular specialized position in the division of labor." [39]

The direction of changes in the occupational orientations of graduate students may be influenced materially by their perceptions of faculty appraisals of their ability. David Gottlieb has presented evidence, from a nationwide survey of the experience of 2,842 students in 25 graduate schools, that the career preferences of graduate students are changed as they move through their professional training in the direction desired by the departmental faculty. Verbal cues from faculty members are influential particularly in respect to the development of a research orientation.

"The strongest changes toward research are found among those students who have been told they will make good researchers. . . . Among the single-minded departments . . . we find that no matter what he has been told the student changes in the direction of research. In fact, the impact of being told you will make a good teacher by a faculty member of a research oriented department is sufficient to bring about a greater change to research than to be told nothing at all. Being told you will make a good teacher by a faculty member

---

39. "The Elements of Identification with an Occupation," *American Journal of Sociology* (January 1956), p. 290.

who values research is, it would appear, most likely to be
viewed as the 'kiss of death' and seen not so much as praise
but as a cue that the student is on the wrong track." [40]

Becker and Carper studied the occupational socialization of
graduate students in physiology, mechanical engineering, and
philosophy.[41] They found substantial differences in the effects
of graduate training: the engineers had already developed an
occupational identity that was strengthened by graduate work;
many of the physiology students had previously hoped to become physicians, and graduate school enabled them to transfer their commitment to physiology; the philosophy students
tended to maintain a "broad and unspecialized intellectual
commitment" rather than to develop an occupational identity.
Howard S. Becker and his colleagues have described in considerable detail the development of occupational identity by
students in a medical school.[42]

Everett C. Hughes has observed that socialization into an
occupation frequently involves the abandonment of earlier
values. As an extreme instance of this he cited the education
of Catholic priests.

"The very process of making a priest is to envelope the candidate in the ecclesiastical world, definitely to limit even the
number of letters he can write to his family, to give him a new
formalized language; in short, to make a new person of him,
with a new definition of his wishes. This does by discipline
what sects attempt to do by conversion; namely, to erase the
person's past so that he may be completely mobilized for
carrying out his mission." [43]

40. "Processes of Socialization in American Graduate Schools," *Social
Forces* (December 1961), pp. 124–31.

41. Ibid.

42. Howard S. Becker et al., *Boys in White* (Chicago: University of
Chicago Press, 1961).

43. Everett C. Hughes, *Men and Their Work* (Glencoe, Ill.: Free
Press, 1958), p. 32. For a more complete account of the occupational
socialization of Catholic priests, nuns, and other religious functionaries,
see Joseph H. Fichter, S.J., *Religion as an Occupation* (South Bend,
Ind.: University of Notre Dame Press, 1961).

When a candidate has passed the requirements established by the faculty of a graduate department or a professional school, including manifesting the appropriate attitudes expected of one who has developed an occupational identity, he will be recommended for employment by the faculty members, particularly those who have worked most closely with him. Thus the relationship is continued. In the words of Becker and Carper:

"The sponsor is responsible to his colleagues for the performance of the person he sponsors, who is in turn responsible to him for his behavior. When a person is sponsored into a first position in the work world after leaving graduate school, he feels obligated to act as a true member of the occupation and to remain within it, because of the trust placed in him by his sponsor. The creation of this obligation solidifies occupational attitudes and loyalties—the individual feels that he must remain what he has become in order not to let down his sponsor —and thus strengthens the identification with occupational title and ideology." [44]

This degree of interdependence does not persist throughout a professional career, although some contact may be maintained with graduate school peers for a considerable period of time.[45]

CONTINUATION EDUCATION

Until quite recently, people have thought of formal education, including education for scientific and professional occupations, as something to be completed prior to entering the world of work on a full-time basis. There is growing recognition that continuing education is essential to maintain occupa-

44. Howard S. Becker and James W. Carper "The Development of Identification with an Occupation," *American Journal of Sociology*, vol. LXI, no. 4, January 1956, p. 298.

45. Theodore Caplow and Reece J. McGee, *The Academic Marketplace* (New York: Basic Books, 1958), p. 143.

tional competence. The medical profession has been a leader in developing short courses, workshops, and seminars, and government officials can now obtain leave with pay to take graduate courses. But, except for the existence of sabbatical leave provisions in some institutions, colleges and universities have not generally made provision for retraining of older faculty members.

In this connection, Earl J. McGrath has stated:

"Only those conscious of the geometrical increase in knowledge relevant to their work and the changing circumstances of practice can avoid beginning to become professionally moribund on the day of graduation. Institutions have the responsibility to cultivate the habit of professional self-enlargement as a part of the normal preparation for the work of a lifetime. They also have the responsibility to make continuing opportunities for professional and general education available to their graduates and others of similar interests in the community." [46]

B. Richard Teare, Jr., has made a similar statement concerning engineering:

"Not only has the character of engineering changed in the last half century; what is equally important to education is its rapid (at present nearly explosive) rate of change. New engineering methods are devised to replace old; new and better materials are sought and found; new devices are invented; operational quantities, such as speed, are increased by an order of magnitude; new areas of knowledge, such as information theory, are discovered or created; even whole new fields, like astronautics, are brought forth. At one time, yesterday's practice of engineering was probably adequate as professional education for tomorrow's engineer, but such is far from true now." [47]

46. McGrath, "Ideal Education," p. 301.
47. B. Richard Teare, Jr., in Henry, *Education for the Professions*, p. 122.

In my opinion, work organizations of all types, including universities, will find it worthwhile to develop systematic provisions for continuation education to modernize occupational skills.[48]

The military services may be a prototype of the pattern of continuation education that will be required. Morris Janowitz has reported that officers are sent back to school at regular intervals to prepare for new assignments; graduates of the Fort Leavenworth Staff and Command School, with an average of thirteen years of commissioned service, had spent a third of their careers in school.[49]

UPGRADING THE OCCUPATIONAL SKILLS OF THE UNEDUCATED

As we said earlier, the uneducated are unskilled and poor. Some are ill or otherwise physically or mentally handicapped. Many have low aspirations and even lower expectations insofar as occupational mobility is concerned. Some are not very intelligent. Others may have ability but, because of defeats suffered in school, in family relationships, or at play, have a low self-appraisal of their abilities; these include school dropouts. Many have sunk into apathy.[50] Altogether, when compared with the talented or even with the solid citizenry who pursue middle-status occupations, they show little promise.

What can be done to rehabilitate and upgrade them? The prospects are not very good, but such hope as does exist rests solidly on education. Among the many problems involved in helping them to rise through education is that many teachers have little interest in working with these rejects, because they know that poor people do not have a very high potential. Some, however, do have latent ability and, if they are moti-

48. Philip Abelson, "Revitalizing the Mature Scientist," *Science* (16 August, 1963), p. 597.

49. Morris Janowitz, *The Professional Soldier* (Glencoe, Ill.: Free Press, 1960), pp. 121–27.

50. *See* Gunnar Myrdal, *The Affluent Society* (New York: Pantheon Books, February 1965).

vated and assisted to overcome the stigma and other damage done by earlier failures, they might become semiskilled workers, clerks, sales workers, or service workers, or even rise into technical or professional occupations.

The problem is not merely one of motivation. There are, in many cases, deep-seated sociological problems attributable to continual exposure to and reinforcement from the values held by their families and friends.

The fact that students from low socioeconomic status (SES) families, including blacks and certain other ethnic minorities, are more likely to fail than other students, has been interpreted by some writers as evidence of administrative discrimination by schools. Patricia Sexton, for example, argues that IQ scores provide teachers with low expectations of scholastic performance by children from low income families, with the result that they are placed in a slow learner group where they are not challenged.[51]

Concern that low IQ scores among persons from low social economic status families may keep such persons from using the educational route to the elite occupations and hence greatly reduce their life chances, has been a major impetus for publicly financed programs of compensatory education such as Headstart and Higher Horizons.

Arthur R. Jensen, an educational psychologist at the University of California at Berkeley has challenged the potential returns from such programs. His argument starts with a reference to the finding of the 1967 Commission on Civil Rights that [52] ". . . none of the (compensatory education) programs appear to have raised significantly the achievement of participating pupils as a group. . . ."

Jensen concluded, on the basis of an exhaustive review of twentieth century research on IQ, that the failure of compen-

---

51. Patricia Sexton, *Education and Income: Inequalities in Our Public Schools* (New York: Viking Press, 1961); *see also* Wilbur Brookover and Edsel Erickson, *Society, Schools and Learning* (Boston: Allyn & Bacon, 1969), p. 17.

52. Arthur R. Jensen, "How Much Can We Boost IQ and Scholastic Achievement?" *Harvard Educational Review*, vol. 39, no. 1 (Winter 1969), p. 3.

satory education programs to raise subsequent educational achievement of participants is due to the hereditary nature of intelligence. He cited with approval the 1905 dictum of E. L. Thorndike:[53] "In the actual race of life, which is not to get ahead, but to get ahead of somebody, the chief determining factor is heredity." Jensen says that the research he examined warrants the conclusion that 80 per cent of individual differences in IQ are due to heredity.[54]

Jensen stated that average IQ varies by social class and argues that some of these differences are genetic "largely as a result of differential selection of the parent generations for different patterns of ability." [55]

A substantial portion of Jensen's article is devoted to a discussion of the differences in IQ between Negroes and whites. He reports that Negroes consistently have IQ scores that on the average are about fifteen points below those of whites and that "as a group, Negroes perform somewhat more poorly on those subtests which tap abstract abilities." [56] Since abstract reasoning ability is crucial to higher education and to success in professional and technical occupations, the conclusion that 80 per cent of IQ differences are hereditary implies that Negroes, as well as whites with low IQs, have little chance of succeeding either in college or in such occupations. It is this implication more than anything else that has disturbed and angered many social scientists and social rights activists.

Jensen's article has revived the long quiescent controversy about the relative importance of heredity and environment as determinants of educational and occupational achievement. It is virtually an article of faith among contemporary sociologists that ethnic, racial, and residential differences in IQ are culture-bound, attributable primarily to social and cultural

---

53. Jensen, "IQ and Scholastic Achievement," pp. 28, 75.
54. Arthur R. Jensen, "Race and the Genetics of Intelligence: A Reply to Lewontin," *Bulletin of the Atomic Scientists* (May 1970), p. 19.
55. Ibid., p. 19.
56. Jensen, "IQ and Scholastic Achievement," p. 81.

influences which tend to be magnified by the urban middle-class content of IQ tests.

If Jensen's thesis is correct, the chances of high educational achievement and subsequent upward occupational mobility of persons from poverty-stricken families cannot be improved much, if any, by compensatory education. This would mean that socioeconomic stratification based upon educational and occupational achievement is caste-like with a substantial hereditary component. At least in the recent past, this possibility has been rejected by most social scientists as well as by Americans in general. It has been rejected at least partly because it runs counter to the ideological position, epitomized by the Horatio Alger myth and the Protestant work ethic, that anyone who works hard can rise in the system.

My opinion, which is based largely on my professional experiences as a sociologist, is that educational and occupational achievements are heavily influenced by social and cultural factors, especially the expectations and appraisals (praise or deprecation) communicated to a person by others whose opinions are important to him (in sociological jargon, his "significant others"). I agree with the conclusion of Brookover and Erickson that while there undoubtedly are limits to the ability of people to learn, few people reach their limit.[57] It follows that scholastic and occupational achievements can be improved even for people with IQ scores that are below the mean. However, it is clear from the failure of large-scale compensatory education programs that effective means for accomplishing this objective have not yet been developed.[58] For the present, therefore, it seems clear, in view of the close connection between educational and occupational achievement, that there are many hundreds of thousands, perhaps millions, of

57. Wilbur B. Brookover and Edsel L. Erickson, *Society, Schools and Learning* (Boston: Allyn & Bacon, 1969), p. 17.

58. Some small-scale programs have reported some success, but at present it does not appear feasible to use their techniques on a general basis. For one example of the influence of teachers' expectations, *see* Robert Rosenthal and Lenore Jacobson, *Pygmalion in the Classroom: Teacher Expectation and Pupils' Intellectual Development* (New York: Holt, Rinehart and Winston, 1968).

persons who have little chance to rise very far in our contemporary occupational system.

The existence of a disparity between the language of the poor and the language used by the teacher may be particularly important. Basil Bernstein has presented convincing evidence that the language structure of the lower classes in Great Britain is not conducive to scholarship or to learning the nuances of social relationships among the middle classes.[59] This problem may not exist to the same degree in the United States as it does in Great Britain, but there is some evidence that it does exist.[60] Deep-seated problems that reside in the culture of local social systems and not merely in the individual cannot be solved without new approaches. More of what is already being done will not suffice, and it is likely to take considerable time as well as experimentation to develop the imaginative approaches required. It is also likely that the application of new approaches may require changes in the attitudes of many community leaders and teachers.[61]

Selected References

Clark, Burton R. *Educating the Expert Society.* San Francisco: Chandler Publishing Co., 1962. Discusses emerging problems of education.

Brookover, Wilbur B., and Erickson, Edsel L. *Society, Schools and Learning.* Boston: Allyn & Bacon, 1969. A short essay on the sociology of education that emphasizes maximization of human potential through education.

59. Basil Bernstein, "Social Class and Linguistic Development: A Theory of Social Learning," in Halsey, Floud, and Anderson, *Education, Economy, and Society,* pp. 288–314.

60. Leonard Schatzman and Anselm Strauss, "Social Class and Modes of Communication," *American Journal of Sociology* (January 1955), pp. 329–38.

61. Michael, *Next Generation,* pp. 104–105.

Education for a Changing World of Work. Panel of Consultants on Vocational Education, U.S. Office of Education, Washington, D.C. This report presents information on vocational and technical education. It led to the Vocational Education Act of 1963.

Halsey, A. H., Floud, Jean, and Anderson, C. Arnold. *Education, Economy, and Society.* New York: Free Press, 1961. A collection of outstanding papers on various facets of the sociology of education.

Venn, Grant. *Man, Education, and Work.* Washington, D.C.: American Council on Education, 1964. Discusses the historical development of vocational and technical education and reviews federal participation up to and including the Vocational Education Act of 1963.

10. Occupational Mobility

Occupational mobility means shifting from one occupation to another. When this movement is between occupational status levels, it is called vertical occupational mobility. If it involves a change to another occupation at the same occupational status level, it is called horizontal occupational mobility.[1] Geographic movement from one area to another is called migration. Among sociologists, especially those who have used occupation as a major indicator of socioeconomic status or class, attention has tended to focus on intergenerational occupational mobility, especially the extent to which the occupational status level of a father determines the occupational status level of his son. Much less attention has been devoted to occupational shifts within individual work histories. Both types of mobility are important to a clear understanding of the sociological factors involved in occupational careers.

Millions of immigrants have improved their economic circumstances and the life chances of their descendants by migrating from Europe to the United States. Until approximately 1920, it was possible for an ambitious immigrant or an ambitious native to settle on a piece of virgin land or to find employment in industry. Many succeeded while others who were less fortunate or less industrious failed. The failures included an unknown but undoubtedly large proportion of the seven million European immigrants who returned to their home countries between 1820 and 1950,[2] as well as a large but

1. These concepts were introduced in the first systematic treatise on social mobility, which was written by Pitirim Sorokin, *Social Mobility* (New York: Harper and Bros., 1927).
2. Walter L. Slocum, *Agricultural Sociology* (New York: Harper and Bros., 1962), p. 91.

unknown proportion of the millions who left American farms to work in urban industrial occupations during the last half century.

The general outlook of most people in the United States has been optimistic. While failures have occurred, these usually have been attributed to personal inadequacies rather than to any inherent qualities in the occupational opportunity structure. Nevertheless, as we have seen, some people now blame social institutions, especially schools, for low occupational placement.

Excepting periods of depression, the prevailing view has resembled the Horatio Alger stories, the expectation that an able individual who works hard inevitably rises from his humble origins to a high-status occupation such as owner of a great fortune, president of a great corporation, or even president of the United States. It has happened: Abraham Lincoln was born in a log cabin, and Charles E. Wilson, former president of General Motors, began as a manual worker. But the odds are against this sort of dramatic upward mobility. Upward occupational mobility frequently occurs, but individuals with high potential ability do not always rise to high status occupations or to high organizational positions.

The recent rediscovery of the existence of widespread poverty in America has focused attention on vertical occupational mobility. Efforts are being made to help the poor, especially the children of the poor, to upgrade their occupational skills so they can earn better incomes and thus participate more fully in the fruits of the "affluent" society.

In this chapter we shall review briefly what appear to be the central findings of selected studies of occupational mobility.

Migration and Occupational Mobility

In the United States occupational mobility is frequently accompanied by geographic migration. American tradition emphasizes the optimistic view that "the grass is greener elsewhere." From colonial times through the present, there have been a number of major currents of migration, including the settlement of the western frontiers, the migration from farms to industrial cities, the migration from the Dust Bowl in the 1930s, the migration of workers to centers of war industry during World War II, and the current movement to Florida and the Southwest. In many cases both push and pull factors were involved. People who lived where there were relatively poor occupational opportunities set out to seek their fortunes elsewhere.

In the last half century the promised land of opportunity has been the industrial cities, where high wages in factories have induced immigrants from foreign countries as well as southern Negroes and other farm youths and young adults to leave their home communities. In recent years we have seen continued migration from farms and from such labor surplus areas as Appalachia and the former textile towns of New England, as well as much intercity migration. States that have gained heavily include California, Texas, and Florida, all characterized by relatively mild climates and expanding employment opportunities in aerospace and other industries.

Many migrants have found better jobs, but this does not always happen. Those most likely to improve their occupational positions are younger whites who are well educated. Those least likely to benefit include older workers, the unskilled, and the uneducated, particularly nonwhites:

"They are the ones with the least resources for moving and least access to information on employment opportunities elsewhere. They are also much less likely than more skilled workers to have firm offers of jobs in other areas. When they do move—possibly as a last resort after a long and fruitless search for work locally—they may go to communities where there is no more demand for their service than there was in their home community. As a result, unskilled workers who migrate are subject to recurring unemployment and tend to make repeated moves. Many return to their home communities to resume the hunt for employment." [3]

3. Lyndon B. Johnson, *Manpower Report of the President* (Washington, D.C.: U.S. Government Printing Office, 1965), p. 146.

A special study by the Bureau of Labor Statistics of the characteristics of migrants who moved between March 1962 and March 1963, together with data from the 1960 census, provides the bases for the following generalizations[4]:

1. Most men who migrated were already employed, and many moved to accept other jobs. However, migration rates were twice as high among the unemployed (11 per cent versus 6 per cent).

2. Most migrants were better educated than those who did not move; 25 per cent of the young men (twenty-five to twenty-nine) who migrated between 1955 and 1960 were college graduates compared with 9 per cent of the nonmigrants.

3. Young men who follow professional and technical occupations have exceptionally high mobility compared to other young men; among such men, twenty-five to twenty-nine in 1960, more than half (51.3 per cent) had migrated between 1955 and 1960 compared to 30.3 per cent of all employed men in this age category and less than a quarter of those employed in blue-collar occupations.

4. Migration rates for nonwhites were much lower than migration rates for whites. For example, among young men who were twenty-five to twenty-nine years of age in 1960, less than one-third of those employed in professional and technical occupations had migrated during the preceding five years, and the migration rate for all nonwhite men in this age category was only 17.1 per cent.

"The low migration rate of nonwhite workers is probably associated with the fact that relatively few of them have had a chance to qualify for the higher skilled occupations. Also, nonwhites less often receive offers of employment in other areas. Altogether, only one out of every five nonwhite men migrants reported that he moved to 'take a job' or 'because of a transfer' between March, 1962, and March, 1963,—just about half the corresponding figure for white men." [5]

4. *Geographic Mobility and Employment Status*, Special Labor Force Report no. 44 (1964) cited in Johnson, *Manpower Report*, pp. 145ff.
  5. Ibid., pp. 147–48.

In spite of the tremendous influx of Negroes into northern and western cities, the data of the 1960 census showed that during the period 1955–60 Negroes had less geographic mobility than whites in every age and educational category.[6] This was true in every major occupational category including professional and technical workers. It has been suggested that the relatively low migration of Negroes in high-status occupations is due to the tendency for high-income Negro families to have several employed members.

"This helps to explain why, contrary to the situation among white families, Negro families at the higher income levels are no more likely to migrate than those with lower incomes. A move by an upper-income Negro family usually involves the displacement of several wage earners who would have to find jobs at their new location in order to maintain the family income."[7]

During the decade of the 1960s, migration of Negroes from the southern states continued at an average annual rate of 147,400. Nevertheless, the South still continues to be the region with the highest proportion of Negroes.[8]

Most Americans of all colors now reside in urban areas and most members of the labor force have nonfarm jobs. In 1971, only 4 per cent of whites and 3 per cent of blacks were farmers or farm workers.[9]

In relation to the great farm-to-city migration, which is still under way, it should be noted that, if migrants from farms are not well-educated, they cannot hope to rise in the occupational world to positions of responsibility, influence, and high pay.

Statistical information from studies of the adjustments of

6. Lyndon B. Johnson, *Manpower Report of the President* (Washington, D.C.: U.S. Government Printing Office, 1964), p. 155.
7. Johnson, 1965, *Manpower Report*, p. 156.
8. U.S. Census Bureau, *The Social and Economic Status of the Black Population in the United States*, 1971, series p-23, no. 42, p. 14.
9. **Ibid.**, p. 66.

rural migrants in nonfarm employment shows that this is exactly what tends to happen. The typical migrant from a farm enters the urban employment market as an unskilled worker, that is, near the bottom of the occupational ladder, and he makes little, if any, upward progress during his work life.[10] The exceptions include principally those who have obtained a good education, plus a few others who have more or less stumbled upon unusual opportunities.

Some writers treat the subject of migration in such a way as to emphasize the injurious rather than the beneficial aspects. Both social and economic costs are involved in changing one's place of residence and one's occupation or place of employment, but this is only one side of the coin. There are advantages, too; although some of these are problematic in the individual case, they are undeniable in the aggregate.

From the standpoint of the society, a mobile labor force such as this country has experienced since the early days of settlement makes it relatively easy to mobilize necessary occupational skills in the geographic locations where the greatest need for such skills exist.

From the standpoint of an individual, taking a job in a new location offers an opportunity for making new friendships and establishing new interpersonal relationships largely unaffected by the mistakes, if any, the person may have made in other work systems or communities. This is particularly advantageous to the young worker who is thus enabled to start in a new work system and a new social environment as an adult rather than as a child. It has advantages, too, for some who are enabled to relegate into the background personal experiences they would like to forget. In addition, by exposing the individual to new values and behavior standards, incentives are provided for changes in values and behavior patterns.

The great mobility of the American labor force is a central element in the relatively ready adoption of social and cultural

10. Elton F. Jackson and H. J. Crockett, Jr., "Occupational Mobility in the United States," *American Sociological Review* (February 1964), p. 9.

change in America. The expectation of moving has focused the attention of many people on a style of life and a manner of interpersonal conduct that facilitates interaction with strangers and promotes the easy development of new interpersonal relationships. As contrasted with Europeans, Americans have long been noted for their hospitality and friendliness and their readiness to accept a stranger at face value until and unless he demonstrates that this trust is misplaced. These attitudes and patterns of interpersonal relationship have developed during the course of the long history of interoccupational and interregional mobility that is characteristic of American workers.

Intergenerational Occupational Mobility

The once strongly held view of the United States as the land of economic and occupational opportunity has been dimmed in recent years. Ely Chinoy, in a review of a number of studies of occupational mobility, comments that this revised view "seems to be widely held among social scientists." [11] Seymour M. Lipset and Reinhard Bendix have expressed grave doubts about the ability of an individual to rise much above the occupational status level of his father.

"If an individual comes from the working class, he will typically receive little education or vocational advice; while he attends school, his job plans for the future will be vague and when he leaves school he is likely to take the first available job he can find. The poverty, lack of planning, and failure to explore fully the available job opportunities that characterize the working class family are handed down from generation to generation. The same accumulation of factors, which in the working class

11. Ely Chinoy, "Social Mobility Trends in the United States," *American Sociological Review* (April 1955), p. 180.

TABLE 6. Current Occupation by Father's Occupation—Noninstitutional Male in thousands. The population in this report includes 718,000 members of the of the armed forces are excluded)

FATHER'S OCCUPATION	TOTAL POPULATION 25 TO 64 YEARS OLD	CURRENT OCCUPATION			
		Professional, technical, and kindred workers	*Managers, officials, and proprietors, except farm*	*Sales workers*	*Clerical and kindred workers*
TOTAL	39,969	4,638	5,958	1,871	2,449
Professional, technical, and kindred workers	1,714	669	286	147	113
Managers, officials, and proprietors, except farm	4,256	866	1,363	363	283
Sales workers	1,450	266	409	205	84
Clerical and kindred workers	1,257	323	205	90	111
Craftsmen, foremen, and kindred workers	6,763	815	1,036	297	487
Operatives and kindred workers	5,675	612	640	230	348
Service workers, including private household	1,720	164	231	93	154
Laborers, except farm and mine	2,376	130	177	80	177
Farmers and farm managers	10,334	503	1,098	235	447
Farm laborers and foremen	1,046	22	72	19	37
Occupation not reported	3,378	268	441	112	208
Per cent whose father's occupation was same		15.3	24.7	11.6	5.0
Per cent Distribution Total	100.0	11.6	14.9	4.7	6.1

SOURCE: Adapted from Tables 1 and 4, Current Population Reports, Series P-23, Department of Commerce, Bureau of the Census, 12 May, 1964.

Population 25 to 64 Years Old, for the United States: March 1962 (Numbers armed forces living off post or with their families on post; all other members

CURRENT OCCUPATION

Craftsmen, foremen, and kindred workers	Operatives and kindred workers	Service workers, including private household	Laborers, except farm and mine	Farmers and farm managers	Farm laborers and foremen	Not in experienced civilian labor force	Per cent same occupation as father
7,693	6,998	2,184	2,562	2,069	678	2,869	23.1
142	168	50	32	20	6	81	41.0
556	341	101	76	39	13	255	34.1
162	142	44	28	23	2	85	15.0
195	106	70	35	16	0	106	9.6
1,843	1,098	323	302	50	23	489	29.4
1,250	1,358	311	395	49	49	433	25.9
341	340	180	102	17	4	94	11.1
498	582	201	313	27	25	166	14.2
1,871	1,946	499	808	1,696	405	826	17.8
197	250	78	129	60	98	84	10.2
638	667	327	342	72	53	250	—
26.1	21.5	9.7	14.1	84.9	15.7	—	
19.2	17.5	5.5	6.4	5.2	1.7	7.2	

No. 11 "Lifetime Occupational Mobility of Adult Males, March 1962," U.S.

creates a series of mounting disadvantages, works to the advantage of a child coming from a well-to-do family." [12]

This position may be called cultural determinism, and its pessimistic tone contrasts vividly with the optimistic tone inherent in the Horatio Alger myth. It has become part of the conventional wisdom concerning the economic handicap incurred by being born into a low socioeconomic status family.

What is the evidence? The most comprehensive information on intergenerational occupational mobility of adult males in the United States was obtained in March 1962 as part of a nationwide survey conducted by the U.S. Census Bureau.[13] Peter M. Blau and Otis Dudley Duncan concluded, after a careful analysis of this sample, that the occupational status level of a father does not predetermine the occupational life chances of his son.[14]

Table 6 indicates a substantial amount of upward mobility, especially among sons of white-collar workers. In fact, sons of clerical workers and salesmen reach professional and managerial occupations nearly as often as do sons of professionals but sons of blue-collar workers have been much less fortunate in attaining high-status occupations. Sons of unskilled manual workers and farmers were least likely to achieve high status. Nearly one out of every four men aged twenty-five to sixty-four years of age in March 1962 was pursuing an occupation classified in the same occupational status level on the census occupational scale as the occupation pursued by the father when his son was about sixteen years old. Sons of professional, technical, and kindred workers were more likely than others to follow occupations similar to those of their fathers, while sons of farm laborers and foremen were the least likely to

12. Seymour M. Lipset and Reinhardt Bendix, *Social Mobility in Industrial Society* (Berkeley: University of Californio Press, 1959), pp. 197-98.

13. U.S. Census Bureau, *Technical Studies: Lifetime Occupational Mobility of Adult Males* (March 1962), series P-23, no. 11 (12 May, 1964).

14. Peter M. Blau and Otis Dudley Duncan, *The American Occupational Structure* (New York: John Wiley & Sons, 1967), p. 200.

follow their fathers' occupations. Looking at the data of table 6 from another point of view, we find that 85 per cent of those who were farmers in March 1962 were sons of farmers, even though only 16.4 per cent of all of the sons of farmers and farm managers were engaged in farming. At the other extreme, only 5 per cent of clerical workers had fathers who followed this occupation.

It is clear that there has been a substantial amount of occupational shifting. Much of this can be attributed to changes in the occupational opportunity structure caused by industrial development, although it is not absolutely measurable.

After analyzing information from this 1962 nationwide survey, Peter M. Blau concluded that sons of fathers in low-status occupations tend to begin their work in an occupation with a status similar to that of their fathers, although many of them later obtain higher-level occupations.[15] Sons of fathers with high-status occupations, on the other hand, tend to begin their work lives in occupations that are considerably lower in status than those of their fathers and then tend to move upward during their work period.[16]

Otis Dudley Duncan analyzed the data of the 1962 nationwide survey of mobility from a different point of view and concluded that upward occupational mobility tended to increase. "As of 1962, there was little immediate cause for anxiety about whether the American occupational structure was providing more restricted opportunities." [17] But Duncan warned that it is hazardous to extrapolate this finding to the future because the data refer to a period of major change that is not likely to be repeated.

"It is well to remember that the . . . data refer to an historical experience in which the transition to complete industrialization was rapidly nearing its end. If the movement off the farms

15. "Occupational Supply and Recruitment," *American Sociological Review* (August 1965), p. 485.
16. Ibid.
17. "The Trend of Occupational Mobility in the United States," *American Sociological Review* (August 1965), p. 498.

has been a major factor inducing upward mobility from non-farm origins in the past, it is not clear what its counterpart may be in an era when few persons originate on farms." [18]

This warning is important for those who are tempted to project historical trends into the future. As Duncan suggests, in considering occupational shifts over a long period of time, it is essential to take into account not only past changes in the occupational opportunity structure brought about by changes in industry and agriculture, such as the revolution in agricultural technology that has led to the tremendous decline in agricultural employment, but also prospective changes that may accompany widespread adoption of automation.

Blau and Duncan found that educational attainment was the most important determinant of upward intergenerational occupational mobility but that better educated Negroes (except for the minority who were college graduates) "fare even worse relative to whites than uneducated Negroes." [19]

There is some basis for hope that these inequities will eventually be corrected. More recent information, noted in chapter 9, shows that the level of educational attainments of Negroes has risen more rapidly than that of whites since 1960. In addition, there is evidence that racial discrimination in employment is not longer as pronounced as it was even a decade ago; in fact, some college and university administrators have accused the U.S. Department of Health, Education and Welfare of fostering discrimination against whites.[20]

The first systematic analysis of intergenerational mobility patterns of American females was reported in December 1971 by Peter G. DeJong et al. These investigators were obliged to use the father's occupation rather than the mother's occupation as their base line. Their data were drawn from six nationwide samples collected by the National Opinion Research Center during the period 1955 to 1965. Contrary to expecta-

18. Ibid.
19. Blau and Duncan, *American Occupational Structure*, pp. 238–41.
20. *Newsweek* (4 December, 1972), pp. 127–28.

tions based on the presumed role conflict experienced by females (homemaker versus worker), comparison of findings with those of Blau and Duncan for males revealed no significant differences between males and females.[21]

Information on occupational mobility in western Europe indicates that intergenerational vertical mobility is not substantially different from that revealed by studies in the United States, a finding contrary to what many have expected.[22]

INTERGENERATIONAL OCCUPATIONAL MOBILITY OF BUSINESS LEADERS [23]

The leadership positions in American business are of special significance, because the men who occupy them make decisions that affect us all. Statistical evidence concerning the origins of men who held top positions in American business in 1952 shows convincingly that most of them came from families in which the father held an occupation that was classified in a higher-status level. More than half of the 8,562 respondents in a study by W. Lloyd Warner and James Abegglen were sons of business executives or owners, and 14 per cent were sons of men who followed various professions—doctors, engineers, lawyers, ministers, teachers, and so forth. Most of the remaining third of the top executives were sons of salesmen, clerical workers, farmers, or manual workers, with a few from other occupations such as military officers and government

21. Peter Y. DeJong, Milton J. Brawer, and Stanley S. Robin, "Patterns of Female Intergenerational Occupational Mobility: A Comparison with Male Patterns of Intergenerational Occupational Mobility," *American Sociological Review*, vol. 36, no. 6 (December 1971), pp. 1033–44.

22. For information concerning occupational mobility in Europe, *see* Gösta Carlsen, *Social Mobility and Class Structure* (Lund, Sweden: C. W. K. Gleerup, 1958); D. V. Glass, ed., *Social Mobility in Britain* (Glencoe, Ill.: Free Press, 1954); and Seymour M. Lipset and Natalie Rogoff, "Occupational Mobility in Europe and the United States," in S. Nosow and W. H. Form, *Man, Work, and Society* (New York: Basic Books, 1962), pp. 362–72.

23. Information concerning the mobility of business leaders presented in this section is based on W. Lloyd Warner and James Abegglen, *Big Business Leaders in America* (New York: Harper and Bros., 1955).

officials. Commenting on the implications of their findings, Warner and Abegglen said:

> "Whatever our national hopes, the business leaders of America are a select group, drawn for the most part from the upper ranks. Only to a limited extent may it be said that every man's chances are as good as the next man's, for birth in the higher occupational levels improves these life chances considerably. If equal opportunity were realized in practice, the business elite and the nation as a whole would share a common background, whereas the composition of the business elite is clearly weighted toward the higher occupational levels of our society." [24]

To answer the question of whether the upper ranks of American business are tending toward closure for men of modest origins, Warner and Abbeglen compared their data with similar information from a study made in 1928 by F. W. Taussig and C. S. Joslyn. The comparison showed that:

> ". . . The system is increasingly open to men from the lower occupational ranks. Not only is there no evidence that opportunity for sons of farmers, laborers, and white-collar workers is decreasing, but movement from these backgrounds into the business elite takes place in greater degree today than a generation ago. The system is not closing and becoming more rigid —in fact it is more flexible and increasingly recruits its leaders from all parts of our society." [25]

Information provided by respondents in the Warner and Abegglen study revealed that top business executives tended to be much better educated than the average man of their age. Further analysis disclosed that educational accomplishments had special significance in connection with the upward occupational mobility of those who had fathers in low-status occupations. Although the business leaders attended a large

24. Ibid., p. 14.
25. Ibid., p. 30.

number of different colleges and universities, over 40 per cent attended one of the following for their first (or only) college-level training: Yale, Harvard, Princeton, Cornell, University of Pennsylvania, University of Illinois, Massachusetts Institute of Technology, University of Michigan, New York University, University of Minnesota, Williams College, University of California at Berekeley, University of Chicago, and Columbia University. Almost one-third of these men went first to Harvard or Yale. This information verifies the idea that certain elite universities provide a disproportionate share of the leaders of American business. Warner and Abbeglen characterized higher education as "the royal road" to elite status for the 1952 business leaders. This seems to be an accurate characterization and will undoubtedly continue to be true. However, increasingly specialized educational accomplishments such as graduate training in business administration will take on much more importance than they have in the past.

Occupational Mobility within Individual Work Histories

Anyone who participates in the world of work builds up a history of work experience. The work history of a particular man who has retired or died after a long work life may show that he has participated in only a single occupation. But, if he lived and worked in the United States in the twentieth century, more than likely he had several occupations. We shall document this observation shortly with empirical evidence obtained from studies made by sociologists and others concerning the patterns of employment of American men during the course of their working years. Unfortunately, comparable information is not available for women, but other evidence indicates that women are much less likely to persevere in the pursuit of occupational careers.

Information from the 1962 nationwide sample survey of occupational mobility of American men aged twenty-five to sixty-four cited earlier reveals that only 23.6 per cent were in the same occupation in which they started and many of the latter were probably young men.[26] This shows that for most men the first job does not represent a lifetime occupational commitment but rather a means of entering the world of work.

Although the majority did not stay in the occupational category of their first job, there were notable exceptions (table 7). Nearly two-thirds of the professional and technical workers and half of those who started out as proprietors, officials, or managers continued in the same occupational category. Other major occupational categories with retention rates above the average were craftsmen, foremen, and kindred workers with 41 per cent and farmers and farm managers with 38 per cent.[27] There was considerable upward mobility between the first and the current occupation, which is not surprising; it is hardly to be expected that inexperienced youths would be able immediately to enter skilled, managerial, proprietary, official, professional, or technical occupations.

As table 7 shows, 6 per cent of those whose current occupations were classified in the manager, official, and proprietary category began in this type of work, while 44.1 per cent of professional, technical, and kindred workers had started in that category. Only among farm laborers had more than half started out in the same occupation. There may be a normal sequence or pattern of progression among occupations in a few cases such as agriculture, where the son of a farmer normally begins as a farm laborer rather than a farm owner-operator or a farm manager, and among craftsmen, foremen, and kindred workers, where a person normally starts as an apprentice.

Leonard Broom and J. H. Smith have suggested that certain occupations which they call "bridging occupations," provide work experience that facilitates movement from one occupational field to another.[28] Among the occupations that, in their opinion, have this quality are butler, soldier, schoolteacher,

26. U.S. Census Bureau, *Lifetime Occupational Mobility of Adult Males*, p. 1.
27. Ibid.
28. Leonard Broom and J. H. Smith, "Bridging Occupations," *British Journal of Sociology*, vol. 14 (1963), pp. 321–34.

peddler, and professional athlete. Although they present no quantitative information, they point out that military officers not infrequently become civilian executives, while military technicians may become civilian technicians and other military men may become guards or public law officers. Broom and Smith believe that teachers are upwardly mobile, especially in developing countries where educated people are in short supply. Athletic stars tend to move into occupations where their reputations have commercial value. It is not difficult to find examples of well-known sports figures who have become wealthy through investing income from endorsement of various products.

In most cases, however, a pattern of relationship is not well established or based upon operating relationships among occupations; instead many occupational shifts among adult members of the male labor force of the United States probably have been based on an opportunistic attitude toward work.

Information concerning the number of occupational changes and the pattern of horizontal or vertical mobility among specific occupations is not available from the census reports, therefore it is necessary to rely on information collected and analyzed by investigators in various places and at different points in time.

Even though the available studies were not all designed with reference to the concept of occupational career as used in this book, it may be useful to review briefly the findings of selected studies.

THE SAN JOSE STUDY, 1937 [29]

Percy E. Davidson and Dewey Anderson studied the work histories of 749 male residents of San Jose, California, aged twenty and over, classifying these men into two age groups, those between twenty and thirty-five and those who were

29. Percy E. Davidson and Dewey Anderson, *Occupational Mobility in an American Community* (Palo Alto, Calif.: Stanford University Press, 1937).

TABLE 7. Current Occupation by Occupation of First Job—Noninstitutional
(Numbers in thousands)

OCCUPATION OF FIRST JOB–	TOTAL POPULATION 25 TO 64 YEARS OLD	CURRENT OCCUPATION			
		Professional, technical, and kindred workers	Managers, officials, and proprietors, except farm	Sales workers	Clerical and kindred workers
TOTAL	39,969	4,638	5,958	1,871	2,449
Professional, technical and kindred workers	3,182	1,990	531	106	146
Managers, officials, and proprietors, except farm	719	123	347	53	38
Sales workers	2,430	277	717	378	246
Clerical and kindred workers	4,229	619	960	384	744
Craftsmen, foremen, and kindred workers	3,666	315	640	138	143
Operatives and kindred workers	10,363	631	1,385	403	556
Service workers, including private household	1,523	115	169	40	76
Laborers, except farm and mine	5,231	301	528	175	258
Farmers and farm managers	1,248	32	79	38	38
Farm laborers and foremen	5,704	111	403	103	156
Occupation not reported	1,674	124	199	53	48
Per cent whose first occupation was in same category		44.1	6.0	20.8	31.0
Per cent distribution Total	100.0	11.6	14.9	4.7	6.1

SOURCE: Adapted from Tables 2 and 5, Current Population Reports, series P-23, Department of Commerce, Bureau of the Census, 12 May, 1964.

Male Population 25 to 64 Years Old, for the United States: March 1962

CURRENT OCCUPATION

Craftsmen, foremen, and kindred workers	Operatives and kindred workers	Service workers, including private household	Laborers, except farm and mine	Farmers and farm managers	Farm laborers and foremen	Not in experienced civilian labor force	Per cent same as for first job
7,693	6,998	2,184	2,562	2,069	678	2,869	29.3
122	73	28	17	28	6	135	65.3
55	37	13	16	12	2	23	49.9
257	305	73	56	21	1	99	16.2
485	414	187	119	50	9	258	18.7
1,415	433	123	144	65	17	233	41.2
2,580	2,663	545	643	203	79	675	27.5
244	319	302	126	6	7	119	21.5
1,122	1,226	348	740	102	65	366	15.2
194	167	58	63	449	63	67	38.0
977	1,124	328	542	1,101	398	461	7.6
242	237	179	96	32	31	433	—
19.0	39.4	15.1	30.0	22.0	61.5		
19.2	17.5	5.5	6.4	5.2	1.7	7.2	

no. 11, "Lifetime Occupational Mobility of Adult Males, March 1962," U.S.

thirty-five and over. This study, made during the depression of the 1930s, showed a substantial amount of instability among the workers; the older men were better established than the younger ones, and, to some extent, this may have been a product of historical events. Many of the older men undoubtedly were well established in their jobs before the depression, whereas many of the younger men had difficulty finding or holding jobs during this period.

A more detailed examination by Davidson and Anderson of the occupational histories of 466 of the San Jose workers showed that there had not been very much upward occupational mobility even after substantial periods of participation in the labor force. Most of them stayed at the same occupational level as the job they first entered.

THE OAKLAND, CALIFORNIA, STUDY [30]

Seymour M. Lipset and Reinhard Bendix analyzed the work histories of a sample of the Oakland, California, middle-status labor force as of 1949. Their study showed that job mobility was the rule rather than the exception. Even though these men were still in the labor force and further changes might be anticipated, the average number of jobs per man was 6.3; among professional workers, who presumably would be the most stable, there had been 4.4 jobs; and among sales workers and semiskilled and unskilled workers the number of different jobs were much higher. The greatest stability in terms of job changes was among business owners and executives. The average number of jobs per respondent classified by occupational status level was: Professional, 4.4; business owners and executives, 3.2; white collar, 4.9; sales, 7; skilled, 4.2; semiskilled, 9.6; unskilled, 10.1; all civilian jobs, 6.3.

With respect to the pattern of occupational changes, Lipset and Bendix found that the shifts were mostly between occupational positions of similar status levels. Relatively little shifting occurred between manual-work and white-collar oc-

30. Lipset and Bendix, *Social Mobility*.

cupations. Such crossing over the boundary between manual and nonmanual occupations as had occurred was temporary rather than permanent in many cases.

Perhaps most significant was the finding that the first job tended to be a good predictor of future occupational mobility. That is, men who started in a low-status occupation tended not to rise very high. Another interesting finding was that proprietors of small businesses frequently had worked previously at manual occupations. Lipset and Bendix suggest that this may be the only practicable choice for upward occupational mobility on the part of a manual worker.

The importance of family background is emphasized by Lipset and Bendix as a factor that greatly influences the subsequent occupational achievements. Their analysis indicates that the socioeconomic level of the family origin as reflected in the father's occupation consists of a configuration of interrelated depressing factors in the case of young people from working-class families and supportive factors in the case of those from prosperous high-level occupation families.

Lipset and Bendix apparently did not analyze the data of their study from the standpoint of occupational career patterns. The focus of their interest was upon occupational mobility, particularly the question of whether sons had progressed upward from the level of their fathers' occupations.

THE OHIO STUDY, 1946 [31]

Delbert C. Miller and William H. Form analyzed job sequences in 276 work histories obtained in Ohio and said to represent the Ohio labor force. This was the most elaborate investigation up to that time. The system of classification used by Miller and Form was essentially empirical and pragmatic rather than theory-oriented.

These investigators were especially interested in ascertaining the extent of job stability among their subjects. They

31. Delbert C. Miller and William H. Form, *Industrial Society* (New York: Harper and Bros., 1951).

defined a stable work period as one during which the worker remains in a job for a period of three years or more. Two other concepts central to their analysis were: (1) the initial work period, which includes part-time work before or after school and summer work by students; and (2) the trial job, defined as one that had been held for less than three years. Their distinction between trial and stable is arbitrary. It takes no account of commitment of the worker to his occupation or job. Since there is no theoretical defense of the breaking point of three years between a trial and a stable job, one might quibble over whether it should have been placed there rather than at two years or four years or at some other point. Nevertheless, the information from the study represents a distinct advance over what was available earlier.

Using these concepts, Miller and Form identified what they call six career families:

1. Early entrance into a stable job.
2. The "normal" job progression to a stable job.
3. Return to a trial job after attaining stability through the conventional pattern.
4. Beginning of the trial work period—mostly younger workers.
5. Return to a trial job after quick attainment of a stable job.
6. Consecutive trial jobs with no stable job as yet attained.

Summary statistics are presented by occupational status levels but not for the total sample. The greatest stability was found among professional workers, 88 per cent of whom reported stable occupational histories. Owners, managers, and officials who reported a high percentage of stable and conventional work histories (approximately 78 per cent). Next in order so far as stability was concerned were the skilled workers and foremen, approximately two-thirds of whom reported stable or conventional work histories. However, 28.2 per cent of the clerks reported occupational histories of the multiple trial pattern, which Miller and Form attribute to the large number of women who do clerical work; they allege that women typically have relatively short work careers.

A considerable amount of instability and insecurity had

occurred among unskilled workers, factory operatives, and semiskilled workers and those who were employed at domestic and personal service work. Since the sample was taken in the city, farmers were not included.

Miller and Form tested the Davidson and Anderson hypothesis that workers tend to remain at the same occupational level as the job first entered. They found considerable support for the hypothesis, although they noted that during the trial work period there is likely to be considerable occupational and residential mobility. Much of this, however, is horizontal rather than vertical in nature.

THE STUDY OF MIDWESTERN URBAN MEN [32]

Joseph Gusfield analyzed the occupational histories of 195 midwestern urban men using a system of classification based partly upon the work of Delbert C. Miller and William H. Form reviewed above. However, the Miller and Form system of classification was supplemented by the addition of a third period called the *established career period* which comprised workers who had been in the same job or occupation for six or more years. This is an improvement over the usage of Miller and Form, but it is still an empirical rather than a theoretical system of classification. Mere time does not seem adequate to establish the existence of a career as we have used the term. There is in addition a normative aspect that implies commitment and the possibility, although perhaps not the achievement, of a steady upward progression toward the pinnacle position.

Gusfield reported that three or more occupations had been pursued by six out of ten of his respondents even though they had not yet completed their participation in the labor force. As might be expected, he found that professionals reported greater stability, with respect both to occupation and to place of work. But even among the professionals, there had been a

32. Joseph Gusfield, "Occupational Roles and Forms of Enterprise," *American Journal of Sociology* (May 1961), pp. 574–80.

considerable amount of mobility. Only 20 per cent of them had worked at only one place up to the time of the study. Trained laborers, mostly construction workers, were the most mobile in terms of place of work, which Gusfield says is "a reflection, probably, of the uniquely independent contracting character of the building trades in the American economy."

Gusfield found that most individuals pursued more than one occupation during their work history. He classified 43.1 per cent of the work histories as *undirected*, characterized by frequent change and impermanence. An additional 27.6 per cent were either *unestablished*, where there was no record of any stable period in a job or occupation, or *disestablished*, where the respondent at least once had had a stable occupation or job but had left it. At the top of his system of classification is the directed career which is characterized by long-term commitment to an occupation. He identified two subcategories: (1) the *immediate establishment* pattern where an early commitment was made to a job or occupation with no changes later in the work history, and (2) the *gradual development* pattern characterized by a shift to the occupation or job after experimentation in some other job, with the current job or occupation the only established job or occupation held.

Gusfield believes that, in the future, persons who follow many nonprofessional occupations will come to resemble those in the professions in the sense that they will develop "an occupational self, unattached to specific organizations." This is an interesting possibility, but the rapid obsolescence of many technical occupations, coupled with the dominant roles of great corporations, large government, and other big organizations, appears to provide influences that may cancel it.

THE 1961 DETROIT STUDY [33]

Harold L. Wilensky studied a sample of 678 white men, aged twenty-five to fifty-five, employed, for the most part, in

33. Harold L. Wilensky, "Orderly Careers and Social Participation," *American Sociological Review* (August 1961), pp. 525–26.

lower middle-class and working-class occupations in Detroit. His sample excluded lower-income and higher-income employees. In the stratum studied, he found that the majority had "disorderly work histories"; only about 30 per cent of his sample had as much as half of their period of participation in the labor force in an "orderly career," defined as a sequence of related jobs through which workers move in a more or less orderly way ascending in the prestige hierarchy as they do so. Wilensky argues that careers in this sense have been regarded for a long time as a source of organizational stability. In fact, as noted previously, work organizations have established career lines for the purpose of providing a stable and satisfied labor force. Managerial and professional career lines are most prevalent. Wilensky suggests that, from the standpoint of the individual, the prospect of a career may lead to the establishment of a "life plan" emphasizing a pattern of deferred gratification in order to achieve long-term objectives.

In coding his data, Wilensky combined direction with orderliness to establish the following categories: (1) progression of an orderly horizontal nature; (2) progression of an orderly vertical nature; (3) progression on the border line of being orderly; (4) horizontal movement from job to job of disorderly nature; (5) movement from job to job either up or down the status scale but disorderly in nature; and (6) only a single job during the entire period of participation in the labor force. On the basis of the application of this system of classification to the work histories of his sample, he concluded that "the vast majority of the labor force is going nowhere in an unordered way. One can expect a work life of nearly unpredictable ups and downs."

Although he excluded most high-income men from his sample, Wilensky observed that the high-income college men who were included more frequently had careers than others did, but he found no distinctive association between orderliness and any other independent variable. He also noted that orderly careers were more frequently found among men under forty and concluded that this may have been the result of the exposure of these older men to the depression of the 1930s.

OCCUPATIONAL MOBILITY OF PROFESSIONAL WORKERS, 1951 [34]

Albert J. Reiss, Jr., reanalyzed the occupational mobility of a sample of 650 white men twenty-five years of age and over in 1951 who had worked in a professional-type occupation at some time during the decade of the 1950s. When interviewed, these men lived in Chicago, Los Angeles, Philadelphia, or San Francisco.

Reiss identified five major types of professions: (1) old established professions of law, medicine, higher education, religion, and esthetics; (2) new scientific and engineering professions; (3) semiprofessions, including nursing, pharmacy, optometry, and social work which "replace theoretical study of a field of learning by the acquisition of precise technical skill"; (4) "would-be" professions, including personnel directors and business managers; and (5) marginal professions, which appears to be a category for technicians.

He found a considerable amount of occupational mobility in all categories during the twelve years prior to 1951. The percentage who changed occupations were as follows: established professions, 29 per cent; new professions, 46 per cent; semiprofessions, 55 per cent; "would-be" professions, 65 per cent; and marginal professions, 52 per cent.

The study indicates that the relatively low occupational mobility of professionals is attributable in large measure to persons in the established professions. A major contribution of the study is that it enables us to note that substantial differences in mobility patterns exist among occupations that are frequently lumped together in the major occupational category "professional, technical, and kindred workers." This lack of homogeneity extends to educational attainments, income, and other characteristics.

34. Albert J. Reiss, Jr., "Occupational Mobility of Professional Workers," *American Sociological Review* (December 1955), pp. 693–700.

THE BLAU-DUNCAN STUDY OF AMERICAN MALES (1962 data) [35]

The principal emphasis in this study was on intergenerational occupational mobility, but some information is also presented about upward occupational mobility from the first job. The authors conclude that a man's educational attainments and his early work experience have a more pronounced influence on upward occupational mobility than his original social status as reflected by his father's occupation. Furthermore, forces that are important in early occupational achievement tend to fade into the past, to be less important as time goes on. Thus, more recent work experiences have greater salience for his subsequent career and such influences as social origin and education have less and less weight.[36]

DISCUSSION

These empirical studies of work histories, although based on limited samples and not entirely comparable in conceptual orientation, provide information that helps us to think more clearly about the meaning of occupational careers. When this information is considered, together with data collected by Warner and Abegglen about the career contingencies of leading business executives, with similar information from case studies and with statistical information collected by the U.S. Census Bureau concerning occupational mobility, we see that the prospect for an orderly work history or an occupational career is not very good for one without a college education. The prospects are best for those who enter one of the professions, followed by those who enter the middle management ranks of business or government. We have little solid information about the skilled crafts, but in the past the skilled construction crafts have provided career opportunities to many

35. Blau and Duncan, *American Occupational Structure.*
36. Ibid., pp. 402–03.

men without higher education. What the future may hold for the crafts no one can say with any degree of certainty.

Except for the reanalysis by Reiss of data for 650 big-city men, the studies that we have examined are deficient even though they provide us with more information than had been available previously. Their deficiency is the virtual exclusion of professional workers, executives, and wealthy businessmen, those most likely to have had occupational careers which correspond to the theoretical model suggested in chapter 1. Wilensky and Lipset and Bendix consciously sought to exclude from their samples both the wealthy and the poor. Miller and Form and Davidson and Anderson apparently did not do this, but since only a small minority of the labor force are executives and professionals, it would appear to be necessary to oversample these occupational fields to provide sufficient cases for analysis when the sample is small.

The general picture that emerges from the studies cited is epitomized by Wilensky's rather depressing conclusion quoted above. Even though this conclusion may be justifiable from the perspective of an orderly model of occupational careers, we need not interpret it as indicative of occupational defeat on the part of most American men. A. J. Jaffe and R. O. Carleton have interpreted the 1930–50 evidence on occupational mobility more optimistically.

"The United States was and still is the land of opportunity. Most men move about from one job to another during the course of their working lives so that they end in occupations often very different from those in which they began. In this process they succeed in climbing the occupational ladder so that very many reach jobs considerably above those in which they began their working careers. The majority of men improve both their economic and status positions." [37]

Much of the upward occupational mobility that has occurred during the last half century is attributable to changes in the

37. A. J. Jaffe and R. O. Carlson, *Occupational Mobility in the United States,* 1930–60 (New York: Columbia University Press, 1954), p. 58.

occupational requirements of industrial firms and other work organizations that have resulted from scientific and technological progress.

The prospects for accelerated occupational change due to the rising curve of technological development, including automation, indicates that young people who enter the labor force during the third quarter of the twentieth century can anticipate a substantial amount of occupational change; this may involve not only redefinition of occupational roles, but actual moving from one occupation to another because of the changing occupational requirements of work organizations. It does not follow, however, that this need be left entirely to chance with the individual pursuing a course on the basis of expediency and opportunism. The rising educational requirements for occupational participation suggest that this would not be a very satisfactory course of action for an individual to pursue. Instead, careful attention should be given to emerging occupational requirements so that individuals faced with the necessity of making occupational changes can obtain the necessary retraining prior to the time when change becomes essential.

Selected References

Blau, Peter M., and Duncan, Otis Dudley. *The American Occupational Structure*. New York: John Wiley & Sons, 1967. Although this study is restricted to males, it is the most comprehensive analysis yet made of occupational mobility in the United States.

Nosow, Sigmund, and Form, William H., eds. *Man, Work, and Society*. New York: Basic Books, 1962. Chapter X, "Occupational Mobility," in this reader in the sociology of occupations presents articles by Richard Centers, W. Lloyd Warner and James C. Abegglen, Natalie Rogoff, Ely Chinoy, and Seymour M. Lipset and Natalie Rogoff, an excellent selection of the literature up to the date of publication.

11. Determinants of Career Aspirations, Decisions and Attainments

Some of the important cultural and situational factors that influence the attainment of educational and occupational status have already been identified. In this chapter, we will examine the influence of specific factors—such as ambition, intelligence, self concept, family background, social and economic status, and reference groups—on levels of aspiration, choice, and achievement of individuals.

Levels of Aspiration

Research on levels of aspiration has been conducted primarily by sociologists. Vocational psychologists have shown little interest in the subject even though Edward K. Strong, Jr., G. F. Kuder, and their followers have made extensive use of closely related information about vocational interests in counseling individuals. The fascination of sociologists with *levels* of aspiration stems from the long-standing preoccupation of sociologists with social stratification.

Sociologists assume, with some justification,[1] that ambition, which may be defined as high aspiration, is a necessary prerequisite to high educational and occupational achievement. Furthermore, early research indicated that persons reared in families with low social and economic status tended to have relatively low levels of educational and occupational aspira-

1. Ruth M. Gasson, A. O. Haller, and W. H. Sewell, *Attitudes and Facilitation in the Attainment of Status* (Washington, D.C.: American Sociological Association, 1972), p. 33.

tion.[2] This was a matter of grave concern to policy makers who were interested in facilitating movement of the economically disadvantaged out of poverty. This concern helps to explain why public funds in substantial amounts were allocated by various federal and state agencies for research to identify the determinants of levels of aspiration.

Young people in our society do not have very realistic perceptions of either the world of work or their own eventual occupational potential. This is not surprising in view of the difficulty of observing the performance of technical and professoinal occupational roles in contemporary society and the associated difficulty of reality testing of capabilities. Yet every little boy knows that he is expected to work when he grows up, and all boys engage in anticipatory activities, including daydreaming. Thus, most normal boys can readily give an answer to questions about their occupational preferences and aspirations at any time. Little girls may think most about homemaking, but they cannot fail to notice that a great many married women work outside their homes; consequently, they, too, generally have done some thinking about possible future occupations.

Aspirations with respect to specific occupations are subject to change as the individual matures and gains additional information about alternative roles and his own ability. At first, aspirations are sheer fantasy (later becoming more realistic), but they must be regarded as tentative until actual entrance into work or until a commitment is made to a scientific or professional occupation that requires long educational preparation prior to work.

The evidence on occupational mobility shows clearly that relatively few adults other than those in high-status occupations, the skilled crafts and farming make long-term career commitments to specific occupations. At the same time, many of them scale their mobility aspirations downward in line with their perceptions of their chances. Yet most of them evidently

2. For a list of relevant studies, *see* Chad Gordon, *Looking Ahead: Self-Conceptions, Race and Family as Determinants of Adolescent Orientation to Achievement* (Washington, D.C.: American Sociological Association, 1972), p. 4.

believe that America is still the land of opportunity for the young, for they have high aspirations for their children.

1. HIGH SCHOOL STUDENTS

High school students are aware of the growing importance and high status of professional, technical, and managerial positions. Study after study has shown that a very high proportion reports aspirations to enter such occupations; Project Talent, a large-scale nationwide study of high school students, found that 62 per cent of the boys and 52 per cent of the girls, who were seniors in the spring of 1960, hoped to enter a professional or technical occupation.[3]

More boys aspired to enter engineering than any other single field (18 per cent); nearly the same percentage said they expected to become engineers. Only 6 per cent preferred to become skilled workers, although 7 per cent expected to enter such occupations. Approximately 5 per cent expressed a preference for schoolteaching, and about 6 per cent expected to become schoolteachers, whereas nearly 5 per cent preferred to become officers in the armed forces and about 4 per cent planned to do so.

Among the girls, about 30 per cent expected to become secretaries, office clerks, or typists, occupations that were preferred by 23 per cent. Nursing, elementary schoolteaching, high schoolteaching, beauty shop work, and accounting or bookkeeping were other occupations which were attractive to the high school senior girls.

Among the seniors who were planning to go to college, the most popular major fields of study for boys were engineering (23 per cent) and business and commerce (14 per cent). Among the girls the most popular fields were education (20 per cent), business and commerce (17 per cent), and health professions (16 per cent).

Many high school students not only aspire to the elite occu-

3. John C. Flanagan et al., *The American High School Student* (Pittsburgh: Project Talent Office, University of Pittsburgh, 1964). Unless otherwise specified, information relating to educational and occupational aspirations of high school students are from Project Talent.

pations but understand that higher education is the "royal road" to such occupations. Project Talent found that among high school seniors in 1960 more than half the boys (53 per cent) and slightly less than half the girls (46 per cent) were planning to go to college immediately after graduation from high school. This compared favorably with information concerning educational aspirations obtained from parents of high school seniors by the Bureau of the Census in October 1959 that 56 per cent of the boys and 49 per cent of the girls were planning to go to college. Follow-up questionnaires sent by the Project Talent staff to graduating seniors revealed that 49 per cent of the boys and 35 per cent of the girls did go to college in the fall of 1960.

The realization of aspirations for higher education is also found in the rapidly rising enrollments in institutions of higher learning. More than 8 million were enrolled in 1972 compared to 3,610,000 in 1960 and 2,659,000 in 1950. There are other indications that the demand for a college education will rise still higher. A recent nationwide survey conducted by the Survey Research Center of the University of Michigan revealed overwhelming public belief in the value of higher education. The authors commented that "many, in fact, believe that a college education is practically the birthright of every American boy and girl." [4]

In a survey of the educational aspirations and expectations of students in thirty rural high schools in the state of Washington in 1964–65, the writer found that 77 per cent of the boys and 72 per cent of the girls had aspirations to attend college while 75 per cent and 65 per cent respectively expected to achieve this goal.

The high proportions of high school students with professional and technical occupational aspirations and expectations have led various investigators to suggest that high school students may not be realistic. For example, the following statement was made by Project Talent investigators:

4. Angus Campbell and W. C. Ackerman, "What People Think About College," *American Education*, vol. 1, no. 2 (February 1965), p. 30.

"There is evidence that high school seniors are unrealistic in their career plans. . . . Despite the fact that the percentage of workers in professional occupations increased more than 45 per cent between 1950 and 1960, it does not appear likely that there will be enough openings for professional workers to accommodate all of those who want to enter them." [5]

This may be a correct appraisal, but judgments such as this that are made on the basis of past experience may have to be modified in view of the prospective occupational requirements in the automated society that apparently lies ahead. Furthermore, it is possible that the availability of large numbers of educated people may actually result in the creation of additional employment opportunities to utilize their skills.

If the occupational preferences expressed by high school students in their responses to questionnaires represented firm choices, the outcome might very well be frustration and unrest. However, there is evidence from a study made in Washington State that these selections are frequently quite tentative. A much wider range of occupations were found to be attractive than might have been inferred from responses to specific questions about career aspirations.[6] (Table 8)

Information has been obtained in a few studies concerning the relationship between occupational aspirations and expectations of high school students that indicate that a substantial proportion of the respondents tend to revise their expectations downward as compared with their aspirations.[7] The same phe-

5. Flanagan et al., *American High School Student*, pp. 5–45.

6. Walter L. Slocum and Roy T. Bowles, "Attractiveness of Occupations to High School Students," *Personnel and Guidance Journal* (April 1968), pp. 754–61.

7. Walter L. Slocum, *Occupational and Educational Plans of High School Seniors from Farm and Nonfarm Homes* (Pullman, Wash.: WAES Bulletin 564, February 1956), and Thomas H. Nunalee, III, and Lawrence W. Drabick, *Occupational Desires and Expectations of North Carolina High School Seniors* (Raleigh: North Carolina State University Department of Agricultural Education and Rural Sociology, Research Series no. 3, 1965). A. O. Haller has argued that the adjectives "idealistic" and "realistic" should always be used with *aspiration* to identify this phenomenon, reserving the concept *expectation* for "those things alter wants of ego." *See* A. O. Haller, "On the Concept of Aspiration," *Rural Sociology*, vol. 33, no. 4 (December 1968), pp. 484–87.

nomenon has also been observed with respect to educational expectations when compared to educational aspirations, although here the downward revision tends to be less drastic.

LaMar T. Empey has presented evidence indicating that occupational aspirations should be evaluated from a relative rather than an absolute point of view. In a 1954 statewide study of high school seniors in the state of Washington, he found that sons of low-occupational status fathers did have lower absolute occupational aspirations than sons of higher-status fathers. However, further analysis disclosed that the sons of low-status fathers had aspirations for upward occupational mobility, but their aspirations tended to be relatively modest. That is, they did not predominantly aspire to professional and managerial occupations but rather to occupations that were one or perhaps two status levels above those of their fathers' occupations.[8]

The orientations of adolescents concerning specific occupations may change materially during relatively short time periods. Data from the nationwide study of 40,000 high school students already cited reveals that three out of four juniors in 1960 had changed their stated occupational objectives when questioned two years later.[9] This makes it clear that verbal reports of occupational aspirations and plans by children and adolescents who have not yet entered the labor force must be regarded as indications of occupational interests rather than as firm declarations of intent. Nevertheless, it is unlikely that persons without ambition for upward occupational mobility would undertake the long and difficult educational preparation necessary to attain a high-status occupation.

2. SCHOOL DROP-OUTS

The high value placed on formal education is reflected in widely publicized advice to teen-agers by high-status person-

8. LaMar T. Empey, "Social Class and Occupational Aspirations: A Comparison of Absolute and Relative Measurement," *American Sociological Review* (December 1956).

9. *Oregonian* (12 November, 1965).

TABLE 8. Career Aspirations and Attractiveness of Selected Occupations, 1966 (Juniors and Seniors in Washington Public High Schools)

Occupation[a]	BOYS			GIRLS		
	Career Aspirations[b] %	Would like Occupation[c] %	Would not like Occupation[c] %	Career Aspirations[b] %	Would like Occupation[c] %	Would not like Occupation[c] %
Professional[e]	66.7			59.0		
Engineer	8.5	64.3	12.7	.3	7.0	74.2
Airline Pilot	4.1	59.1	17.5	.0	16.7	57.2
Lawyer	3.8	48.2	28.3	.8	34.0	56.6
Mechanical Draftsman	2.5	42.5	27.3	.0	7.3	76.6
Radio Announcer	1.1	39.7	29.9	.3	27.5	45.3
College Professor	.5	35.4	40.9	.5	29.3	49.7
Medical Lab Technologist	—d	34.6	39.4	—d	39.2	42.8
Computer Programmer	—d	32.4	40.3	—d	24.6	53.0
Psychologist	.2	31.6	39.5	.9	56.1	28.2
Physician	3.6	30.6	42.5	2.9	28.4	49.1
X-Ray Technician	—d	28.3	40.9	—d	31.4	46.9
Veterinarian	1.5	27.2	46.5	.7	53.1	29.2
Dentist	1.5	27.0	48.3	.0	13.9	65.7
Recreational Programs Supervisor	.1	26.2	40.8	.2	39.3	33.6
Commercial Artist	1.2	26.0	47.0	3.7	40.9	37.8
Certified Public Accountant	1.2	24.6	46.6	.2	23.5	52.2
Reporter on Daily Newspaper	.3	21.0	47.4	.9	30.8	45.6
Agricultural Research Scientist	.0	20.6	46.6	.0	11.1	65.9
Social Worker	.2	20.5	57.9	4.3	69.7	14.6
Elementary School Tteacher	6.2	18.0	60.6	15.8	59.0	27.1
Physical Therapist	2	17.0	49.7	1.4	44.3	34.5
County Agricultural Agent	.0	15.1	67.2	.0	7.7	72.6
Minister, Priest, Rabbi	.4	11.0	67.1	.1	11.6	62.8
Dietician	.0	4.1	72.8	.4	29.8	43.7
Home Demonstration Agent	.0	3.5	77.7	.2	26.9	51.7
Nurse (RN)	.0	2.6	84.8	7.0	44.3	38.7
Managerial[e]	9.6			2.9		
Owner and Operator of Small Business	—d	52.0	21.2	—d	37.0	35.9
Factory Manager	—d	45.3	21.9	—d	5.5	76.3
Manager of Department Store	—d	40.7	29.5	—d	35.0	39.8
Banker	—d	33.4	33.7	—d	19.1	53.9
Manager of a Loan Company	—d	26.8	39.7	—d	11.3	61.8
Clerical[e]	.5			15.8		
Bookkeeper	.0	16.2	57.8	1.1	34.2	47.9
Bank Teller	.0	15.0	52.5	.0	31.4	43.4
Hotel-Motel Clerk	.1	11.4	64.4	.0	29.6	42.1
Secretary	.0	2.7	77.8	11.7	62.1	21.3
Sales[e]	1.9			3.0		
Automobile Salesman	.1	28.0	44.1	.0	2.7	83.1
Life Insurance Salesman	.2	19.9	52.4	.0	5.3	76.2

246

Table 8.

Occupation[a]	BOYS			GIRLS		
	Career Aspirations[b] %	Would like Occupation[c] %	Would not like Occupation[c] %	Career Aspirations[b] %	Would like Occupation[c] %	Would not like Occupation[c] %
Sales Person in Retail Store	—[d]	18.5	52.3	—[d]	39.1	35.5
Sales Person of Farm Supplies	—[d]	9.9	65.6	—[d]	1.8	81.7
Craftsmen[e]	13.4			.7		
Automobile Mechanic	4.1	44.4	34.6	.0	5.1	82.2
Electrician	.8	39.8	31.6	.0	3.7	81.3
Foreman in Factory	.2	33.5	33.1	.0	2.5	80.9
Carpenter	1.0	29.3	41.2	.0	3.3	82.6
Plumber	.0	7.6	63.9	.0	1.1	88.8
Tailor or Dressmaker	.0	3.2	78.1	.0	36.5	39.0
Operatives[e]	1.2			.2		
Truck Driver	.2	31.1	45.7	.0	3.6	83.8
Welder	.4	25.9	49.8	.0	1.4	89.4
Machine Operator in Factory	.0	24.2	47.4	.0	2.9	84.0
Taxi Driver	.0	13.8	64.4	.0	6.5	79.8
Service[e]	3.4			14.9		
Police Officer	1.0	33.4	38.0	.0	17.0	65.9
Cook (Restaurant)	.8	25.7	50.3	.1	26.6	51.0
Aide in Child Care Center	—[d]	11.9	64.7	—[d]	72.1	13.3
Restaurant Host or Hostess	.0	8.7	66.0	.0	43.4	30.8
Airline Stewardess	.0	4.9	80.9	7.2	70.7	13.8
Waiter or Waitress	.0	4.8	74.2	.0	33.3	41.3
Hair Dresser or Cosmetologist	.0	3.5	83.5	6.1	58.0	24.6
Janitor	.0	3.1	83.5	.0	1.7	88.6
Nurse's Aide	—[d]	2.6	84.0	—[d]	45.1	34.7
Maid—Motel or Hotel	.0	.8	89.1	.3	10.0	72.5
Laborers[e]	1.2			.0		
Warehouse Worker	.3	8.1	66.4	.0	.8	87.1
Farmers[e]	1.7			.2		
Farm Operators	1.7	20.1	51.8	.2	9.4	74.9

[a] Occupations are presented within major census categories and arranged in descending order of per cent of boys who would "like it."

[b] Percentages are based on responses of 1,387 boys and 1,448 girls who named a career goal.

[c] Percentages are based on the number who rated each occupation.

[d] This occupation appears in the list of 61 occupations but not in the census occupational code which was used in coding occupations for which students expressed career aspirations. Consequently, no data are available concerning aspirations.

[e] Includes all occupations aspired to which were coded in this category, not just those listed in this table.

Table 8 reprinted by permission from *Personnel and Guidance Journal* (April 1968), pp. 756–57.

alities, such as professional athletes, to complete high school. The U.S. Office of Education has joined in the effort to keep students in school by financing innovative programs of various types and by publishing statistics concerning high school graduates and dropouts from time to time. The percentage of persons seventeen years of age who were high school graduates has risen from 29 per cent in 1929-30 to 78 per cent in 1969-70. The following table shows the breakdown of high school dropouts in 1970 by age, sex, and race.[10]

TABLE 9. Percent of high school dropouts among persons 14 to 19 years old, by race and sex: United States, 1970.

	Negro		White	
Age	Male	Female	Male	Female
1	2	3	4	5
TOTAL, 14 to 19 years old	15.9	13.3	6.7	8.1
14 years old	0.9	2.9	1.4	1.1
15 years old	3.3	2.7	2.0	2.4
16 years old	10.9	11.1	5.0	6.7
17 years old	16.0	13.7	7.6	10.2
18 years old	29.8	27.8	13.6	14.1
19 years old	44.1	25.8	12.9	15.7

NOTE. Dropouts are persons who are not enrolled in school and who are not high school graduates.

SOURCE. U.S. Department of Commerce, Bureau of the Census, *Current Population Reports*, series P-23, no. 38.

It will be noted that among persons nineteen years of age the dropout rates of Negro boys were more than three times those of white boys while those of Negro girls were 1½ times those of white girls.

The occupational aspirations of the dropouts were not learned, but information concerning actual employment in 1959 of males showed that the unemployment rate was high (nearly double that of high school graduates), and most of

10. *Digest of Educational Statistics,* 1971 edition, op cit., p. 51.

those who were employed worked at low-status occupations; only 7 per cent were in white-collar jobs.[11]

3. COLLEGE UNDERGRADUATES

As we might expect, nearly all college students aspire to high-status occupations. A nationwide study of the educational and occupational aspirations and expectations of 33,982 June 1961 graduates of 135 colleges and universities, revealed that nearly eight out of each ten (77 per cent) expected to enter a professional or scientific occupation.[12] The largest single field, attracting almost one third of the seniors, was primary and secondary education. An additional 12 per cent anticipated future employment by a college, university, or junior college so that "somewhere between 40 and 45 per cent of the seniors expect to be employed in education."

Physical and biological sciences were named by 7.5 per cent and engineering by 8.3 per cent. The social sciences attracted 4 per cent and the humanities 6.5 per cent. Medicine was named by 2.8 per cent and other health professions (dentistry, nursing, optometry, pharmacy, physical therapy, and so forth) by an additional 4 per cent. Law was chosen by 3.9 per cent, and business and administration of various types (including public relations, accounting, advertising, public administration, military, secretarial, and other commercial and business fields) was reported by 18.2 per cent. Only 1.5 per cent chose agriculture or related fields.

With respect to the future educational plans of the 1961 college seniors, James A. Davis observed that:

11. James D. Cowhig and Charles B. Nam, *Educational Status, College Plans and Occupational Status of Farm and Nonfarm Youth,* October 1959, Census Series ERS(P-27), no. 30 (August 1961).
12. Unless otherwise specified, data in this section are from James A. Davis, *Undergraduate Career Decisions* (Chicago: Aldine Publishing Co., 1965), and James A. Davis, *Great Aspirations* (Chicago: Aldine Publishing Co., 1964).

"Perhaps the biggest compliment the graduating seniors paid to higher education was that they wanted more of it. . . . Only one fourth had no plans to go to graduate school at any time, while almost one third were planning to go the next fall. A college graduate is more likely to go on to graduate school than a high school graduate is to go to college."

Although 83 per cent of the 1961 college seniors were favorable toward graduate study, and 77 per cent expected to enter graduate school, only 20 per cent of them had been accepted for graduate study in the fall of 1961 at the time of the study in June 1961. The remainder expected to enter graduate school at some later date. Other studies confirm that many of those who do go to graduate school do not enter immediately after college graduation.[13]

Davis has pointed out succinctly some of the undesirable consequences of postponement of entry into graduate school:

"Granted that engineers and business administrators can be quite effective without advanced degrees or that school teachers may actually benefit from having practical experience before they begin their Master's degree work, the advantages of immediate and extensive graduate training for the major professions in the arts and science fields are overwhelming. Without graduate training, entry into the major professions is barred and work in the arts and sciences can be only at a low level.

"Even postponement of advanced training takes a toll. From the viewpoint of the student, the older he is when he begins graduate study the fewer working years he will have as a thoroughly trained professional and the greater the chance that he will have a family to support during his studies." [14]

Analysis of the reasons for postponement by students who were not planning to continue into graduate school immedi-

13. Elbridge Sibley, *The Education of Sociologists in the United States* (New York: Russell Sage Foundation, 1963), p. 40.
14. Davis, *Great Aspirations*, pp. 61–62.

ately led Davis to conclude that internal motivations (primarily lack of interest or preference for practical experience) were important for 70 per cent. Financial obstacles were cited by 43 per cent; between 18 and 20 per cent of those who wished to go to graduate school but did not expect to enter immediately regarded finances as the major obstacle—however, more than half of these had not applied for a stipend.

Although the occupational preferences and aspirations of college undergraduates are undoubtedly more stable than those of high school students, many are uncertain about their occupational plans when they enter college and change their objectives before they graduate or withdraw. Approximately half of the June 1961 graduates reported "some meaningful career shift or development during college." Davis has classified fields of study with respect to gains or losses in students as:

"(1) *Gainers:* Business and education, the two fields with low losses, high gains and net increases; (2) *Losers:* Medicine, engineering, the physical sciences, and 'other professions,' the fields with high loss rates and recruitment rates that do not replace the losses; (3) *Traders:* The social sciences, the biological sciences, law, and the humanities, the fields with high loss rates and recruitment rates that compensate for the defections."

College students are generally forced into a tentative career choice because they are required to declare a major field of study not later than the beginning of their junior year. This may satisfy the college, but it does not necessarily satisfy all students. In a study at what was then called the State College of Washington, the writer found that 40 per cent of the 1953 seniors were not certain that they had chosen the most suitable major.[15]

15. Walter L. Slocum, *Occupational Planning by Undergraduates at the State College of Washington* (Pullman, Wash., WAES Bulletin 547, February 1954).

4. ADULTS

Adult workers tend to become emotionally involved in whatever occupation they happen to be working at. This is reflected in reports that high proportions of workers prefer their current occupations and neither aspire nor expect to rise to a higher-level occupation.[16]

In spite of these verbal reports indicating satisfaction with current jobs, the evidence concerning occupational mobility examined in chapter 10 indicates that a very substantial amount of shifting from one occupation to another does occur, and it seems reasonable to suppose that aspirations for improving the conditions of one's employment must play a major part in connection with such shifts.

What happens to aspirations for upward occupational mobility as a person grows older? Chris Argyris, a social psychologist, has taken the position that the needs of mature individuals for self-realization are frequently thwarted by procedures and policies designed to insure conformity with organizational goals.[17] Persons who are unable or unwilling to conform to organizational norms may leave, reduce their aspirations and sink into apathy, or try to fight back. Fighting an organization seldom produces desirable results from the standpoint of the rebel.

High occupational aspirations cannot be realistically sustained over a period of time without recognition and encouragement, which is difficult to obtain because of the vigorous competition for organizational positions of power and influence. Due to the pyramidal nature of most formal work organ-

16. A number of such studies have been reviewed in F. Herzberg et al., *Job Attitudes: Review of Research and Opinion* (Pittsburgh: Psychological Service of Pittsburgh, 1957).

17. Chris Argyris, *Interpersonal Competence and Organizational Effectiveness* (Homewood, Ill.: Dorsey Press, 1962); *see also* his "Understanding Human Behavior in Organizations," in Mason Haire, ed., *Modern Organization Theory* (New York: John Wiley & Sons, 1959), pp. 118–19.

izations, relatively few can be promoted. The chosen few tend to be persons who have always been successful. The others even those who have achieved some success, tend to revise their aspirations downward.

Discrimination against older workers is widely practiced in American industry and even in government. Industrial workers displaced after reaching age forty frequently have considerable difficulty finding new positions commensurate with those they have lost, and they have virtually no chance of entering higher level occupations. These features of the employment opportunity structure are well known; hence, adults who are employed in particular occupations, especially those with low or middle status, apparently tend to readjust their aspirations downward in accordance with their perceptions of opportunity.

John E. Dunkelberger found in a study of male household heads in low income areas of the rural South that these men had high latent aspirations but relatively low expectations. He said, "They were very realistic about the world in which they lived. They were aware of the facts of their situation; and they had lowered their level of aspiration to a point consistent with their prospects for achievement." [18] These men tended to center their hopes concerning upward occupational mobility on their children. Nearly all of them aspired to high status-level occupations for their sons. A similar finding has been reported by Ely Chinoy, who found that automobile workers had relatively low aspirations for themselves but high aspirations for their sons.[19]

Robert Presthus has suggested that most of the workers employed by corporations might be placed into one or another of the following three categories on the basis of their career aspirations:

18. John E. Dunkelberger, *Intensity of Job Mobility Aspirations Among Household Heads in Low Income Area of the Rural South* (Ph.D. dissertation, State College of Mississippi, Mississippi State University, Department of Sociology and Anthropology, June 1965), p. 176.
19. Ely Chinoy, *Automobile Workers and the American Dream* (Garden City, N.Y.: Doubleday & Co., 1955), p. 126.

(1) *Upward-mobiles.* This category includes executives and others who desire to have executive careers. The executives receive "disproportionate shares of the organization's rewards in power, income, and ego reinforcement." They tend to accept the values and goals of the corporation and conform to its behavior norms, showing proper deference to those in authority.

> "Like the Navy's gentlemen, the upper-mobile is never intentionally rude. This is a luxury he cannot afford, since like firmly held views, such self-indulgence is of limited career utility." [20]

Although there are relatively few upward-mobiles, their importance can hardly be underestimated. They make the important decisions, establish rules, and supervise others.

(2) *The indifferents.* This category, according to Presthus, includes the great mass of corporate employees. They have given up any hopes that they may have had of rising to executive positions and, instead, seek security and sufficient income to enable them to live the kind of life they desire away from the job.

> "The indifferent . . . tends to find his real satisfactions in extravocational activities. While the upward-mobile 'carries his job home with him,' the indifferent separates his work from his 'personal' experiences, and work is often repressed as something unpleasant. The pay check is what counts." [21]

(3) *The ambivalents.* These are introverted persons who have intense intellectual interests and poor interpersonal skills. They are sensitive to the need for change and hence are inclined to be very critical of the organization. They seldom have enough power or influence to bring desired changes into being. Yet, Presthus says, they do want success and consequently experience status anxiety. Since they are unable to conform sufficiently to organizational norms to achieve favorable recognition, they tend to become neurotic.[22]

Presthus does not present any quantitative data concerning the number of workers who might fall into these categories; he

20. Robert Presthus, *The Organizational Society* (New York: Random house, 1965), pp. 167, 171.
21. Ibid., p. 225.
22. Ibid., p. 264.

acknowledges that some corporate employees would not fit readily into this classification scheme. Nevertheless, it has merit in connection with our consideration of organizational careers because it emphasizes the importance of personality factors.

As we saw earlier, formal education is likely to become very important as a means of assisting adults to keep abreast of changing occupational requirements. Consequently, it is important to ask what aspirations adults have for education.

Evidence from a recent nationwide National Opinion Research Center study of 11,957 households indicates that very substantial numbers of adults do participate in some type of learning activity; it was estimated that 17 million adults had enrolled in formal courses on a part-time basis while 2.5 million were full-time students and an additional 9 million had studied independently during the twelve-month period prior to June 1962.[23]

The authors, Johnstone and Rivera, concluded that there is a large latent demand for adult education:

"The most important conclusion to be derived from this study is that America is likely to experience an adult education explosion during the next few decades. The typical adult student today is young, urban, and fairly well-educated, and this is exactly the type of person who will be around in greatly increased numbers in the very near future." [24]

The study makes it clear that adults with relatively poor education and low-status occupations apparently seldom aspire to participate in programs of continuing education unless they are able to visualize some immediate tangible advantage. They are not interested in education for its own sake.[25]

23. J. W. Johnstone and Ramon Rivera, *Volunteers for Learning* (Chicago: Aldine Publishing Co., 1965).
24. Ibid., p. 19.
25. Ibid., p. 22.

Determinants of Occupational Aspirations

Interests developed through actual work experience, emulation of role models, reading, watching television or movies, and other ways are very important in generating occupational aspirations. Values transmitted to a person by his reference groups, including his family and his age peers, and through the educational process, together with unique personal experiences, are important in guiding and crystallizing occupational preferences. The specific mixture of these factors differs for individuals from different socioeconomic strata. There is also clear evidence of substantial differences between the sexes; as noted earlier the culture at present orients girls primarily toward marriage and family life rather than toward occupational careers.

Economic, psychological, and sociological factors all affect occupational aspirations, preferences, and choices, and, in some cases, one or another of these factors may be dominant. In nearly every case, however, multiple influences are involved. It is thus important to recognize the significance of the interaction among background and situational factors and self-assessment.

1. PERSONAL VARIABLES

The significance of many personal variables is obvious. For example, occupational choices by adolescents are relevant at the age when educational preparation for a specialized occupation must begin or when they are ready to enter the labor force. Age is important later in connection with timetables for entry into or promotion within certain career lines and in connection with retirement. Further, as noted earlier, the widespread discrimination against older job seekers affects expectation.

Physical characteristics are important in our society only for a few occupational roles such as "professional" athletes, law enforcement officers, and manual laborers. Good general health, on the other hand, is a prerequisite for most full-time occupation roles.

The sex of the individual is important because clearly defined occupational sex roles exist; most employed women work in occupations defined as women's work, occupations that are normally followed by few, if any, men. The central importance of marriage and family life to women has great occupational significance. While a large and growing proportion of women do enter the labor force at some time during their adult lives, their participation is expected to be intermittent and supplementary to their homemaking activities. This may lead many parents to discourage their daughter's aspirations to enter high-status occupations. Women are seldom regarded as serious competitors for high rank in most professions, although there are outstanding exceptions. There is much truth in the comment by Leona E. Tyler:

"Girls are less able or perhaps less willing than boys are to think about the choosing of a career without reference to other considerations. A girl may see it as more important that she be acceptable to the kinds of people who matter to her, so that the kind of man she wants to marry will be likely to propose to her than that she find just the occupation that best fits her talents and aptitudes." [26]

A person's own appraisal of his ability and aptitude has very great importance in the occupational choices of those who think in such terms. The self-concept reflects one's estimate of what other persons think of him. This has been accepted by sociologists as a self-evident proposition, at least

26. Leona E. Tyler, "The Future of Vocational Guidance," in M. S. Viteles, A. H. Brayfield, and L. E. Tyler, *Vocational Counseling: A Reappraisal, in Honor of Donald J. Patterson* (Minneapolis: University of Minnesota Press, 1961).

since Charles Horton Cooley coined the phrase "the looking-glass self," which provides a dramatic characterization of the process through which ideas of self develop out of a person's perceptions of the attitudes others have with respect to him.[27]

Relatively little empirical research has been done, either to validate the general proposition or to learn the specific ways in which self-appraisal of abilities and aptitudes affects occupational aspirations and decisions. A recent exception is a study made in Massachusetts by Robert E. Herriott, who found that intellectual self-concept, as measured by a scale that he developed, was significantly related to educational aspirations when seventeen other variables were held constant.[28] Wilbur B. Brookover has also developed an instrument for measuring educational self-concept that is employed in a longitudinal study in Lansing, Michigan. His data indicate that "self-concept of ability is a significant factor in achievement at all levels, 7th through 10th grades." [29]

2. PERCEIVED INTERPERSONAL RELATIONSHIPS

Delbert Miller and Willaim H. Form have suggested that older persons who are admired serve as primary work models with whom the child identifies himself by role taking.[30] This appears to be a correct interpretation, but in addition to serving as examples, adults may assist an adolescent through the role of adviser.

No major studies have focused on educational and occupational role models, although fragmentary information appears in the publications of a number of investigators. The impor-

27. Charles Horton Cooley, *Human Nature and the Social Order* (New York: Scribner's, 1902), pp. 151–53.

28. Robert E. Herriott, "Some Social Determinants of Educational Aspirations," *Harvard Educational Review*, vol. 33, no. 2.

29. Wilbur B. Brookover et al., *Self-Concept of Ability and Academic Achievement* (East Lansing: Bureau of Educational Research Services, College of Education, Michigan State University, October 1965), p. 201.

30. Delbert Miller and W. H. Form, *Industrial Sociology* (New York: Harper and Bros., 1951), p. 521.

tance of role models is largely a matter of faith among sociologists. William H. Sewell and Alan Orenstein, for example, in a recent paper suggest, but without documentation, that an explanation for the lower aspirations of low-status youths is the nature of their role models. "Intimate adult contacts [of such youths] are restricted to those in lower-status occupational positions." [31] A longitudinal study by Alan Bell of 101 males suggests that while fathers may be important role models for their adolescent sons, other persons tend to be chosen as role models when the sons grow older.[32]

Research indicates that most high school and college students recognize that their personal relationships with other people have played an important part in helping them make their occupational plans. In a 1953 Washington study, for example, three out of every four high school seniors acknowledged that some person had influenced their occupational planning in a helpful way, and one out of every three reported negative influences. Parents headed the list of those exercising helpful influence, with teachers in second place, close friends their own age in third place, and vocational counselors fourth.[33]

These findings suggest that adults may be of assistance to an adolescent faced with occupational decisions not only by providing him with examples but by communicating with him directly and giving him advice, thus helping him to clarify his understanding of the requirements, advantages, and disadvantages of various occupational fields and roles. The hazard in this is the limited experience of the adult. Biased advice based on inadequate information may be worse than none and those with the most restricted horizons may be the most positive.

31. William H. Sewell and Alan Orenstein, "Community of Residence and Occupational Choice," *The American Journal of Sociology*, no. 5 (March 1965).

32. Alan P. Bell, "Role Modeling of Fathers in Adolescence and Young Adulthood," *Journal of Counseling Psychology*, vol. 16, no. 1 (1969), p. 35.

33. Walter L. Slocum, *Occupational and Educational Plans of High School Seniors from Farm and Nonfarm Homes* (Pullman, Wash.: WAES Bulletin 564, February 1956).

3. GENERAL SOCIAL AND CULTURAL FACTORS

The discussion up to this point has implied that occupational decisions are made at the conscious level. This is true to some extent, but we must remember that occupational decision-making takes place within a social and cultural context. Any specific decision may be influenced by such general factors as societal values, the state of technological development, or the relative prosperity of the economy, all of which may influence the occupational opportunity structure. To illustrate the significance of societal values, relatively free choice of an occupation is an expectation in contemporary American society. Americans expect a young man to select his own occupational field from the occupations open to young men. He is expected to do it at the appropriate time and to be accountable for the decision he has made.

Young women also have considerable freedom of choice, but their range of selection tends to be restricted to "women's work."

As we have noted previously, there are many barriers to realization of occupational aspirations of young people of either sex. One cannot simply decide to be a doctor and become one automatically. Specific and lengthy formal education is required for entry into medicine and many other professional fields. A few occupations still require apprenticeships, and there are a few, such as farming, that may be largely hereditary, although not actually closed to others.

4. REFERENCE GROUP VALUES

Sociologists and social psychologists generally agree that values, particularly the values of reference groups (those groups with which the individual is associated or with which he desires to associate himself), exert significant influence on the socialization of a person. The values of reference groups—one's own family, the adolescent's peer groups, and the college students' fraternities and sororities, or other friendship groups—are internalized and in this way influence his attitudes and his actions. Decision-makers are not necessarily aware of such influences at the conscious level even though they may be transmitted through personal contacts. Reference group values operate subtly and information about them usually cannot be obtained directly.

In a study of the educational aspirations of rural high school students in the state of Washington, I found some support for the hypothesis that the higher the perceived educational orientation of a student's reference group the higher his own educational aspirations. The study also provides limited support for the hypothesis that the educational values of family of origin are less influential than peer group values insofar as level of educational aspirations of respondents are concerned, when there is a difference between the value positions of these two reference groups.[34]

Evidence from midwestern studies indicates clearly that farm boys who plan to farm differ in their value orientations from those who do not plan to farm.[35] Iowa farm boys planning to farm were found to prefer work with things (machinery or tools) and enjoyed physical work activities more than boys not planning to farm.[36]

Ralph H. Turner investigated the influence of selected values on the occupational ambitions of a sample of students at ten high schools in Los Angeles and Beverly Hills, Cal-

34. Walter L. Slocum, "The Influence of Peer-Group Culture on the Educational Aspirations of Rural High School Students," Washington State University (unpublished paper presented at the Rural Sociological Society Meetings, Chicago, August 1965).

35. Lee G. Burchinal with Archibald O. Haller and Marvin J. Taves, *Career Choices of Rural Youth in a Changing Society* (Minneapolis: University of Minnesota Agricultural Experiment Station Bulletin, 548, November 1962); Donald R. Kaldor, Eber Eldridge, Lee G. Burchinal, and I. W. Arthur, *Occupational Plans of Iowa Farm Boys*, (Ames: Iowa State University of Science and Technology, Research Bulletin 508, September 1962); and Murray A. Straus, "Personal Characteristics and Functional Needs in the Choice of Farming as an Occupation," *Rural Sociology* (September-December 1956), pp. 257–66.

36. Lee G. Burchinal, "Who is Going to Farm?" *Iowa Farm Science* (April 1960).

ifornia. He concluded that there was some evidence of relationship between values and socioeconomic background of the family of the student, but that the magnitude of the associations was small.[37] He found "instances of high ambition among students from the lowest backgrounds,"[38] and concluded that there were distinctive handicaps in the lower socioeconomic status neighborhoods, stating:

> "The peculiarity of social organization among boys in the lower neighborhoods may be stated comprehensively as a pattern of future-orientation without anticipatory socialization. Ambition and academic success are valued, but the distinctive values appropriate to the destination of the highly ambitious are not learned along the way."[39]

Morris Rosenberg has presented information on the relationship of values to occupational choice based on a nationwide study involving more than 4,500 college students.[40] He has defined values, following Robin Williams, as "things in which people are interested—things which they want, desire to be or become, feel as obligatory, worship, enjoy."[41] Rosenberg had this to say:

> "When an individual chooses an occupation, he thinks there is something 'good' about it, and this conception of the 'good' is part of an internalized mental structure which establishes priorities regarding what he wants out of life. It is therefore indispensible to an adequate understanding of the occupational decision process to consider what people want or con-

37. Ralph H. Turner, *The Social Context of Ambition* (San Francisco: Chandler Publishing Co., 1964), pp. 76, 77.

38. Ibid., p. 134.

39. Ibid., pp. 136–37.

40. Morris Rosenberg, *Occupations and Values* (Glencoe, Ill.: Free Press, 1957).

41. Robin Williams, *American Society* (New York: Alfred A. Knopf, 1951), p. 375.

sider good or desirable, for these are the essential criteria by which choices are made." [42]

Rosenberg concluded that members of this nationwide sample were interested in work as more than simply a means of making money. ". . . Not money and status, but, rather, self-fulfillment, interpersonal satisfactions, and security receive the greatest emphasis." However, students tended to consider two or more values as having been important in connection with occupational choice and three configurations of related values were identified:

1. Orientation toward helping people (manifested by those who tended to regard work as an opportunity for gratification from relationships with others).

2. Orientation toward extrinsic rewards (more interest in work as a means for obtaining money rather than for its own sake).

3. Orientation toward self-expression (manifested by those who thought of work as providing opportunities for expression of talents and creative abilities).[43]

Rosenberg noted also that his data indicate that occupational choice affects the values of the chooser because the individual who has chosen a profession is likely to regard himself as one who is to become a doctor, a teacher, an engineer. Because he has incorporated these images in his self-concept, he tends to develop "a picture of the attitudes, values, and behavior which are appropriate for a member of this occupation. . . . This image of his *future* occupational status is likely to influence the student's *present* attitudes, values, and behavior." This is a manifestation of occupational commitment that Robert Merton has called *anticipatory socialization*.[44]

Rosenberg also made the point, which is also consistent with studies made elsewhere, that students desire work that inter-

---

42. Rosenberg, *Occupations and Values*, p. 6.
43. Ibid., pp. 11–13.
44. Ibid., p. 24.

ests them and that provides them with an outlet for special abilities rather than being primarily concerned with money and security.[45]

On the basis of information from many studies, differences in educational and occupational aspirations of adolescents may be due, at least in part, to the distinctive values associated with various social systems.

5. ECONOMIC FACTORS

Economic circumstances of the family of an adolescent undoubtedly influence his occupational aspirations and expectations substantially. The goods and services available to members of our society are distributed through a complicated system of wholesale and retail establishments, and poverty severely limits the degree to which members of a family can participate in the fruits of the affluent society. The necessity of adjusting one's self to lower levels of consumption than the norm further operates to reduce aspirations and expectations because of its negative effect on self-appraisal. Herbert Spencer and some other early thinkers held that poverty tends to motivate people to upward occupational mobility, but the reverse seems more frequently the case today.[46]

In a study in Iowa, Donald R. Kaldor and his colleagues found that both economic and noneconomic factors tended to be involved in the choice of farming as an occupation. Those who planned to farm came from families that were better able to provide financial assistance, especially boys who were "certain" about their occupational plans.[47]

45. Ibid., p. 25. *See also* Burchinal et al., *Career Choices of Rural Youth*, and Walter L. Slocum, "Some Sociological Aspects of Occupational Choice," *The American Journal of Economics and Sociology* (January 1959), pp. 139–48.

46. For examples of earlier attitudes toward poverty, see excerpts from writings of Herbert Spencer, William Graham Sumner, Thomas H. Huxley, John Stewart Mill, and Andrew Carnegie in Robert E. Will and Harold G. Vetter, eds., *Poverty in Affluence* (New York: Harcourt Brace & World, 1965), pp. 58–64.

47. Kaldor, et al., *Occupational Plans*.

Perceptions of the differing economic rewards of particular occupations do influence the occupational preferences of adolescents. However, some are attracted to a greater extent than others by economic incentives, and studies have repeatedly indicated that other aspects of occupational roles, such as prestige and work that is considered to be interesting, are also important.[48]

6. SCHOOL EXPERIENCE

Lee G. Burchinal, in his review of the factors influencing occupational choices of rural youth, calls attention to the importance of both formal and informal school experiences.[49] He observes that communication skills and specialized knowledge are attributable primarily to formal education and says that "expectations of success and development of competency and of educational and occupational aspiration levels result, at least in part, from formal learning experiences and perceptions of teachers' evaluations." [50]

Robert A. Ellis and W. Clayton Lane found that 85 per cent of a sample of Stanford University undergraduates from lower socioeconomic status homes perceived high school teachers as having influenced them to go to college; 33 per cent named a high school teacher as the most influential person.[51]

Some investigators have noted generally higher levels of educational and occupational aspirations among those who earned higher grades and were more active in extracurricular activities, especially those who had held leadership positions.[52]

---

48. James A. Davis, *Great Aspirations* (Chicago: Aldine Publishing Co., 1964), p. 12, and Slocum, *Occupational and Educational Plans of High School Seniors from Farm and Nonfarm Homes.*
49. Ibid., pp. 17–18.
50. Burchinal, et. al., Career Choices of Rural Youth, p. 17.
51. Robert A. Ellis and W. Clayton Lane, "Structural Supports for Upward Mobility," *American Sociological Review* (October 1963), pp. 743–56.
52. Slocum, *Occupational and Educational Plans of High School Seniors from Farm and Nonfarm Homes;* E. Grant Youmans, *The Educational Attainment and Future Plans of Kentucky Rural Youths* (Lexington: Kentucky Agricultural Experiment Station Bulletin, January, 1959).

James S. Coleman found indications that, while the peer group culture tended to depress intellectual activity by giving highest status to athletic stars rather than to scholars, some of his schools emphasized only athletics and others emphasized both athletics and scholarship.[53]

7. WORK EXPERIENCE

There is no adequate substitute for actual experience in a work situation to provide an adolescent with an opportunity for testing his aptitudes and interests against the requirements of an occupational field or a specific occupational role. Actual work provides the best opportunity for an individual to discover the satisfactions and disadvantages of an occupational role, although these are not always immediately apparent. While experience, unless interpreted within a purposeful frame of reference, may not provide significant learning, the challenge presented by an actual employment situation provides sufficient stimulation, according to respondents in studies made in the state of Washington,[54] to warrant making available to adolescents work experiences that they will consider meaningful and significant rather than routine and casual. Unfortunately, only routine and casual work experience are, for the most part, now available to young people. This is due to a combination of circumstances, including legal prohibitions against the employment of child labor in production except for farm work, and even there to some extent; the lengthened period of normal schooling; governmental regulations, such as social security and unemployment compensation; and the cost of industrial accident insurance and the risk involved in employing others unless heavy public liability insurance is carried. These measures have all been developed primarily as protection for workers, but the partial result has been to destroy meaningful employment opportunities for

53. James S. Coleman, *The Adolescent Society* (New York: Free Press of Glencoe, 1961), chapter IX, "Scholastic Effects of the Social System."
54. Slocum, "Some Sociological Aspects of Occupational Choice."

persons not yet ready to be a permanent part of the labor force.

In addition, the impact on the labor force of recent technological developments have undoubtedly eliminated many employment opportunities for younger people.

8. OCCUPATIONAL INFORMATION

A recent study (conducted by Lois DeFleur and Ben Menke) of the knowledge of 300 Washington high school boys about seven occupations present in their region revealed a low level of knowledge; in fact, these boys ". . . were able to discuss less than half of the relevant points about seven common occupations in their section of the state." The investigators also concluded that there had been very little increase in occupational knowledge while in high school.[55]

Providing employment opportunities that actually give adolescents a thorough insight into the operation of complex technical or professional occupations is exceedingly difficult. In such cases, actual employment is not feasible. Nevertheless, some things can be done to help counselors and teachers provide adolescents with better information than is now available, including systematic statistical studies of occupations, case studies, biographies, and autobiographies. Information once collected on a scientific basis must be kept up to date as the requirements change with the further application of technology and the discovery of new scientific information, but this could be accomplished through monographs, popular articles, and motion picture and television scripts as well as through lectures. The emphasis, however, should be broadened from the "bare bones" technical type of description found in such works as the *Dictionary of Occupational Titles* to include sociological and social-psychological aspects.

55. Lois B. DeFleur and Ben A. Menke, "Learning About the Labor Force: Occupational Knowledge Among High School Males," forthcoming in *Sociology of Education*, spring 1974.

The importance of providing reliable information about employment prospects, job requirements, and potential rewards and satisfactions to those who want to make rational occupational decisions should be evident. Substantial information has been compiled about various occupations, but much of it is concerned with the requirements for manipulating material rather than emphasizing satisfactions, interpersonal relationships, and matters of this kind.[56]

9. CONCLUSIONS

Idealistic aspirations may be regarded as daydreams or preferences which are not limited by lack of opportunity, ability, or other resources; if the dreamer does not regard them as viable objectives, they are unlikely to have any serious consequences for achievement. Idealistic aspirations may be stimulated by television, by reading, by role models, by praise from "significant others," or in other ways.

Realistic aspirations are undoubtedly generated in the same manner but presumably reflect appraisals of resources available to meet the costs involved in reaching the desired educational or occupational objective.

Research shows that the level of realistic aspirations of high school and college students is influenced especially by measured intelligence,[57] self-appraisal of ability to perform

56. *See* Bureau of Labor Statistics, U.S. Department of Labor, *Occupational Outlook Handbook* (Washington, D.C.: U.S. Government Printing Office); Bureau of Employment Security, U.S. Department of Labor, *The Dictionary of Occupational Titles* (Washington, D.C.: U.S. Government Printing Office); and Robert Hoppock, *Occupational Information* (New York: McGraw-Hill Book Co., 1963).

57. William H. Sewell, Archie O. Haller, and Murray A. Straus, "Social Status and Educational and Occupational Aspiration," *American Sociological Review* (22 February, 1957), pp. 67–73; William H. Sewell and V. P. Shah, "Socioeconomic Status, Intelligence, and the Attainment of Higher Education," *Sociology of Education* (Winter 1967), pp. 1-23; Ralph H. Turner, *The Social Context of Ambition* (San Francisco: Chandler Publishing Co., 1964).

perceived roles,[58] family values,[59] and family socioeconomic status,[60] and by having received encouragement from parents or teachers.[61] More concretely, *realistic aspirations are most likely to be high for students with high intelligence, high scholastic achievement, and high self-concept of ability, who have knowledge of and identification with high-status occupations, with family value orientations toward college education and elite occupations, who have received encouragement from parents and teachers, who have high family SES and a belief that a favorable opportunity structure will exist. The negatives of these factors lead, of course, to low expectations.*

Occupational Decision-Making

In view of the crucial importance of work for males in our society, a young man's choice of an occupation must be regarded as a major decision even though he may not consider it as such when he takes a job. As we have already seen, occupational decisions, for most men, have a way of coming unstuck. Very few remain throughout their work life in their first occupational field and still fewer remain in the first occupational position. Much occupational mobility is unquestionably due to the rapidly changing occupational requirements of industrial firms and other types of work organizations. But at least some portion of it must be attributed to members of

58. Walter L. Slocum, "Sociological Aspects of Occupational Choice," *The American Journal of Economics and Sociology* (January 1959); Julienne Ford and Steven Box, "Sociological Theory and Occupational Choice," *The Sociological Review* (November 1967), p. 289.

59. Walter L. Slocum, "Educational Aspirations and Expectations of Students in Rural Washington High Schools," *Washington Agricultural Experiment Stations Bulletin 690* (January 1968).

60. Sewell and Shah, "Socioeconomic Status," 20, 23; Empey, "Social Class and Occupational Aspirations"; Donald R. Kaldor and Donald G. Zytowski, "A Maximizing Model of Occupational Decision-making," *Personnel and Guidance Journal* (April 1969), pp. 781–88.

61. Slocum, "Educational Aspirations and Expectations."

the labor force who want to find more interesting work, to gain more prestige, to obtain better pay, or to live in another geographic location.

Relatively few American women pursue long-term occupational careers, although nearly all of them work for pay at one time or another. It is possible that the current drive for equality between the sexes, spearheaded by women's liberation groups, may change the bases for participation of both men and women in the world of work to the extent that more women and fewer men will have career aspirations and experiences. Consequently, it seems necessary to consider occupational decision-making by both sexes. In most respects, the decision-making processes appear to be similar, although some of the cultural and social factors involved are obviously much different. Since most of the relevant research and theory development up to the present time deals with men, the following discussion of decision-making norms and processes will, of necessity, be primarily oriented to men.

A tentative, probing, searching attitude is also characteristic of the occupational preferences and aspirations of adolescents. Occupational decisions are made and remade many times by most adolescents before they actually enter the labor force. This pattern cannot be regarded as entirely dysfunctional, in view of the record of adult occupational mobility; the increasing emphasis upon extended formal education prior to entry into the world of work, however, may make early firm decisions essential for those who hope to enter scientific and professional occupations. Educational choices frequently limit, but do not necessarily determine, occupational choice.

Although the emphasis in our society on the acceptance of responsibility by individuals for occupational decisions is the normal situation for us, it is not the normal situation for all of mankind. In so-called primitive societies—those little communities where all of life is lived out in a small territorial space, where people are illiterate, and where life is short—anthropologists have found that life is closely governed by restrictive traditions, and there are few decisions of the kind confronting us in our society. With reference to the Pakistani village, which is a social system of this kind, Inayat Ullah, a Pakistani sociologist, has said:

"The real individual in the sense of Western urban society does not exist in the village. He [the villager] is an inalienable part of multiple groups which completely overshadow his individuality. He is not master of his own will, an architect of his own fate. The various decisions in different fields of life are made by groups for him, and he rarely feels the need to challenge them." [62]

Inayat Ullah might have said that in his Pakistani village occupation is inherited because for the most part this is still the case. The son of a potter becomes a potter; the son of the landlord succeeds to his father's exalted position; the son of the lowly agricultural laborer is himself a laborer. Furthermore, there was until recently little disposition on the part of Pakistani or Indian villagers to aspire to escape from this static tradition-bound situation.[63]

Occupational inheritance is not part of the American tradition. Our ideology tends to emphasize the other polar extreme, the Horatio Alger myth, the idea that any boy, regardless of how humble his beginnings, may rise to the highest occupational status level. We also accept the corollary that he can do so on the basis of his own merit, ideally his devotion to hard work.

We are closer to the free and rational choice model than we are to the caste system, but there are many imperfections in

62. Inayat Ullah, "Democracy in Rural Communities in Pakistan," *Sociologus*, vol. 9, no. 1 (1959), pp. 36–47.

63. *See* Kingsley Davis, *The Population of India and Pakistan* (Princeton, N.J.: Princeton University Press, 1951); Walter L. Slocum, Jamila Akhtar, and Abrar Fatima Sahi, *Village Life in Lahore District* (Lahore, Pakistan: Social Sciences Research Center, Punjab University Press, October 1959); and M. T. Ahmad, *Systems of Social Stratification in India and Pakistan* (Lahore: Punjab University Press, 1972), pp. 125–31.

the operation of this free choice model. Like the Pakistani villager, we are governed by the general norms of our society and by the special norms of our families and the other social systems to which we belong or to which we aspire to belong. In addition, many situational factors influence our decisions. The notion that the typical American is a free individual unaffected by others in his decision making is a myth. We do not see much arbitrary use of power, but the influence of social pressure, though subtle, is very effective. Family and peer group expectations influence us more than we like to admit. Like the Pakistani villager, we live out our lives in groups and comply with group norms. Only in some respects are our norms less rigid than those of the villager in an underdeveloped country.

Occupational choice and participation may be one of our more flexible areas, but it should be borne in mind that we do not tolerate such deviations as failure on the part of boys to choose an occupation at the appropriate age or of unemployed men of employable ages to seek employment. Thus the norms of our society say, in effect, "Young man, you are free to choose an occupation and to make preparation for it; having made preparation, systematic or otherwise, you are free to try to find employment in it. You are not free, if you are to be classified as a normal individual, to elect not to work at some gainful occupation." This expectation extends through the entire period from termination of formal education until approximately age sixty-five. The occupational ideology that we have called the work imperative or the Puritan ethic requires, in the ideal case, single-minded devotion to performance of the expectations of the occupational role.

Our society has been called an employee society because most members of the labor force work for wages or salary. At the same time we still tend to idealize the independent entrepreneur, the businessman rather than the employee. At least on an ideological level, this tends to complicate to some extent the occupational decision-making of adolescents. As we noted in chapter 2, a small minority of adolescents and young adults have apparently rejected the societal norms that require regular employment of males who have completed their formal education. These young men have relieved themselves, at least for a time, from the necessity of making occupational decisions, especially decisions involving careers.

The person faced with making his first occupational choice decisions generally sees the occupational opportunity structure very dimly. Like everyone else, he is a product of his experience and able to interpret information only in terms of his experience, which includes the values and behavior norms transmitted to him by his parents, his schoolmates and other age-peers, his teachers, and others who are important to him. Generally he has little information about the content, requirements, rewards, or disadvantages of technical and professional occupations, those that are most prestigeful and thus carry the greatest rewards in our society. He has a small and declining opportunity for reality testing and thus can seldom discover through actual experience the extent to which he has aptitudes and interests for particular occupations. How, for example, does the high school son of an economist learn enough about his father's occupational roles to test in any realistic way the motivation he may have to follow in his father's footsteps? The antinepotism rule of the university where his father is employed keeps him from obtaining employment in his father's department, at least under the direction of his father, and other members of the department may also be reluctant to employ him even when they are able to do so because someone might say that favoritism was involved. Most bureaucracies have similar rules, and this to some extent negates the advantage that the son of a professional person has over the son of a nonprofessional in making his occupational choice decisions. As this illustration suggests, adolescents must make major occupational decisions on the basis of inadequate information. Furthermore, much of the information that does come to their attention is less meaningful than it might be because they do not have the background to interpret it properly.

Theories of Occupational Decison-Making

There is no comprehensive paradigm or theoretical model of occupational decision-making that is accepted by substantially all social scientists in the sense that Newton's view of the physical world was once accepted by physical scientists. Nevertheless, there are many partial or middle-range theories. It is not feasible to undertake an exhaustive examination of the relevant theories,[64] but attention will be called to those about which there seems to be substantial agreement and also to some other ideas which appear to be promising.

1. DEVELOPMENTAL THEORIES

Vocational psychologists have done a great deal of empirical research and theory building relating to the vocational development of the individual, with particular emphasis upon middle-class children and adolescents. The work of Donald Super, Anne Roe, John Holland, and their students and colleagues is based upon developmental and personality psychology.[65]

Both men and women pass through typical life stages that have well-known and generally accepted timetables. These timetables establish expectations for certain types of behavior by members of both sexes during certain age periods. The transition points between the periods, as well as the periods themselves, are determined somewhat by physical develop-

---

64. *See* Samuel H. Osipow, *Theories of Career Development* (New York: Appleton-Century-Crofts, 1968) and Edwin L. Herr, *Decision-Making and Vocational Development* (Boston: Houghton Mifflin Co., 1970).

65. Donald E. Super, *The Psychology of Careers* (New York: Harper & Row, Publishers, 1957); Anne Roe, *The Psychology of Occupations* (New York: John Wiley & Sons, 1956) and J. L. Holland, *The Psychology of Vocational Choice* (Waltham, Mass.: Blaisdell Publishing Co., 1966).

ment but to an even greater extent by the customs and traditions of American society and of the lesser social systems existing within it. The early stages of life are widely regarded as the time for learning the basic norms, folkways, and technology. Increasingly this occurs through participation in formal education within the school systems, although social training in the family is extremely important. The period between completion of school, which occurs in the late teens or early twenties, and old age, which is identified for employment purposes as age sixty-five, is regarded as the period for productive work on the part of men and for homemaking, childbearing, and child-rearing on the part of women although the home-maker's role is increasingly supplemented by participation in the labor force by many women for varying periods of time. As the person reaches old age, he is expected to retire from active work.

These broad periods can be subdivided into many smaller stages. Eli Ginzberg and his associates postulated three stages of occupational choice for youths on the basis of their study of a relatively small sample of sons of upper-middle status workers in New York:

1. The fantasy stage extending from age six to about age eleven, during which boys thought of themselves as spacemen, cowboys, and so forth.

2. The tentative stage from eleven to about age eighteen or nineteen, the period when boys tended to vacillate from one occupation to another in their thinking.

3. The realistic stage beginning at about age eighteen or nineteen and continuing until actual entry into employment.[66]

Other investigators have also found the concept of stages useful in studies of occupational decision-making.[67]

Thus, we may accept the view that there are culturally established timetables for certain types of behavior, including occupational decision-making and preparation. In general, as

66. Eli Ginzberg et al., *Occupational Choice* (New York: Columbia University Press, 1951).
67. Cf. Edwin L. Herr, *Decision-Making and Vocational Development*, pp. 10–14.

Ginzberg has suggested, early occupational thinking in elementary school and perhaps in junior high schools tends to be fantasy based; as the individual grows older and approaches actual entry into the labor force, his occupational aspirations and choices become more realistic. In high school, educational and occupational aspirations and plans are less fantasy-based and more realistic than in elementary school. At that time decisions must be made concerning the course of study; these in turn may greatly affect the range of occupational choices. A person who does not take the college preparatory curriculum, for example, has little, if any, chance for later entry into college, and in some high schools, particularly the larger ones, vocational courses exist to prepare the student for actual participation in certain occupations. Those who withdraw before completion of high school or on high school graduation are faced with the problem of obtaining employment. For the dropouts this is likely to be employment in unskilled, clerical, or sales work or service work. At the college and university level, the undergraduate is normally required to choose a major field of study no later than the beginning of his junior year. If he chooses engineering, he must make his choice as a freshman; this is also true of some other fields. Approximately 60 per cent of those entering college eventually obtain baccalaureate degrees, although many finish their work at a different institution.[68]

College dropouts are not considered much better qualified than those who have only a high school diploma. Consequently, many occupations are closed to them.

Except in engineering, elementary schoolteaching, and a few other fields, the baccalaureate degree is not regarded as adequate professional preparation. Those who choose, while undergraduates, to pursue one of the learned professions (or medicine, law, or the ministry) must enter graduate school, medical or law school, or theological seminary for extended

68. Robert E. Iffert, *Retention and Withdrawal of College Students*, U.S. Office of Education, Bulletin 1958, no. 1 (Washington, D.C.: U.S. Government Printing Office, 1957).

specialized training at the graduate level. Graduate education is almost entirely oriented toward a specific occupation.

Thus the opportunity to choose certain occupations may be largely determined by the decisions that a person makes as he moves through the educational system as well as by his scholastic record. Although some opportunities do exist for correcting unfortunate decisions, many decisions are in effect irreversible because of rather rigid requirements for decisions to be made at specific stages in the timetable. For example, the curriculum requirements for premedical education effectively foreclose the choice of medicine by one who has not elected the premedical course as a college freshman. Of course, in some fields, such as philosophy, the timetable provides for much later choices with little, if any, penalty for earlier indecision.

For present purposes, the essential ideas of the developmental theories can be stated in the following proposition: *Career decisions of young people who are oriented toward work are developmental in character and move from fantasy toward realism in a predictable sequence with ascertainable age boundaries which reflect cultural timetables for maturation.*

Most developmental theories deal with the choice of a preferred occupation by children, adolescents, and young adults. Nevertheless, the basic concept appears to be applicable to the entire period of a person's participation in the world of work.

As noted earlier in the discussion of occupational mobility, American men and women do not necessarily pursue one occupation throughout their work lives or work permanently for one organization. Mobility, involving movement from one occupation to another or from one work organization to another, has characterized employment patterns in the United States for a long time.

Consequently, the work history of an American may be characterized by new occupational decisions from time to time. These may be conceptualized as forks or branches that lead in different occupational directions. Some branches lead to the top of an occupational career line; some lead in horizontal directions; others may lead downward. At each of these turning points crucial decisions must be made. Some of these are made primarily by the person who is pursuing an occupational career; others are made by his colleagues in the work organization, by his supervisors, and by his family.

Examples of occupational turning points are the attainment of permanent tenure by a civil service employee or a member of a university faculty, promotion to the next higher occupational or organizational rank, leaving an occupational position in one work organization to accept another, discharge for unsatisfactory performance of an occupational role, and leaving civilian life for military service.

There are culturally approved timetables for adults as well as for children and youth. Most upward occupational mobility occurs during the early stages of the work history; this is also true of movement from one work organization to another.

2. VOCATIONAL APTITUDE THEORIES

Efforts by psychologists to assist vocational counselors to match people and occupations led to the creation and widespread use of tests designed to ascertain occupational interests and aptitudes. This approach, sometimes called the trait-factor or actuarial theory is characterized by Herr as ". . . the oldest, most persistent, and most straightforward of the approaches pervading theory, research and practice in vocational development." [69]

The evidence can be summarized in the following proposition: *Individuals differ in ability but each individual ordinarily has the capacity for success in more than one occupational role or field.*

3. NEED THEORIES

Anne Roe, E. S. Bordin, and associates, and John L. Holland have theorized that certain types of occupations tend to be

69. Herr, *Decision-Making and Vocational Development*, p. 18.

selected because they satisfy certain needs which are attributable to personality differences.[70] These theories emphasize classification of decision makers by personality type or by category of need and seek to relate these typologies to different occupational field.[71]

The central proposition that emerges can be stated as follows: *Personality needs which vary by type of personality can be satisfied better by some occupations than others.*

4. ECONOMIC THEORIES

Theories advanced by economists can be classified into two major categories: macro and micro. The macro theories deal with supply and demand for labor, including the relationship of wages to supply and, in the past few years, the economic value of education which economists label "human capital." These theories are, of course, important in the appraisal of occupational outlook. It is virtually impossible, at least for a sociologist, to identify the major contributions of macro-economists in a few propositions and I will not attempt to do so.

The single micro-economic theory of occupational behavior that has come to my attention is a rational view based on principles of economic decision-making drawn from farm and business management theory.[72] The major proposition is: *A person will tend to choose the occupation which offers the greatest return for his resources (skills, abilities, personal qualities, financial worth, borrowing capacity, and so forth).* This assumes rather more knowledge than most people have, and it also assumes a high degree of rationality in occupational decision-making. Within these limits the proposition appears to have utility.

70. E. S. Bordin, Barbara Nachmann, and S. J. Segal, "An Articulated Framework for Vocational Development," *J. Couns. Psychol.*, vol. 10 (1963), pp. 107–116; Holland, *Psychology of Vocational Choice*; Roe, *Psychology of Occupations.*

71. Herr, *Decision-Making and Vocational Development*, p. 23.

72. Donald R. Kaldor and Donald G. Zytowski, "A Maximizing Model of Occupational Decision-making," *Personnel and Guidance Journal* (April 1969), pp. 781–788.

5. SITUATIONAL THEORIES

A number of people, including some sociologists,[73] have argued that occupational choices are made accidentally. An individual may believe that accident in the sense of complete operation of the laws of chance has occurred, but this explanation is too simple. When people explain their occupational choices as accidents, they seem to mean that they have been influenced by some powerful stimulus beyond their control. The major flaw in this hypothesis, as Professor Eli Ginzberg has pointed out,[74] is that there are countless stimuli in the experiences of every person that might influence occupational choice, while only a few actually do so. As Ginzberg has said:

"It is a special case of a naive 'chance theory' of history which holds that there is no way to account for historical events in causal terms. Actually the error lies in the historian's inability to relate the observable events or processes so that they become meaningfully related." [75]

It does not follow that situational factors are unimportant. The evidence indicates that most people make their occupational decisions on the basis of information available to them and that for most people significant knowledge about jobs tends to be situational in character. Seymour M. Lipset, Reinhard Bendix, and F. Theodore Malm discovered, for example, that for the largest bulk of workers in the Oakland, California, labor force in 1949 the first job was the only job that was known about at the time of first employment.[76] Thus, for some young men occupational choice does not precede actual ac-

73. Miller and Form, *Industrial Sociology*, pp. 521–22.
74. Ginzberg et al., *Occupational Choice*, p. 20.
75. Ibid., pp. 20–21.
76. "Job Plans and Entry into the Labor Market," *Social Forces* (March 1955), pp. 229–30.

ceptance of a job. In fact, it seems probable that a great many people, perhaps most of those who do not aspire to careers in one of the elite occupations, simply accept whatever employment happens to be available when they enter the labor force and thus drift into the world of work without making explicit decisions to select or reject alternative occupations.[77]

Perceptions of opportunity by young people are vague at best but as circumstances change, as in the recent shift from a shortage of college graduates to surpluses in nearly all professional fields, some feedback does occur and revised estimates of the situation may trigger choices of lower-status occupations.

6. SELF CONCEPT THEORIES

Self-appraisal of ability to perform anticipated occupational requirements and of the congruence of occupational roles with other aspects of one's self-concept are considered by many psychologists and sociologists as important bases for choice or rejection of specific occupations.

Donald Super has been given credit for initial development (1951) of the theory that ". . . the occupational choice is an effort to implement the individual's self-concept." [78] Since that time, Super and his colleagues have refined the theory; their basic idea is that a person tends to choose occupations with characteristics that are compatible with his conception of himself as developed through personal experience.[79]

F. L. Field, C. D. Kehas, and D. V. Tiedeman have proposed that decision makers select courses of action which

77. *See* George Katona, "Rational Behavior and Economic Behavior," *Psychological Review*, vol. 60 (1953), pp. 307–318, and Peter M. Blau, et al., "Occupational Choice: A Conceptual Framework," *Industrial and Labor Relations Review*, vol. 9 (July 1956), pp. 531–543.

78. Charles L. Wheeler and E. F. Carnes, "Relationships Among Self-Concepts, Ideal-Self Concepts, and Stereotypes of Probable and Ideal Vocational Choices," *Journal of Counseling Psychology*, vol. 6, no. 15 (1968), p. 530.

79. Cf. D. E. Super, R. Stareshevsky, N. Matlin, and J. P. Jordaan, *Career Development: Self-Concept Theory* (New York: College Entrance Examination Board, 1963).

conform to their conceptions of (1) "what they are like; (2) what they can be like; (3) what they want to be like; (4) what their situation is like; (5) what their situation might become; and finally (6) the way they see these aspects of self and situation as being related." [80]

Consideration of an occupational field or an occupational role by a person not yet in the labor force (or of an alternative occupational role by one who has a job) primarily consists of imagining how one would meet the requirements, perform the duties, enjoy the rewards, and endure the disadvantages of the field or role. Self-appraisal of one's own abilities is central, but self-appraisal includes evaluation of the actual or presumed approval of other people who are important to the person making the decision. This process will be called *playing at* an occupational role and it may be distinguished from *role taking*, which involves an understanding of the role of another specific person. Because the process is usually covert, it is not really *role-playing*, as Donald E. Super has called it.[81] To put it another way, the decision-maker imagines how it would appear to him and to his parents, to his girl friend, or to others who are important to him if he were a policeman, or a professor, or a prize fighter, or something else.

Playing at the more exotic roles as preadolescents frequently do may be considered fantasy. As noted earlier, Ginzberg and his associates identified the period between six and eleven years of age as the period of fantasy choices.[82] During this period, the small boy (or girl) may play at being a cowboy, a spaceman, a movie star, or some other exotic role, but at this stage he has no opportunity for any reality testing of such a role. In their discussion of this fantasy period, Ginzberg and his associates have called attention to the inability of young

80. F. L. Field, C. D. Kehas, and D. V. Tiedeman, "The Self-Concept in Career Development: A Construct in Transition," *Personnel and Guidance Journal*, vol. 41 (May 1963), pp. 769–770.

81. Donald E. Super, "A Theory of Vocational Development," *The American Psychology* (May 1953), p. 190. *See also* Slocum, "Some Sociological Aspects of Occupational Choice," pp. 139–48.

82. Ginzberg et al., *Occupational Choice*, p. 60.

children to handle time perspectives in the same manner as adults do.[83] This distinction is important and may be interpreted, within the sociological frame of reference, as indicating imperfect socialization with respect to the values and perspectives of adult society.

As the child matures, his social training proceeds in accordance with the cultural timetables that guide development at various ages. He is able to understand more clearly the requirements of the adult world and begins to develop a concept of himself as someone who resembles adult role models. This *self-concept* may have important occupational components, especially for boys. Leona Tyler has suggested, for example, that occupational choice has an "identity-fixing quality." [84]

Nearly all of the self-concept theories, as well as the need theories, emphasize selection of occupations that are compatible with the self-concept and which satisfy personality needs. It seems reasonable that perceptions of lack of compatibility with self-concept may be a major factor in *rejection* of occupations.

It is obvious that many more occupations are rejected than selected. At the outset of life, all occupations are at least theoretically open to any child. The process of narrowing the choice to a single occupation or, at most, a relatively small number, involves time, many cultural and social factors (some of which an individual may be completely unaware), and the influence of "significant other" persons—all of which may be reflected in self-concept.

Leona E. Tyler has pursued the idea for a number of years in her researches on the psychological constructs involved in occupational choice patterns. In a recent study comparing patterns of choices in three countries, Tyler and her colleagues employed a card-sorting technique that required their ninth grade subjects to select some occupations as "possibilities for a person like you" and to reject others as "out of the question

83. Ibid., p. 65.
84. Leona Tyler, *The Work of the Counselor* (New York: Appleton-Century-Crofts, 2d ed., 1961), p. 290.

for a person like you." [85] They concluded that girls were more likely to reveal their occupational interest by the pattern of occupations rejected,[86] whereas boys were more likely to show theirs through the occupations selected.[87]

Edward Gross has discussed rejection as an aspect of the choice process, emphasizing that the rejection of unwanted occupations enables a person to move away from undesirable situations.[88]

In a 1955–56 study of the educational and occupational plans of Washington high school students, Slocum found that 27 per cent of his respondents reported that they had been advised to avoid one or more occupations.[89] In a 1965–66 statewide study, Slocum and Bowles reported that when asked to rate the desirability of each of a list of 61 occupations, girls most frequently rejected those occupations traditionally classified as men's work while boys most frequently rejected those regarded as women's work.[90]

Broadening the occupational decision-making paradigm to include rejection of undesired occupations opens up a number of questions previously restricted by most investigators to positive choices.

Failure to achieve satisfactory progress in school is likely to lead to a low self-appraisal of scholastic ability and subsequently to rejection of occupations perceived to have a substantial intellectual content. Rejection of applicants for employment by prospective employers may also lead to rejection of certain occupations.

85. Leona E. Tyler, N. D. Sundberg, P. K. Rohila, and M. M. Greene, "Patterns of Choices in Dutch, American, and Indian Adolescents," *Journal of Counseling Psychology*, vol. 15, no. 6 (1968), pp. 522–529.

86. Ibid., p. 528.

87. Ibid., p. 528.

88. Edward Gross, "A Sociological Approach to the Analysis of Preparation for Work Life," *Personnel and Guidance Journal*, vol. 45, no. 5 (January 1967), pp. 416–423.

89. Walter L. Slocum, *Occupational and Educational Plans of High School Seniors from Farm and Nonfarm Homes* (Pullman: Washington Agricultural Experiment Station, 1956, Bulletin 564, p. 123).

90. Slocum and Bowles, "Attractiveness of Occupations," pp. 759–60.

7. RATIONAL APPROACHES

Although the idea of vocational counseling rests on the assumption that occupational choice is basically rational in nature, it does not necessarily follow that all aspects of the imagined occupational field or occupational role receive systematic and rational evaluation; rather, some aspects tend to be magnified, even glamorized, while others are minimized if considered at all. Economists who have analyzed economic decision-making have traditionally assumed a rather high degree of rationality on the part of decision-makers. However, studies by rural sociologists have revealed that other factors than economic considerations have been of great importance in economic decisions by farmers.[91]

The economist Eli Ginzberg and his associates apparently believe that a high degree of rationality exists in occupational decision-making by adolescents; they state that every occupational choice is a compromise between interests, capacities, values, and employment opportunities.[92]

A fully rational occupational choice is one that is arrived at on the basis of a systematic and objective evaluation of such factors as personal aptitudes and capacities, values and interests, and the prospective rewards and disadvantages associated with various occupational fields and occupational roles.

Many occupational choices are not fully rational in the full sense of this definition. On the other hand, many adolescents do obtain some information about their aptitudes and capacities through vocational tests, through part-time work experiences, and in other ways. Furthermore, some secondary schools and some colleges and universities present courses including considerable information about factors that must be

91. E. A. Wilkening and Donald Johnson, "A Case Study in Decision Making Among a Farm Owner Sample in Wisconsin," paper presented at the Rural Sociological Society Meeting (August 1958), p. 14; *see also* Kaldor and Zytowski, "Occupational Decision-Making."

92. Ginzberg, et al., *Occupational Choice*, pp. 5, 186.

taken into account in occupational decisions. These experiences assist adolescents to test their presumed interests.

We may hypothesize that there is a continuum of rationality with respect to occupational decision-making, some decisions being made solely on the basis of impulse and some being fully rational in the sense of the definition above. At the present time, however, on the basis of information available from empirical research involving high school and college students, most occupational choice decision-making by adolescents (and probably also by adults) is properly classified as either mixed or nonrational.

Rationality in occupational choice is a desirable objective both from the standpoint of individual decision-makers and of the society as a whole. A decision-maker can improve his decisions on the basis of objective information about his aptitudes, through reality testing of his interests, and through knowledge of the occupational outlook for specific occupational fields and roles. In this respect, early occupational decisions resemble economic decision-making more closely than the choice of a marriage partner, which is generally accompanied by a high degree of emotion.

However, occupational turning-point decisions by adults also involve important noneconomic considerations.

A person who becomes deeply committed to an occupational role that involves important responsibilities and provides favorable recognition for achievement may encounter problems of an emotional nature when adjusting to a new occupational role that involves working out new interpersonal relationships and learning the values and behavior standards required for successful role performance in a new work organization.

Failure on a job, particularly failure involving dismissal for unsatisfactory performance, may have drastic consequences for occupational careers, resulting in termination of employment, not only in a particular organization but in the occupation. One who has been branded as a failure in an occupational role has trouble obtaining the recommendations that are usually necessary to obtain employment in the same occupation elsewhere.

One of the most important career turning points is the decision to accept or reject a tempting offer to move to another place to take another position. For a faculty member, for example, this may mean transferring to another university, to a government department, or perhaps to a private business firm. Positions in government or business may involve leaving one's professional field as well as the university. The possible consequences of such a move must be judged against available alternatives, the advantages must be weighed against the disadvantages. If a professor has held his current position for any length of time, if he has risen in the professorial career line in his department, if he has established his roots in the community, if he owns property, if his children have established close relationships with neighbor children, if his wife does not wish to move, then he has powerful reasons to stay. On the other hand, he may feel that his department chairman and his dean did not give him as big a salary increase as he should have had last year, and perhaps the offer is really tempting in terms of its potential rewards. A higher prestige position with higher pay or even with prospects of higher pay in a university of more prestige is difficult to reject. In any case, the decision to move to a new position or to stay put is not simple.

The privilege of trying out a new position with a firm commitment to return to his present position is seldom available to a professor, although this kind of consideration is sometimes given to men whose services are greatly desired by their current employer. In such cases, a professor may be given a leave of absence to serve in another position, although this is ordinarily done with the understanding that he will return for a period of at least one year.

Similar considerations are involved in the decision of an executive or a technician to move to another place to take another position, although specific circumstances differ in each individual case, and there may be some general differences when occupations are compared.

As noted earlier, occupational decision-making is seldom, if ever, a one-time event. Rather, the selection of an occupational field consists of a series of decisions, some of which are, for practical purposes, irreversible while others are tentative and subject to reconsideration and later reversal or confirmation.

The occupational decisions of children, adolescents, and young adults from economically deprived families are characterized in most cases by a rather high degree of opportunism with little if any long-range planning and, except for those entering the skilled crafts or trades, relatively little commitment to an occupation. For those from middle- and upper-income families, the situation is quite different. In these cases, cultural expectations exist for the selection of an occupation involving a career, usually one of the professions, or a career in a business organization, but the occupational requirements may appear sufficiently formidable to the individual to be forbidding. As in the dating situation, where serious commitments may not be admitted even to oneself at an early stage because of the fear of rejection by the other, so in the case of an early commitment to an occupation such as a profession, the commitment may be tentative and its further development contingent upon receipt of encouragement from important figures within the occupation.

At the college level, the student is required to select his major field of study no later than the beginning of his junior year and in some cases at the beginning of his freshman year. How firm are these choices? A study made at the State College of Washington in the middle fifties revealed that roughly 40 per cent of the graduating seniors were not certain they had chosen the most suitable field.[93] This is consistent with information presented by Morris Rosenberg that 60 per cent of college students who wanted to enter a particular occupation in 1950 had changed their minds two years later.[94] These data provide striking confirmation of the fluidity of occupational decision-making even among college students who may

93. Walter L. Slocum, *Occupational Planning by Undergraduates at the State College of Washington* (Pullman, Wash.: WAES Bulletin, 547, February 1954).
94. Rosenberg, *Occupations and Values*, p. 62.

be presumed to be the most stable category among adolescents. Such changes in occupational aspirations are consistent with occupational mobility data presented earlier that show that job changing continues for many throughout the work life. In this respect early vacillation may be functional for the person, but there may be serious consequences for specific work systems and for the economy at large, and these data raise serious questions about the functions of the school system in relation to preparing for an occupation. The best course for those who have not made a commitment to a specific profession such as engineering (for which, incidentally, Rosenberg found very little shifting) would be a broad base of studies that would provide a foundation for a flexible response to occupational opportunities and vocational interests.

Determinants of Achievement*

Achievement of high status requires ability, ambition, and effort. In addition, appropriate educational and occupational

* This discussion is based primarily on relevant research findings. It should be borne in mind that these empirical studies of occupational aspirations, choice, and attainment were designed by the investigators to provide information about selected facets of the relevant attitudes, backgrounds, and personal experiences of samples of individuals (usually males) who were selected from specific school classes or other convenient populations. Most of the studies obtained data by using structured questionnaires rather than observation or interview techniques, and the specific questions asked were dictated by the professional orientations of the investigators. Thus, the findings, though voluminous, are fragmentary and disjointed. There was a heavy concentration of emphasis, in both sociological and psychological research, on high school and college populations. Some recent follow-up studies of these samples provide what should be regarded as preliminary information about the impact of selected factors on early occupational attainment.

The great bulk of the specific studies (perhaps 98 per cent) have been made in the United States. They are largely devoid of any historical perspective. Consequently, generalizations based on the findings should not be regarded as universal principles to be applied without modification to other cultures or historical periods. The available data pertains primarily to the identification and analysis of relationships among factors that are

opportunities must also be available in school systems and work organizations.

Most of the systematic information that is available concerning the determinants of achievement is in the form of inferences based upon the statistical association of selected variables with the attainment of various levels of education and/or occupational status. A successful career in a high-status occupation is the model against which other occupational achievements are judged. Nevertheless, in our society it is necessary to have a successful educational career first. Consequently, we will first look at educational achievements.

1. EDUCATIONAL ACHIEVEMENTS

The operation of the educational system in the United States has been described as a contest for grades and other rewards.[95] At this point we may ask: Who usually wins this contest? Is it open in the sense that anyone can win or are the chances of success higher for some contestants than for others?

Without discounting the crucial contribution of effort to achievement, it appears from the research that the probabilities of success (for example, high marks and a college degree) are higher for students who have certain personal and social characteristics than for others.[96] These include level of educa-

---

important in explaining the vocation-related behavior of American boys and young men who have been students during the past twenty years or so. In view of the fact that technological and societal change is apparently still accelerating, caution must be used in extrapolating generalizations from data that are space-found, time-bound and culture-bound. In spite of these limitations, the data are the best that are available and, in my opinion, can provide better bases for individual action and social policy than personal experience or intuition.

95. Ralph H. Turner, "Sponsored and Contest Mobility and the School System," *American Sociological Review*, vol. xxv, no. 6 (December 1960), pp. 855–67.

96. The levels of association between indicators of educational association and any single independent variable are not high enough in any studies to explain as much as half of the variation.

tional aspiration,[97] intelligence, as measured by various tests (IQ),[98] high marks in previous education,[99] family socio-economic status (SES),[100] level of parents' educational achievements,[101] and favorable and early recognition by teachers and parents of scholastic achievements.[102] However, there is some evidence that the influence of family SES tends to decrease as educational level of boys increases." [103] This suggests that the influence of style of life as reflected by the socio-economic level of the family of origin may have its greatest impact at the point of entry into the school system.

Summarizing the evidence in directional terms: *successful educational careers are most probable for boys with high aspirations and above average IQ, who have previously received high marks, who have been socialized in families with high SES and high educational standards, and who conform to teachers' expectations concerning scholastic performance.* Failure is, of course, associated with low scores on these variables.

Comparable data are not available for females, but there is no reason to believe that the relationships would be substan-

97. Gasson, Haller and Sewell, *Attitudes and Facilitation*, 1972, p. 19. 19.

98. Sewell and Shah, "Socioeconomic Status," p. 19; ———, "Parents' Education and Children's Educational Aspirations and Achievements," *American Sociological Review* (April 1968), p. 206; R. M. Hauser, *Socio-Economic Background and Educational Performance* (American Sociological Association, 1971), pp. 149–51.

99. Cf. Marion F. Shaycroft, *The High School Years: Growth in Cognitive Skills* (Pittsburgh: School of Education, University of Pittsburgh, 1967); Walter L. Slocum, unpublished data, 1971.

100. Sewell and Shah, 1967, "Socioeconomic status," p. 19; Richard H. Hall, *Occupations and the Social Structure* (Englewood Cliffs, N.J.; Prentice-Hall, 1969), p. 346; Hauser, *Socio-Economic Background*, p. 149.

101. Sewell and Shah, "Parents' Education," p. 208; Hauser, *Socio-Economic Background*, p. 149.

102. Slocum, "Educational Aspirations and Expectations," p. 14; Gasson et al., *Attitudes and Facilitation*, p. 19.

103. Sewell and Shah, "Socioeconomic Status," p. 19; *see also* Hauser, *Socio-Economic Background*, p. 155.

tially different. Girls usually receive higher average marks in high school than boys.[104] Fewer graduate from college, but that is probably due to the tendency for girls to be oriented towards careers as homemakers rather than as regular full-time workers in some elite occupation.

Educational careers tend to have a cumulative nature; that is, early success leads to continued success and failure to further failure. Two processes are at work, and they tend to reinforce each other. The first is the incorporation of success or failure into the self-concept of the student, and the second is the tendency of teachers to expect the student's performance to conform to his previous achievement level.

2. EARLY OCCUPATIONAL ATTAINMENTS

The jobs that young men and women are able to find when they first enter the world of work on a regular basis frequently are different from those that they would have preferred. In many cases, they accept the first job available, often one that they learn about from a relative or friend who knows of a position that is open. As we have already learned, few remain in the entry occupation or work organization. Nevertheless, for most men the status level of the first occupation tends to be only a little below the highest level achieved and the entry level is affected materially by type of schooling and educational achievements such as diplomas, degrees, and cumulative grades (GPA).[105]

Other factors found by research on early occupational attainment of men to be positively associated with a high-status

104. Slocum, "Educational Aspirations and Expectations."
105. Bernard Berelson and Gary A. Steiner, *Human Behavior: An Inventory of Scientific Findings* (New York: Harcourt, Brace & World, 1964), p. 471; Glen Elder, "Occupational Level, Achievement Motivation, and Social Mobility: A Longitudinal Analysis, *Journal of Counseling Psychology,* 15 (January 1968), p. 347; Peter Blau and O. D. Duncan, *The American Occupational Structure* (New York: John Wiley & Sons, 1967); Walter L. Slocum, unpublished data from a follow-up study of former high school students, 1971; Gasson et al., *Attitudes and Facilitation,* p. 19.

occupation include high family SES, [106] urban more than rural residence,[107] ability,[108] ambition,[109] receipt of advice from numerous individuals,[110] and anticipatory socialization into the values and norms of a desired occupation.[111]

This information, together with relevant information about opportunity, leads to this proposition: *The probabilities of initial placement in a profession or other high-status occupation are highest for able, ambitious men who have been socialized by reference groups that value upward mobility; who have had successful and relevant educational careers; who have personal characteristics that are valued in the higher status occupation; who accept the higher status occupation as a reference group; and who have had timely employment opportunities.*

3. UPWARD CAREER PROGRESS

Most workers enter occupational career lines at or near the bottom. There is a tendency for those in the professions and corporate management to enter while relatively young but only after a successful educational career that is considered by employers to insure appropriate preparation.

Studies of career mobility are less numerous than studies of occupational mobility, perhaps because of the extensive use of occupational status as an indicator of social class in numerous studies by American sociologists. In this discussion, attention will be directed only to upward career mobility by managers and organizational professionals, including scientists.

106. Joseph Kahl, *The American Class Structure* (New York: Holt, Rinehart and Winston, 1957), p. 272; Berelson and Steiner, *Human Behavior*, p. 468; Gasson et al., *Attitudes and Facilitation*, p. 19.

107. Berelson and Steiner, *Human Behavior*, p. 470; Lee Taylor, *Occupational Sociology* (New York: Oxford University Press, 1968), p. 208.

108 Elder, "Occupational Level, Achievement Motivation, and Social Mobility," p. 328.

109. Ibid., p. 344; Gasson et al., *Attitudes and Facilitation*, p. 19.

110. Taylor, *Occupational Sociology*, p. 205.

111. Berelson and Steiner, *Human Behavior*, p. 487; Robert K. Merton, *Social Theory and Social Structure* (Glencoe, Ill.: Free Press, 1957), p. 265.

Evidence from studies of career mobility indicates that career opportunities are affected by occupational and organizational growth and decline,[112] that rapidity of career progress may be restrained by organization timetables,[113] that sponsorship by a prestigious person leads to upward career mobility by protege,[114] and that meritorious performance of roles as judged by colleagues and/or superiors is required.[115]

In addition to these findings, there are some additional findings that appear to emphasize the importance of specific professional norms. Thus, Reif found that early discovery and publication of important scientific findings yields high visibility which leads to rapid upward career mobility for a scientist,[116] and Caplow and McGee allege that upward mobility of "cosmopolitan" professors in major universities is based primarily upon publication of scholarly books and articles.[117] Among managers, there is a strong tendency to promote men who conform to the organizational image of the "right man for the job," [118] while in some organizations, membership in a "leading clique" or personal characteristics unrelated to ability or performance such as religious affiliation, ethnic background, race, or "social connections" may determine who is promoted among competitors with comparable occupational qualifications.[119]

112. Barney G. Glaser, *Organizational Careers* (Chicago: Aldine Publishing Co., 1968), p. 193.

113. Norman H. Martin and Anselm L. Strauss, "Patterns of Mobility Within Industrial Organizations," *Journal of Business* (April 1956), p. 205.

114. Martin and Strauss, 1956, "Patterns of Mobility," p. 208; Diana Crane, "Scientists at Major and Minor Universities: A Study of Productivity and Recognition," *American Sociological Review* (October 1965); Glaser, *Organizational Careers*, p. 194.

115. Walter L. Slocum, *Occupational Careers* (Chicago: Aldine Publishing Co., 1966); Erwin Smigel, *The Wall Street Lawyer* (New York: Free Press of Glencoe, 1964), pp. 136–38.

116. Fred Reif and Anselm Strauss, "The Impact of Rapid Discovery Upon The Scientist's Career," *Social Problems*, 12 (Winter 1965), pp. 297–311.

117. Theodore Caplow and Reese McGee, *The Academic Market Place* (Garden City, N.Y.: Doubleday & Co., 1961).

118. Glaser, *Organizational Careers*, p. 194.

119. Melville Dalton, "Informal Factors in Career Achievement," *American Journal of Sociology* (March 1951); Orvis Collins, "Ethnic

This information may be stated as a proposition: *Upward career mobility in an elite occupation that is pursued in organizations is most probable for an able, ambitious man who was socialized in a family with high SES and upward mobility orientations, who has "desirable" personal characteristics, who has had a successful and relevant educational career, who performs occupational roles superbly as judged by occupational and organizational norms, who has a prestigious sponsor, and who has timely opportunities for promotion.*

The proposition as stated does not adequately cover the use of bargaining with employers by men who have outstanding achievements; however, it is not inconsistent with this "higgling," as economists call it. Bargaining for promotion sometimes occurs among professors,[120] and although it does not appear to have been reported for managers, it undoubtedly occurs among them also.

A Paradigm of Career Aspirations, Choice and Achievement

Two polar typologies of occupational behavior have been reflected in the literature reviewed. These might be called the *rational* model on one extreme and the *situational* model on the other.

The first model is based on the view that man is a purposive being who is able to control his own destiny, that he can choose his course rationally, and that he is able, by his own efforts, to achieve his desired goals—"to do his own thing." In this model, ambition leads to choice, and, for those who have the necessary ability and other resources, choice leads to

Behavior in Industry: Sponsorship and Rejection in a New England Factory," *American Journal of Sociology* (January 1946); William Kornhauser, "The Negro Union Official: A Study of Sponsorship and Control," *American Journal of Sociology* (March 1952); Glaser, *Organizational Careers*, p. 193; Lloyd W. Warner and James Abbeglen, *Big Business Leaders in America* (New York: Harper and Bros., 1955).

120. Caplow and McGee, *Academic Market Place*; David G. Brown, *The Mobile Professors*, American Council on Education, 1968.

preparation and achievement. Thus a person to some extent is seen as able to create his own opportunities.

The other model views man as the creature of his social environment. It regards him as restricted to occupations of certain types because he has been socialized by specific reference groups and schools which largely determine his self-concept of ability and level of realistic aspiration. In this model, as the name implies, choice is determined largely by situational factors; one tends to drift into available employment for which his cultural background and educational experiences make him a candidate. He then proceeds to adjust his ambition to his occupational achievements.

Both of these models are caricatures. The truth appears to lie somewhere between the two extremes.

In my opinion, we may confidently expect more of a "payoff" for a rational approach to career planning in the future than there has been in the past. If this is a reasonable expectation, the rewards to people who don't pursue such an approach to occupational choice and preparation will be substandard both in terms of satisfaction and income. At the same time, we cannot overlook important influences of the social environment on ambition, opportunity, and achievement.

A summary view of the influences and processes involved in attainment of occupational status by individuals in contemporary America would include the following:

1. Human behavior occurs within or with reference to groups, organizations, communities and/or societies which we may refer to collectively as social systems.

2. Social systems have distinctive configurations of culture, including language, values, behavior norms, and technology.

3. Members of a social system (and persons who adopt it as a reference group) are socialized so as to act in accordance with or at least with reference to the values, norms, and other cultural aspects of the system. Socialization involves interpersonal contact, communications received from mass media, reading, and so forth.

4. Members of social systems are accorded differential prestige, socioeconomic status, privileges, and power. Generally

the status structure is like a pyramid with relatively few high-level positions.

5. Most individuals have the potential for success in more than one type of educational or occupational behavior, but few are so talented that they are without limits. The individual's capabilities depend on his intelligence, his experience, and his motivation.

6. The social aspects of the self develop over time through interaction, including perceived appraisals of self by members of social systems who are important to a person (his "significant others").

7. Individuals tend to repeat behavior for which they are rewarded and to discontinue behavior for which they are not rewarded. Thus, praise from significant others will reinforce desired achievements.

8. Career decision-making is developmental, moving from fantasy toward realism as a person grows older and more mature.

9. The processes of status attainment are sequential; it would not be far off the mark to say that success leads to success and failure to failure. This may be termed the Matthew effect after Matthew 25:29: "To everyone who has will more be given and he will have abundance, but to him who has not even what he has will be taken away."

10. A person who makes a rational occupational choice will tend to choose a career for which he thinks he has available resources.

11. Behavior is affected by perceptions of the relevant situation; thus, a *job seeker* may take whatever job is available whereas a more sophisticated *career planner* will obtain information about occupational outlook and requirements and make appropriate preparation before seeking a specific position.

Summarizing, we may say that *the educational and occupational aspirations, expectations, and achievements of individuals are determined by the complex interaction of personal, cultural, and social system factors as mediated through experience in concerete situations, and that rational choice and subsequent actions are based at least in part on perceptions of rewards and costs.*

Selected References

Borrow, Henry, ed. *Man in a World at Work.* Boston: Houghton Mifflin Co., 1964. A collection of essays on various topics of concern to vocational counselors; the fiftieth anniversary volume of the National Guidance Association.

Flanagan, John C., et al. *The American High School Student.* Pittsburgh. Project Talent Office, University of Pittsburgh, 1964. A monumental report on the characteristics and educational and occupational aspirations of a nationwide study of 547,000 high school students. Project Talent has been set up as a longitudinal study; consequently, additional data can be anticipated from time to time.

Ginsberg, Eli, et al. *Occupational Choice.* New York. Columbia University Press, 1951. A pioneering exploratory study of the occupational decision-making of a small sample of upper middle-class boys in New York. Presents the widely adopted concept of stages of choice.

Herr, Edwin L. *Decision-Making and Vocational Development.* Boston: Houghton Mifflin Co., 1970. A comprehensive review of psychological theories of occupational choice.

12. Career Strategies

Consideration of strategies reminds us of the schemer or the manipulator. We may think of Dale Carnegie's promise to teach us "how to win friends and influence people" or even of Machiavelli, but the actual development of a career strategy involves much more fundamental considerations. In view of the central importance of the work role in our society, especially for men, it might not be inappropriate to think of career planning as the development of an overall moving perspective towards occupational participation. Paraphrasing "life plan," the term used by Karl Mannheim, some may even regard career planning as the construction of a lifetime occupational plan.[1] This is an ambitious, though rarely attained goal.

Little latitude exists for individual variation in a rigidly structured society where life is governed by strict traditional norms as in the case of village India and Pakistan. In marked contrast, in an industrialized and urbanized society such as our own, the individual is expected to choose an occupation from a number of existing alternatives or even to create his own unique career. This latitude provides flexibility and opportunity for the exercise of initiative and ingenuity, but it also creates uncertainty and insecurity. In a rapidly changing occupational opportunity structure, family tradition provides relatively little, if any, guidance.

There is considerable evidence that the great majority of American men in recent generations have followed an opportunistic policy, seeking jobs that became available at a par-

1. Karl Mannheim, *Man and Society in an Age of Reconstruction* (New York: Harcourt, Brace & Co., 1940).

ticular time and place, and moving when opportunity beckoned.

What guidelines are there for a person to use at the beginning or near the beginning of his work life? Unfortunately, not many; those that do exist are undoubtedly oversimplified.

As we have seen, the social ethic apparently has not replaced the Protestant ethic as an effective career strategy for those who reach the top in the elite occupations. Unrelenting concentration and long hours devoted to the job are essential, but hard work is not sufficient by itself to guarantee upward career mobility. Competent role performance is also required. But occupational role expectations vary enough between work organizations so that behavior adequate for promotion in one might be unsatisfactory in another. Even a strategy designed after careful study of all available information concerning relevant occupational and organizational career patterns may not insure that any particular individual will reach the top. Instead, upward career mobility will surely cease at some point for the great majority. Furthermore, many members of the labor force can anticipate increased leisure. Consequently, attention to developing nonwork interests and roles seems appropriate even for persons who have aspirations for successful executive or professional careers.

A person planning his career may find it useful to review the experiences of others for clues concerning effective career strategies, but he should remember that the past is not necessarily an adequate guide to the future. History rarely repeats. Instead, circumstances change in ways that require adaptive changes on the part of persons, groups, and societies. After the so-called "robber barons" of the late nineteenth century made their fortunes, the laws were changed to close the loopholes they had used. Perhaps more important is the fact that most attractive occupational careers now take place within formal work organizations, increasingly in large organizations.

At present, the impact of the upsurge of science and technology on occupational roles has supplanted earlier influences. In the military services, for example, education enabling an officer to cope successfully with technical problems has largely superseded aristocratic origin and has challenged seniority as a basis for upward career mobility.

In universities, research and subsequent publication have replaced teaching as a major criterion for promotion, and administration has fallen from favor as a career goal.

The neophyte should not regard these changes as final. It is highly probable that occupational values will continue to shift, although it is hard to predict exactly what will happen. In scientific fields recognition should continue to accrue to innovators rather than to those who slavishly follow a formula; the weight of history indicates, however, that those who challenge deep-rooted occupational norms may anticipate harsh treatment such as that given General Billy Mitchell, Joseph Lister, Robert Koch, and Galileo.

In view of the presence of competition for scarce rewards in the world of work, it may be useful to conceptualize educational, occupational, and/or organizational achievements (status) as the result of a ladder-climbing game or contest with many competitors; nevertheless, while all are concerned about rewards, all do not necessarily seek the same rewards nor play according to the same rules—for example, some professors are cosmopolitans, others are locals, and there may be more than one career ladder for both. Career contests are played on a continuing basis in many settings, including educational systems, occupational associations, and work organizations.

Except for the "cosmopolitan" professionals and the self-employed, career games are played primarily within a specific university, business firm, government agency, or other work organization. Each game involves competition (usually a polite contest) with others for grades, for scholarships and prizes, for promotion to higher rank, for pay raises, and for other forms of recognition. The rules for judging the competition are never specified as clearly as the rules for recreational games such as football, bridge, or poker. In fact, *the rules of a career game are usually only partially known to the competitors when they make crucial decisions. This leads to incorrect decisions and sometimes to remorse and frustration.* Some of the rules are relatively general within a major society while others appear to be restricted to specific occupations, work organizations, and/or periods of time.

In a meritocracy, upward career mobility is supposed to be based primarily upon high achievement as evaluated in terms of occupational and/or organizational standards. However, sponsorship and interpersonal social skills may sometimes be as important as occupational competence (expressed as intellectual or manual skills) in upward mobility in a particular work organization. The degree of competition among work organizations for competent specialists and executives also affects career progress; persons with rare skills that are in great demand obviously have greater bargaining power than others.

Getting Started in a Career

As noted earlier, not everyone aspires to an elite occupation nor to a high organizational position. Some of those who would like to have the rewards that go with such status are not willing to work hard or do the other things that are necessary, and some may be ignorant of the requirements for attainment of high status. The following suggestions concerning strategy are directed primarily to career seekers.

1. SELECTING AN OCCUPATION

Ideally, the choice of an occupation should be made early enough so that information about occupational requirements can be used in making appropriate educational preparation. The performance of veterans of World War II and of other adults in college, suggests that having a definite vocational objective tends to improve a student's motivation for scholarship.

It is clear from the work of vocational psychologists that,

while individuals may have the ability to succeed in more than one occupation, the range of ability of most individuals is not unlimited. Consequently, it is important for a young person to identify his or her special abilities. Self-appraisal of ability to perform some occupational skills can be made on the basis of feedback from teachers, parents, and other adults. However, the complexity of the modern occupational structure renders such sources relatively impotent because of the limited range of knowledge possessed by any specific person. A more rational approach would be to make use of aptitude testing services which are available in many schools and most colleges.

A substantial amount of useful information about occupational requirements and prospects is available in libraries. The *Occupational Outlook Handbook*, cited earlier, is probably the best general source. More specific information can be obtained from publications issued by various professional associations. An excellent way of collecting additional timely and pertinent information is to interview knowledgeable persons who have attained responsible positions as occupational specialists and prepare an occupational monograph. A list of relevant topics follows:[2]

An Occupational Monograph

1. *Introduction:* A general description of the occupation and of major work organizations in which it is found, and future prospects based on information in the *Occupational Outlook Handbook* and/or other publications.
2. *Subjective dimensions of the work:* Opportunities for self-fulfillment, social contribution, and exercise of influence or power versus subordinate status.
3. *Objective dimensions of work:* Location, pay and fringe benefits and specific operations to be performed.
4. *Occupational Role Models:* Characteristics of successful persons in the occupation.
5. *Educational preparation:* General preparation, specific

2. This approach has been used successfully by my students. The version of the outline presented here incorporates revisions suggested by students.

occupational training and anticipatory socialization into occupational culture.

6. *Entrance:* Selection procedures, initial socialization into occupational subcultures, and procedures for gaining acceptance.

7. *Occupational culture:* Values and norms governing occupational performance and implications of the occupation for style of life.

8. *Typical career patterns:* Career lines, timetables, and criteria for tenure and promotion and probability of demotion.

9. *Retirement:* How long must an employee work to qualify, what is the retirement age, what are the costs, and what are the benefits?

Important considerations in making a rational selection among alternative occupations are (1) the compatibility of personal aptitudes, interests, values, and needs with occupational requirements, (2) the outlook for long term careers, (3) barriers to entry and upward mobility, and (4) availability of resources needed to meet training expenses and other costs.

2. FINDING A VACANT POSITION

As we have already learned, for many people, job hunting is a haphazard process based on scanty information from friends and relatives about possible openings. Even graduate students rely heavily on their professors to find jobs for them, using their network of informal relationships with other professors.[3] Some job seekers use the services of private and/or public employment agencies, file formal applications with personnel offices of large corporations, respond to advertisements, and/or take civil service examinations. Even where

3. Cf. Robert E. Love, "Getting your first job: a view from the bottom," *American Psychologist*, vol. 27, no. 5 (May 1972), pp. 425–30.

there is actually a national job market (as for professors), no comprehensive listing of vacancies is now available. Thus, a job seeker can apply only for positions that he is able to learn about. Usually this is not a large number. Few job hunters aggressively seek to develop a substantial list of vacancies but instead accept what appears to be the best of the options available, frequently the only one they know about.

3. MAKING APPLICATION

College placement officers and employment agencies have developed a considerable body of folklore concerning tactics to be used in the presentation of self in an employment interview. I will not offer any specific suggestions concerning dress or deportment or about the details of how credentials and other qualifications can best be presented. College undergraduates should consult their placement office for advice.

One of the relevant lessons that can be learned from sociology is that an individual who seeks to become a member of a work organization is more likely to be invited to join if he is believed to have skills or other qualifications that will contribute to achievement of the goals of the organization, and if his values are perceived to be compatible with those dominant in the organization.

This suggests that a candidate should learn as much as possible about organizational goals, values, and occupational requirements so that he can direct attention of recruiters to those aspects of his education, experience, and other qualifications that meet the relevant specifications.

Specific requirements concerning education, moral character, health, and sometimes other attributes must be met before a person is considered qualified for a position in an organization. Doctors, dentists, and lawyers cannot begin their professional careers until they have passed examinations and obtained a license to practice. This is also true of civil engineers, and teachers in the public schools must have a valid teacher's certificate. But scientists, university professors, administrators, and most members of the newer professions do not obtain licenses. Whenever they have completed their formal education they are ready to begin as soon as they can find suitable employment.

In all cases, ability and aptitude for performing desired occupational roles are sought, and, for most elite occupations, specific educational preparation is required. In addition, some organizations seek to obtain recruits with particular personality traits and values.

4. ENTERING A WORK ORGANIZATION

Since most occupational careers are experienced within work organizations, it seems worthwhile to discuss entry at some length. Among professionals, the first position is very important because the reputation established there is likely to accompany the person throughout his career. Similar problems are encountered each time a person enters a new work organization, although he may enter as a qualified specialist who has held a closely comparable position in another work organization. This is true because each work organization is unique in some respects, and a new member must gain acceptance as a person as well as a performer of a particular occupational role, which does not mean that only those with a particular type of behavior may succeed. It is possible for persons with objectionable personal traits to become effective members of work organizations, but generally speaking, they find easier acceptance if the organization members regard their personal characteristics favorably.

A recruit is usually a stranger, and a stranger, by definition, is someone whose values, behavior norms, and other personal characteristics are unknown. Members of the social system he seeks to enter may be distrustful and suspicious until and unless he can demonstrate that he shares their essential values and behavior norms and is thus a person who can be trusted. In tribal societies, the problem of dealing with the stranger was sometimes solved by killing him. In modern urban industrial society, various tests are applied to determine rapidly who is and who is not a prospective member. For example, a candidate with low socioeconomic rank is not welcome in a role that carries relatively high rank. In fact, the poor, the ignorant, the uneducated, the uncouth will not be considered for positions that demand well-educated, polite, gentlemanly people with well-developed interpersonal skills.

5. ORGANIZATIONAL SOCIALIZATION

Successful entry into a work organization begins with the appointment to a position. Gaining acceptance as an effective member of the work organization and its subsidiary social systems, including informal work groups, now confronts the recruit.

Our discussion of education for occupations, indicated that some occupational culture patterns may be learned in the university or professional school. This is seldom, if ever, possible insofar as organizational culture patterns are concerned; to a marked degree, these are unique to individual concrete work organizations. Consequently, the person joining a new work organization has to learn not only the specific occupational roles of his organizational position but also organizational values and behavior norms, and, despite emphasis in corporations and other bureaucratically organized work systems on impersonal procedures, the new member must obtain acceptance as a person.

Work systems differ greatly in the nature and length of the trial period. Closed systems, characterized by a distinctive ideology and close social relationships, pose somewhat different problems for the new members from those posed by open systems, which may permit more freedom in the sense of variation from the organizational norms. During the probationary period, particularly in relatively closed systems, a recruit is evaluated by supervisors on the basis of his performance of the occupational roles assigned to him; he is also evaluated as a person by his immediate colleagues.

Particularly in old, established organizations with well-defined ideological positions and routine operations, the new recruit may be viewed as a potential rival. Consequently, he may be subjected to harassment of various kinds. In situations of this kind, an inadvertent statement or act during the first few days or weeks may effectively destroy the possibility of obtaining acceptance as a full member. In other cases, the situation is quite the opposite, and the new recruit is encouraged and assisted to meet the problems confronting him, and his initial mistakes and blunders are viewed tolerantly. To a considerable extent, the social atmosphere is influenced by the state of the labor market, but long-term institutionalized organizational norms are also involved.

An unskilled or semi-skilled worker who enters a work organization may encounter little emphasis on conformity to ideological norms, with the emphasis placed instead on the nature of the performance of operations involved in the occupational role and on relationships with others in his work group. However, a person recruited into a unionized work organization has to establish relationships with the union as well as with management and fellow workers, and his probationary period may involve both the employer and the union.

The professional has other problems, especially one who enters an established department or group of professional peers. In his case, consideration is given to the extent and nature of his socialization as a professional as evidenced by the possession of degrees, academic achievements including school grades, organizational membership and offices, and recommendations from leading members of the profession. For a professional, recruitment into and early socialization in the profession precedes entry into a specific work organization.

6. ATTAINING JOB SECURITY

Formal tenure or permanent status is available only in certain types of work organizations such as schools, colleges, railroads, and government agencies. We have already discussed tenure from the perspective of the work organization (chapter 4).

A considerable degree of job security is attainable in most well-established organizations. The governing principle appears to be what we called *centrality* in chapter 4. Stated in other terms, an employee whose contributions are regarded as essential to the proper functioning of the organization will have the most secure tenure. Those who are promoted usually have considerable job security, except for presidents and other top executives who serve at the pleasure of a board of directors. Nevertheless, it does not necessarily follow that all employees who attain permanent status or tenure are likely to be promoted. This is especially true for civil service employees and public schoolteachers who attain tenure after a relatively short probationary period of either six months or one year.

Career Mobility

In contrast to occupational mobility, which consists of shifting from one occupation to another, career mobility in-involves moving from one occupational stage to another. This may involve promotion to a more responsible position, demotion, discharge, moving to another organization, or retirement.

Career mobility in contemporary industrialized urbanized society may be likened to a contest in which the top positions are achieved rather than inherited. The rules governing competition differ somewhat from one profession to another and sometimes from one work organization to another, but talent, compliance with role expectations, and long hours are usually required in all.

In the elite occupations, few of the starters reach the top. Those who do have distinguished careers have unusual influence in their fields, in their work organizations, and sometimes in the society as a whole. Furthermore, their brilliant performance of occupational roles provides inspiration to associates and to young people who may accept them as role models and aspire to emulate their achievements.

The existence of distinctive occupational and organizational subcultures requires appropriate modifications in career strategies. In his discussion of the means employed by ambitious European civil servants to attain high office, Brian Chapman reported that a Frenchman might succeed by using methods that would disqualify him from consideration in Germany.[4] On a smaller scale and to a lesser degree this is probably true of different work organizations and of different occupations within a particular national state. That is, differences among organizational and occupational subcultures, while not so pronounced as the differences between nations, may be substantial. We have already noted that socialization into the culture of the major professions begins in the university and continues after actual entry into the world of work. The incorporation of occupational values into the self-concept may make it difficult for a person who changes occupational careers to achieve upward career mobility commensurate with his expectations.

In some work organizations, a promotion cannot be made until and unless a vacancy occurs in a higher position in the "table of organization," particularly in many governmental agencies and business organizations and in the administrative career lines of educational systems. In contrast, scientific and professional workers are usually promoted in accordance with evaluation of their own professional development. Thus, a university department may have more full professors than associate professors rather than a strictly pyramidal structure.

In hierarchical organizations, the adequacy of performance is customarily evaluated by administrative superiors. In scientific and similar professions, competence is also evaluated by other members of the profession—the scientific peer group. As Theodore C. Caplow has said, an essential element in obtaining a promotion is favorable evaluation by one's superiors.[5] In most organizations organized on a bureaucratic basis, promotions are supposed to be based on merit, but subjective

    4. Brian Chapman, *The Profession of Government* (London: George Allen and Unwin, 1959), p. 283.
    5. Theodore Caplow, *The Sociology of Work* (Minneapolis: University of Minnesota Press, 1954), p. 68.

elements such as personal preferences inevitably enter to some extent. Personal relations skills may be fully as important as occupational competence in some organizations. Sponsorship by an established figure in the occupation is very helpful, although not essential in all cases.

Although merit, as evidenced by the individual's performance in compliance with occupational norms, has great importance, seniority is also considered. Thus, established senior men will have greater reputations and receive higher salaries and other rewards than able young men. This is true of universities, the military services, business corporations, and government agencies. Cases where extremely able young men have been promoted ahead of older men are known, but these are exceptions rather than the customary procedures.

Together with performance, seniority, and ability, being at the right place at the right time frequently has an important bearing on successful career mobility.

1. MILITARY OFFICERS[6]

Prior to the tremendous expansion of the armed forces in World War II, personal reputation, as well as seniority, was important in a successful officer's career. For example, General George C. Marshall and other senior officers kept lists of officers who were considered potential commanders, which were utilized in promotions as needs developed.

Although this practice probably persists to some extent, the vast size of the contemporary military establishment makes it impossible to rely on it completely; in 1962, there were 343,000 officers on active duty. Officers are now rated more or less continuously by their superiors, peers, and subordinates, and these efficiency reports are incorporated in the "file" the personnel office maintains for each officer. This file is consulted

---

6. Information concerning career patterns of military officers has been drawn from Morris Janowitz, *The Professional Soldier* (New York: Free Press of Glencoe, 1960), and Morris Janowitz, ed., *The New Military* (New York: Russell Sage Foundation, 1964).

in connection with recommendations by officer selection boards for promotion.

There is a definite timetable for promotions; in peaceful times, an officer who is overage for his rank will be retired early unless he is an occupational specialist who is not expected to advance further. This policy of "up or out" means that few officers can have a lifetime military career; many are obliged to pursue "second careers."

The tremendous size and complexity of the modern military establishment has introduced new occupational requirements for officers as well as for enlisted men. Thus, there are many new career lines and promotion to high rank is not necessarily dependent upon ability to command combat operations. Nevertheless, the "elite nucleus" is made up of a small group of men who have made an intense lifelong commitment to military leadership. Most of the officers who have ever reached the top 0.5 per cent of the hierarchy have been graduates of the military academies, and most of them have complied with conventional career expectations. However, some have attracted attention for unconventional behavior, including U. S. Grant, "Stonewall" Jackson, and "Jeb" Stuart during the Civil War and Douglas MacArthur, "Bull" Halsey, George Patton, Jonathan Wainwright, James Doolittle, and Curtis Le May in World War II.

An outstanding example of being born at the right time has been cited by Morris Janowitz in *The Professional Soldier*. Men who graduated from West Point or Annapolis in the years immediately prior to World War I had greatly enhanced opportunities for reaching the rank of general or admiral, because they were able to obtain field experience during World War I and were the appropriate age during World War II when opportunities for promotion were at a peak.

An officer may request assignments that he believes will enhance his chances for promotion.

"Early in his career he learns that the road to the top, at least to the level of one or possibly two stars, is not through assignment to the specialized technical services, but by being an unrestricted line officer . . . the aspiring officer believes that the prescribed career is in the combat arms, although the fortunes of particular weapon systems change with technological progress. He believes it is important to have command duty, and to be involved in operations when assigned to staff duties. Informal communications play an important role in the allocation of these desired assignments, especially for the middle-level officer who has built a reputation for his skill and potentiality for promotion. At the highest levels, of course, colleague reputation and informal contacts outweigh personnel records as a basis of making assignments." [7]

Promotion is also influenced by records made at various military schools to which an officer is assigned. Some of these, such as the Industrial College of the Armed Forces, are open only to carefully screened officers (and a few civil service executives from government departments involved in relationships with the Defense Department). [8]

2. BUSINESS EXECUTIVES

Little systematic information is available concerning career mobility in the so-called middle-management range in business organizations. Most studies have focused instead on the characteristics and career patterns of men who have reached top positions.

Mabel Newcomer has reported that the majority of big business executives in 1950 had long periods of service in their companies before reaching the top; slightly more than one in five had never worked for another company. She found that many of these executives had been selected by their predecessors, which suggests that sponsorship is of some importance. She also reported that approximately six out of each ten presidents and board chairmen had previously been vice-presidents of their companies. The principal factors in obtaining top executive office cited by Newcomer were: inheritance,

7. Janowitz, *The Professional Soldier*, p. 147.
8. *Business Week* (5 February, 1966).

13.8 per cent; founded the organization, 6 per cent; investment, 7 per cent; success in another company, 18.2 per cent; working up within the company, 50.8 per cent; all other factors, 4.2 per cent.[9] These so-called factors are so broad that they give few clues to the career strategies actually pursued by top business executives.

W. H. Whyte, Jr., has described the *social ethic*, his concept of the ideas that young executives in business corporations had in the early 1950s concerning strategies for executive careers in organizations. According to Whyte, the social ethic emphasizes the development and exercise of human relation skills as a teamwork approach rather than the traditional Protestant ethic of individual hard work as a basis for upward career mobility.[10] The social ethic appears to be an application of the idea developed by David Riesman in *The Lonely Crowd* of the "other-directed" man who looks primarily to others for cues. But Whyte's impressionistic essay unfortunately does not provide much information about the actual prevalence of the social ethic.

It cannot be denied that the evaluation of a person by others, especially his superiors, has great importance in upward career mobility. Interpersonal skills may frequently play a considerable part in this evaluation, particularly in executive positions. Whyte has observed, however, that the top executives of the great corporations are not "well-rounded" men but rather able individuals who have risen to the top by strategies other than those emphasized by the social ethic.[11] Support for this point of view is also found in the report by W. L. Warner and James C. Abegglen of a study of more than 8,500 top leaders of American business in 1952. They found that sociability was not the strongest quality of the American busi-

9. Mabel Newcomer, *The Big Business Executive: The Factors That Made Him, 1900–1950* (New York: Columbia University Press, 1955). *See also* Mabel Newcomer, "The Big Business Executive," in W. Lloyd Warner and Norman H. Martin, eds., *Industrial Man* (New York: Harper and Bros., 1959), pp. 130–36.

10. W. H. Whyte, Jr., *The Organization Man* (Garden City, N.Y.: Doubleday, 1956), pp. 121–66.

11. Ibid., pp. 155–65.

ness elite. Rather, the leaders were men of strong character with a tremendous capacity for putting in long hours and the ability to make tough decisions. They could and did say "no" when it was called for.[12] This may indicate that the formula described by Whyte in *The Organization Man* does not lead to the top in business corporations. In fact, there is very grave doubt that it leads to the top in any elite occupation.

A study[13] of 1,003 rising younger executives in 150 large corporations, which was published in 1964, revealed that singleness of purpose and hard work were still dominant norms; a third of them reported that they even devoted all of their "leisure" reading to material relevant to their jobs. The respondents averaged 39.5 years of age and a fourth of them had already worked for three to five different companies, which indicates that many of them do not make long-term organizational commitments. The study portrays these younger executives as innovative and aggressive in presenting and defending their views; few of them appeared to be "yes men." [14] Since they had already risen several steps, this suggests that many companies reward such behavior rather than the conforming group-oriented behavior of the social ethic. One should not conclude that tact is not necessary in presenting a challenge to existing practices or policies or that timing is unimportant in gaining acceptance for such ideas.

A recent study of Sexton Adams and Don Fyffe analyzed the strategies used by managers to gain promotions in three corporations.[15] They concluded that performance of the type called for by the Protestant work ethic by itself would not lead to promotion but on the contrary might render an otherwise acceptable candidate unpromotable. In fact, they concluded that persons of this type, whom they classified as "technicians" are not promoted primarily because they are not

12. W. Lloyd Warner and James C. Abegglen, *Big Business Leaders in America* (New York: Harper and Bros., 1955).

13. Walter Guzzardi, Jr., *The Young Executives* (New York: The New American Library, 1964), pp. 42, 46, 72, 73, 74.

14. Ibid.

15. Sexton Adams and Don Fyffe, *The Corporate Promotables* (Houston, Texas: Gulf Publishing Co., 1969).

sensitive to the social requirements for promotability in their work organization.[16]

The exact nature of these expectations differs somewhat from company to company, but the common core is to be found in an executive's central function, which is to make "correct" decisions. Executives who make decisions concerning products, facilities, personnel, financing, and other matters that turn out to be correct most of the time in terms of the interests of the corporation will win promotions. In business corporations, an executive is judged mainly by the outcome of his decisions as reflected in the profit or loss shown on the bottom line of the balance sheet for his plant, store, division, or company. Of course, he is also judged on matters such as managerial style, but style is likely to be less important than profitability.

Successful executives are able to get others to follow their leadership. In some cases this may involve manipulation in the sense of exploitation, but this approach is likely to lead to failure in the long run.[17] However, persons with managerial styles ranging from virtual dictatorship to "noncontroversial conformity" may gain promotions in different types of organizations.[18] The former is more likely to get ahead in corporations characterized by great emphasis on efficiency and "cost effectiveness," and the latter in corporations that place more emphasis on the creation of a favorable social climate as a basis for motivating employees to support organizational objectives. According to Sexton and Adams, a *dictator* relies on fear as a basis for motivation and uses punishment for failure and a system of rigid controls to insure compliance with orders while a *noncontroversial conformist*, who relies on rewards, is highly skilled in interpersonal relations, sociable, and well liked by others.[19]

Among managers who have taken graduate university training in business administration (those who have earned a

16. Adams and Fyffe, *Corporate Promotables*, pp. 175–76.
17. Ibid., pp. 173–74.
18. Ibid., pp. 110–27; 146–61.
19. Adams and Fyffe, Ibid., pp. 158–59.

master's degree in business administration), advancement to higher level positions is most rapid in medium-sized firms.[20]

Membership in the proper clique may be instrumental in bringing a candidate for promotion to the attention of higher officials.[21] Sponsorship by a highly-placed executive is also likely to be helpful.[22]

3. ENTREPRENUERS

The successful entrepreneur is an American folk hero. The model is found in the Horatio Alger myth, which glamorizes the idea that a man of ability can rise by his own efforts from a humble beginning to become the owner of a great fortune. This has actually happened, but it did not happen often even in the past and it is virtually impossible now for a poor man or woman to move up the old entrepreneurial ladder by earning, saving, and shrewd investment.

Relatively few of the 3,474,274 self-employed workers in nonfarm occupations in 1970 were entrepreneurs, if we define entrepreneur as a person who creates or otherwise gains control of large economic resources. Capitalist is another name for a business entrepreneur. The self-made millionaire is the primary model.

There are few millionaires. In 1969, only 865 people in the United States had incomes of a million dollars or more, although, of course, a much larger number owned assets worth a million dollars or more. According to a survey released by *Fortune* magazine early in 1968, there were then 153 Americans whose wealth was estimated to be $50,000,000 or more. Howard Hughes and J. Paul Getty were described as billionaires and Bob Hope, who came from a poor English family, was listed in the $150,000,000 category.

Many of the super-rich, including the Rockefellers, the

---

20. Ronald E. Herrington, David C. Dionne, et al., *The Young Businessman: Small Company or Large?* (New York: Hobbs, Dorman & Co., 1967), p. 192.
21. Adams and Fyffe, p. 58.
22. Ibid., pp. 61–64.

Mellons, and the Kennedy brothers, inherited great wealth, but others like Edwin Land of Polaroid invented new products, struck oil, made a "killing" on the stock market, got in on the "ground floor" of a growth industry, or, like Bob Hope, invested large earnings in real estate.

The classical career model of the entrepreneur emphasized saving and scrimping as means of accumulating initial capital. It seems plausible that this is still an important approach for those who start without substantial resources at their disposal. There apparently are no systematic studies of the stages and typical turning points in the careers of entrepreneurs, but, on the basis of biographical, autobiographical, and anecdotal materials, it appears that the essential features are somewhat as follows:

(1) Save or inherit initial capital.

(2) Establish a business or invest in property. Live frugally and accumulate more capital. Above all, keep the capital working, use other people's capital as much as possible and take advantage of tax loopholes.

(3) Enlarge the business operations or invest the capital in more property, including stocks. Create a corporation, being careful to retain control.

Apparently, many aspiring capitalists fail because they think they are rich before they are. They sell something and have money. Then they spend the money for consumer goods—but, actually, they are spending capital rather than profit. As a self-made millionaire revealed in his autobiography in the *Saturday Evening Post* of 30 December, 1967, a new business won't support the owner immediately; it has to be protected at first like a tender plant.

A study of successful manufacturers made by the Bureau of Business Research at Michigan State University concluded that entrepreneurs do not get ahead because they practice the social ethic. Rather they are tough, selfish people who tend to be impatient, intolerant and uncharitable—altogether an unattractive profile if one considered them as potential friends.[23]

23. Orvis F. Collins, D. G. Moore, with D. B. Unwalla, *The Enterprising Man* (Bureau of Business and Economic Research, Michigan State University, 1964), p. 244.

In view of the continuing decline in self-employment (from 26.1 per cent in 1940 to 10.2 per cent in 1970) it might appear that entrepreneurial careers will soon become extinct. Don't believe it. The essence of the entrepreneurial function is the creation of new enterprises by taking risk and mobilizing technology, financial resources, and people. In earlier times most radically new enterprises were created by venturesome individuals like Henry Ford who took great risks and reaped great rewards if they were successful; many, of course, failed. Betty C. Churchill reported in 1955 that more than half of all new businesses fail within the first two years and two-thirds fail within four years.[24] Many new businesses are formed by persons whose previous experience was in some blue-collar occupation.

In spite of what may appear to be declining opportunity, the number of new millionaires has increased rather than declined. Thus, it appears that entrepreneurial opportunities still exist.

Large corporations still need and pay a premium for entrepreneurial talents. Donald Schon reports that the private entrepreneur has been supplanted to some extent by what he calls the "product champion" who is supplied with resources by central management and assisted in establishing new product lines which may compete with existing products.[25] For example, General Motors is reported to have assigned development of the Wankel rotary engine to the hydromatic division rather than to any of its divisions that make piston engines.

4. WALL STREET LAWYERS[26]

In the large Wall Street law firms the pinnacle of the career is a partnership. After a man's entry into the firm, it normally takes from seven to twelve years before he is promoted to

24. Betty C. Churchill, "Age and Life Expectancy of Business Firms," *Survey of Current Business*, December 1955.
25. Donald A. Schon, *Technology and Change* (New York: Dell Publishing Co., A Delta Book, 1957), pp. 153–71.
26. Erwin O. Smigel, *The Wall Street Lawyer* (New York: Free Press, 1964), chapters 4 and 5.

partnership, if he is made a partner. Even though initial selection is rigorous, only a few eventually become partners. Others leave, some in the first year or two, the others as soon as they sense that they are not likely to be offered a partnership. Since only the better students from the top law schools are recruited in the first place, it is clear that the selection process is very rigorous indeed. These lawyers work extremely hard, long hours; but this is taken for granted, and selection is evidently based on the quality of performance as evaluated by the partners.

5. CRIMINAL LAWYERS[27]

Arthur Wood's study, which compared criminal lawyers with civil lawyers in five cities, showed that the fewer of the latter than of the former had difficulty getting started. This was apparently due primarily to the fact that 70 per cent of the civil lawyers but only 30 per cent of the criminal lawyers had joined a law firm at the outset of their careers.[28] Visibility, a reputation for winning cases, is essential for solo practitioners. Wood found that many disliked criminal practice and that on the average criminal lawyers were less successful from a financial point of view than civil lawyers.

The successful criminal lawyer is different. According to Wood, he loves his work and enjoys the thrill of a trial. He likes to defend the accused.[29]

This characterization suggests that personal value orientations and personal style are important components of success. In addition, most successful criminal lawyers must establish the proper "connections" with powerful political figures and judges. Wood illustrates this by quoting comments made by two of his interviewees. One, who was outside the "machine," alleged that favoritism is practiced by prosecutors, detectives

27. Arthur L. Wood, *Criminal Lawyer* (New Haven, Conn.: College & University Press, 1967).
28. Ibid., p. 46.
29. Ibid., p. 65.

and bondsmen. The other, described as a former member of the "machine" emphasized the necessity for a lawyer to keep on good terms with the judges if he wants to be successful.[30] Wood found that some criminal lawyers in cities with political machines do not participate in them. These lawyers, he reports, tend either to be highly successful or relative failures. The former are usually well-known lawyers who have considerable legal talent and expertise.[31]

6. FEDERAL EXECUTIVES

Promotion opportunities for executives in the competitive civil service are largely determined by the existence of vacancies in the approved tables of organization rather than in accordance with the individual's personal timetable. Considerable administrative discretion exists in the selection of personnel for promotions, and the decision is ordinarily actually made by the immediate supervisor of the vacant position. If the nominee has appropriate training and experience, the nomination is ratified routinely by the superior of the initiator and then by the agency personnel department. However, procedures for promotion are not uniform among the eighty agencies and thousands of field installations. A single agency may have several plans for different occupations or locations; one may require group appraisal of qualifications, while another may depend entirely on supervisory recommendations.[32]

W. Lloyd Warner has commented favorably concerning the characteristics and motivations of the typical career civil service executive:

"He possesses lofty aspirations, the majority of which stem from external influences, from heroic figures or models, and

30. Wood, *Criminal Lawyer*, p. 169.
31. Ibid., p. 178.
32. *Federal News Clip Sheet No. 28* (February 1964), U.S. Civil Service Commission, Washington, D.C.

from demands made upon him by the system and by his role as a career man.

"Achievement orientation is strong." [33]

Warner believes that federal executives accept responsibility for their own success or failure. "The federal executive functions on his own. His success or failure is dependent on him; if he finds the system lacks challenge, the fault is his, not the system's." [34]

In addition to promotions from one GS grade to another, increases within grade are also provided. They go to employees whose work is at an acceptable level of competence at the following intervals: every year for the first three rates, every two years for the next three rates, and every three years for any remaining rates. Within-grade increases may be given more frequently to employees who do high quality work. There is some overlapping between the salaries of persons in different grades, and it should also be noted that persons reduced in grade during Reduction-in-Force (RIF) are not put in the first step of the lower grade but are given a salary near their old rate. Increases for meritorious service are given occasionally as a reward for exceptional service. Usually a merit increase consists of one step in the grade occupied by the person.

7. SCIENTISTS IN A GOVERNMENT RESEARCH ORGANIZATION

Barney G. Glaser found that the standard career pattern of scientists in a large government medical research organization involved a considerable amount of mobility in its early stages.

"The scientist moves among university departments, or affiliated research groups, sometimes doing a stint in a government, nonprofit, or industrial research organization, always seeking

33. W. Lloyd Warner, Paul P. Van Riper, Norman H. Martin, and Orvis F. Collins, *The American Federal Executive* (New Haven, Conn.: Yale University Press, 1963), p. 195.

34. Ibid., p. 230.

better research conditions and more interesting, more prestigious, and, perhaps, more profitable positions." [35]

Promotions in this research organization were based upon recognition from professional colleagues for achieving high-quality basic research. Evaluation of suitability for promotion was made by a promotion board upon referral of the individual by the institute director.[36]

Employees of this organization considered it an appropriate place to follow a career in science, because it had a record of thousands of significant discoveries in medical research and at least one Nobel laureate. Even so, Glaser found that the typical scientist did not make a career commitment to the organization until he reached the supervisory level. Prior to that time, their commitments were to their scientific discipline.

"As investigators go through the organizational career, they tend—*as validated scientists*—to choose as bases of operations in the organizational structure those different footholds that are best suited to resolving typical career concerns. . . . Once established, the investigators turn to developing a following of potential subordinates among close professional associates. At this stage they also make the crucial decision to commit themselves to the organizational career, because of their chance to make supervisor, because of their research independence, and because they judge the organization to be a prestigeful organization in the scientific world. After achieving a supervisory promotion, they tend to settle down for the remainder of their careers among the largest group of professionals in their discrete field." [37]

8. COLLEGE AND UNIVERSITY PROFESSORS

All recognized professions and many other occupations are represented in higher education. However, while the subject

35. Barney G. Glaser, *Organizational Scientists: Their Professional Careers* (New York: Bobbs-Merrill Co., 1964), p. 3.

36. Ibid., p. 5.

37. Ibid., p. 95.

matter content obviously varies between occupational fields, the main occupation of most professors consists of resident teaching. In universities, and some colleges, research may be a major role. The career model for teachers in most institutions of higher learning is the university professor. Most college and university deans, vice-presidents, and presidents were once professors, but administrative work above the departmental level can be classified as a distinctive occupational career line.

All professors are specialists. Consequently, acceptance into the graduate training program of a university department or into a professional school or college is the first step. This is most probable for candidates who have outstanding scholastic records in appropriate courses.

Grades and other forms of recognition tend to be awarded on the basis of achievement as judged by the standards of excellence that exist in each discipline or profession. In this competition, which continues throughout a professional career, success tends to be cumulative: the most talented students go to the higher-ranked graduate departments and professional colleges; while there they are likely to be selected for sponsorship by the top professors. These sponsor-protégé relationships may lead to appointment to the best positions and to continued recognition. Diana Crane found in a study of scientists in universities that the attainment of eminence is associated with the eminence of the sponsor and with the prestige of the institution where the doctorate was earned.[38]

The second step in the career frequently involves a part-time appointment as a teaching assistant or research assistant. These positions give the encumbent experience in teaching or doing research under the supervision of a professor. During the 1950s and 1960s when there was a severe shortage of many types of scientists, many graduate students in scientific fields received federally financed traineeships or other stipends which permitted them to complete their graduate studies more rapidly.

38. Diana Crane, "Scientists at Major and Minor Universities," *American Sociological Review* (October 1965), pp. 699–713.

Completion of the Ph.D. or a comparable professional degree is now required by many universities for appointment as an assistant professor; candidates who have completed all degree requirements but the dissertation (ABD's) are still able to obtain entry appointments.

In high-status colleges and universities candidates tend to locate positions through informal networks of communication between professors rather than through employment agencies.[39] Candidates apply to the department rather than to a central personnel office.

In many colleges and universities, qualifications for promotion are reviewed in accordance with the timetable for professorial advancement in the institution without regard to any definite quota or table of organization.

Seldom, if ever, is a faculty member promoted more than one academic rank at a time. The period of time elapsing between promotions may occasionally be quite short, but usually a specified period of time must elapse before an individual can be considered for the next higher rank within that particular university. At Washington State University, for example, a person is expected to serve five years as assistant professor before he is considered for promotion to associate professor. The almost glacial pace of academic promotion sometimes leads to solicitation of and acceptance of offers from other institutions involving higher academic ranks and more salary.

This is usually handled in accordance with subtle rules of etiquette. The assistant professor who is discontented with his status and wants either a promotion or a big pay raise or both seldom confronts his department chairman or dean and demands such rewards. Instead he builds up his list of publications and when he thinks he has enough articles in the proper

39. Cf. Theodore Caplow and Reese J. McGee, *The Academic Marketplace* (New York: Basic Books, 1958); David G. Brown, *The Mobile Professors* (Washington, D.C.: American Council on Education, 1967); and Walter L. Slocum and Melvin DeFleur, "On Making It in Academe: The Successful Professor in The Graduate Department," *Research Studies* (Pullman, Wash.: Washington State University, vol. 40, no. 1, March 1972).

journals, he contacts a well-placed peer or a former professor and indicates, more or less casually, that he might consider a move. These sponsors may mention his name favorably to the recruitment officer or chairman of a department that has an opening. This may stimulate interest, perhaps even an offer. With the offer in hand, he approaches his department chairman and says something like this: "I like it here but I have to think of my future. I have this offer from —— but I thought I should find out first what my prospects are here."

The answer will usually indicate clearly what his prospects are in his present department. If the chairman has an unfavorable evaluation of the aspiring faculty member, he may simply say, "Congratulations! When will you be leaving?" If the chairman would like to keep the faculty member, he may try to get a definite commitment from the administration for a big pay raise and/or promotion. If that is not feasible, because of university policy or budget limitations, he may say that he will do whatever he can to meet the competition at the next date that adjustments in pay and rank are made.

Apparently professors of all ranks keep an eye on the job market, perhaps to keep their employers from forgetting their claims when annual salary adjustments are made. David G. Brown reports that 98 per cent of a sample of social scientists in the southeastern United States said that they were interested in learning of employment opportunities that they might be qualified for.[40]

Some interesting findings from a 1965 study of 13,000 college teachers follow:[41] Most professors of all ranks considered themselves free to move. Job changing brought increases in rank and/or salary for most movers. The probability of moving in a given year was 19.5 per cent if under 30 and 1.2 per cent if over 60. Those who publish are more likely to move. Those who are married are more likely to move. A previous contact, espe-

40. David G. Brown, *The Market for College Teachers: An Economic Analysis of Career Patterns Among Southeastern Social Scientists* (Chapel Hill, N.C.: University of North Carolina Press, 1965), p. 67.
41. Brown, *The Mobile Professors*, pp. 23–61.

cially the thesis advisor, was instrumental in finding a new job for 65 per cent of the movers. By the time a man becomes a full professor he will have moved three times on the average. The most frequent reason for leaving was having been given a negative evaluation by a department chairman.

During the 1960s the shortage of well-qualified faculty gave ambitious professors with good credentials a distinct advantage in this bargaining process. With the turnaround in supply of and demand for Ph.D.s that has occurred since 1969, the situation has changed so that it resembles that of the 1950s— that is, the individual has less bargaining power and the institution has more.

A recent development, due in large measure to pressure by the U.S. Department of Health, Education, and Welfare on colleges and universities, has been a marked improvement in employment prospects for females and for members of ethnic and racial minorities who have Ph.D.s. This also means, of course, that the prospects of new Ph.D.s who are white males have worsened since there are not enough desirable openings to provide employment as assistant professors for all new Ph.D.s. This does not necessarily mean that Ph.D.s will be unemployed, but it is highly probable that some of them will have to accept jobs in community colleges and in other work organizations which are not ordinarily regarded with favor by persons with Ph.D.s.

Rarely is mere passage of time considered adequate for promotion to the next higher academic rank. Achievement as a teacher, a committeeman, or a research worker or a combination of these are given greater weight than time alone. Theodore Caplow and Reece J. McGee have alleged that although most faculty members are hired to teach, their performance is evaluated very largely on the basis of their publications, especially whether they have published in the leading professional journals in their fields. A decade ago they stated:

"It is neither an over-generalization nor an over-simplification to state that in the faculties of major universities in the United

States today, the evaluation of performance is based almost exclusively on publication of scholarly books or articles in professional journals as evidence of research activity." [42]

This observation is still basically valid, in my opinion; however, other evidences of professional esteem—large research grants, invitations to serve as consultants to important agencies, and prizes—are also taken into account.

The strong emphasis by colleges and universities on performance as a basis for tenure, promotion, and differential pay raises has general acceptance among faculty members. It is regarded as the only acceptable way to get ahead. Consequently, the upwardly mobile professor is likely to be a "work addict." The Puritan work ethic is the norm for it is widely believed that, while hard work alone is not a substitute for high ability, even a genius would be unable to win a Nobel Prize without putting in long hours.

On the basis of responses from ninety-three research chemists, Anselm Strauss and Lee Rainwater reported that professional productivity is the main attribute emphasized with very little emphasis on interpersonal skills, political maneuvers or luck.[43]

With respect to the timetable of promotions, most men with the doctorate now begin their college or university teaching as assistant professors. Instructorships are usually reserved for those who have not yet obtained the doctorate. Those who are successful in meeting the requirements can expect to become associate professors after four or five years, and after another five years or so they may become full professors.

In many universities during the past ten or fifteen years, annual pay increases have become common. Thus, a professor who has reached full rank may still continue to pursue an upward career course, achieving greater recognition and higher income without actually achieving higher organizational rank.

42. Caplow and McGee, *Academic Marketplace*, p. 83.
43. Anselm Strauss and Lee Rainwater, *The Professional Scientist* (Chicago: Aldine Publishing Co., 1962), p. 84.

College and university professors who take outstanding professional colleagues as their occupational reference group have been called cosmopolitans or itinerants. Those persons have been contrasted with the local or the home guard, whose occupational reference group is his own department in a particular university or other work organization.. The locals tend to be loyal to a particular university or department; they find satisfaction in serving on committees and may pay relatively little attention to the professional peer group outside of the particular college or university.[44]

A cosmopolitan professor is oriented primarily to an occupational career whereas a local professor sees his career opportunities lying primarily within a particular work organization. Both the cosmopolitan and the local may have occupational careers, but the cosmopolitan's may involve moving from one university to another while staying in the same occupation. For the local, it may take the form of moving up through the ranks of instructor to professor within a particular university. The more deeply committed a person becomes to a particular organization, the more his future career progress depends on administrative evaluations by his immediate superiors. To an increasing extent, career progress in a particular institution of higher learning is depending on favorable evaluation by professional colleagues outside the institution. If this trend continues, the prestige of teaching and committee work may decline still further.

It is not unusual for men to obtain the doctorate at about age thirty, although some do so younger. The normal age of retirement is sixty-five to seventy, so that at the age of fifty the average academic career is approximately half over. Those who have reached this age have relatively few opportunities to move to permanent positions in other universities unless they

44. Alvin W. Gouldner, "Cosmopolitans and Locals, Toward an Analysis of Latent Social Roles," *Administrative Science Quarterly* (1958), p. 2; Everett C. Hughes, *Men and Their Work* (Glencoe, Ill.: Free Press, 1958); and Robert K. Merton, "Patterns of Influence, Local and Cosmopolitan," *Social Theory and Social Structure* (New York: Free Press of Glencoe, 1957).

have achieved outstanding reputations in their fields; even these move much less frequently after age fifty than when they are younger.[45] Slowing down of mobility with advancing age is determined to a large extent by the culture. As observed earlier, there is widespread discrimination against employment of older men in all occupations. Furthermore, older men are more likely to have established community ties that tend to discourage migration.

9. TEACHERS IN PUBLIC SCHOOLS

With more than 17,000 different school districts and more than 2.5 million teachers in the United States, it is virtually impossible to specify a detailed typical pattern of upward career mobility. However, it appears that the fiercely competitive emphasis upon attainment of tenure, promotion, and salary increases through individual merit, so characteristic of universities, is seldom found in the public schools. For classroom teachers, recognition in terms of better salary is most frequently achieved through a combination of seniority and additional formal education, especially a master's degree. There also is a considerable movement of experienced teachers from school systems with low salary schedules to school systems with more attractive schedules.

In large school systems with districtwide salary schedules that emphasize seniority, lateral movement from one school to another may be regarded as upward mobility even though salaries are identical. For example, in a study of the careers of Chicago public schoolteachers, Howard S. Becker found that new teachers were frequently assigned to the slums and tended to regard transfer to a "better" school in a "better" neighborhood as a career goal.[46]

For many men and a few women teachers, upward mobility means moving into the administrative career line. Preparation

45. Caplow and McGee, *Academic Marketplace*, p. 87.
46. Howard S. Becker, "The Career of the School Teacher," *American Journal of Sociology* (March 1952), pp. 470–77.

for such a move involves additional formal education in the area of school administration and a special certificate.

Superintendents in the larger school systems are usually selected from members of the American Association of School Administrators. Membership in this organization is restricted to persons with two or more years of appropriate graduate study in one of eighty universities accredited by the National Council for Accreditation of Teachers' Education, with preference given to members who have earned a doctorate.

The importance of continued education to career mobility of teachers and school administrators is without parallel among professionals except for military officers.

Arrested Career Mobility

As we have already noted, most of those who embark upon careers in scientific, professional, and executive occupations do not reach the top. At some point, upward mobility is arrested by demotion, discharge, resignation, or simple failure to progress.

The pyramidal nature of business management suggests that few executives can expect to become corporation president or board chairmen. Fred H. Goldner discovered that the possibility of a demotion had been accepted by many management men in one large industrial corporation as a normal risk in an executive career; 63 per cent of the headquarters executives in this firm foresaw the possibility of demotion.[47] However, many of these same men believed they also had a good chance of being promoted. In the organization studied, some men who were demoted were subsequently promoted, and the organization evidently tried to soften the shock of demotion by treating the event ambiguously.[48] Goldner found that those who were

47. Fred H. Goldner, "Demotion in Industrial Management," *American Sociological Review* (October 1965), pp. 714–24.
48. Ibid., p. 720.

demoted sometimes adapted to defeat by enlarging non-occupational roles.[49]

Relatively few studies have been made of the personal and social implications of demotion and other forms of arrested career mobility. Many previously ambitious persons are able to cope successfully with the problems while others may experience severe trauma as the following case illustrates:

Earl Jones (a fictitious name) was an executive with one of the major oil companies. During World War II he served in the army, rising to the rank of colonel. His company regarded him with sufficient favor and they supplemented his army salary so that his total income was the same as it had been when he entered the service. Upon his return from the service, he returned to his old desk in a large Oklahoma city, and he and his wife resumed the social activities which had been interrupted by military service. They owned a beautiful home in an exclusive section of the city and belonged to exclusive clubs. About eight years after his return from military service he was transferred to a post out in the oil fields. This required the Joneses to dispose of their home. However, Mrs. Jones continued to spend a large part of her time in the city, rather than in the small town. They joined the country club attended by the wealthier residents of the town, and their social life during the week consisted of nightly activities at the club and frequent weekend trips to a good-sized city located approximately 350 miles distant.

After approximately three years at this location, Mr. Jones was called into the personnel office. The personnel officer said, "We have a wonderful proposition for you." Earl said that his first thought was, "They are going to offer me a job as general manager or perhaps even president." Instead, they told him that they were going to retire him early and offered him a choice of financial plans covering the period until he attained age 65 in approximately 10 years. In order to be eligible, he had to agree not to accept employment with any other major oil company, with any transportation company, with any chemical company, or with any one of the large number of

49. Ibid., p. 723.

other companies to which his experience would be valuable. He said, "If you ask them, they will tell you that I requested retirement. Perhaps the paper that I signed did constitute a request," he said, "but I certainly did not voluntarily request it, and it came as such a shock to me that I did not even choose the financial plan most advantageous to us. Instead of taking one that provided the highest annual compensation during the period, I chose a plan at a lower rate that would provide my wife with half of this amount in case of my death during the period. I completely forgot about our insurance program, which would have amply provided for her, and I did not fully consider the implications of the virtually complete cessation of these payments after age 65. On that date," he said, "I am left with $135 per month from the oil company plus a small amount from the Social Security Administration."

Earl Jones has been able to obtain employment in a small business. Before seeking this employment, he and his wife tried life in a Latin American country where they had heard it was possible for Americans to live cheaply and enjoy life. They did not find it interesting, and they reported that it was not possible for people to live cheaply if they tried to live in accordance with the customary American standard of living.

When interviewed seven years after his enforced separation, Earl Jones was still bitter about his treatment, still tense, but inclined to try to see the matter from the point of view of the corporation. He said, "It makes sense from the standpoint of the corporation. They saved a great deal of money by doing this to me and a substantial number of others about my age in similar positions. They were able to cut down substantially on their administrative overhead, and the new men they replaced us with were better trained, more flexible, and, of course, much lower paid." Jones alleges that many of the major oil companies follow similar types of management reductions.

So much for Mr. Jones. What were the consequences for Mrs. Jones? Of course, they were immediately dropped by their previous associates. In view of the high self-concepts of these people, there is little doubt that they avoided further contacts with former corporation associates. Especially during the period prior to Earl's acceptance of the business job, when he was trying to figure out what went wrong, they were thrown together more than had ever happened before except perhaps

on their honeymoon. Mrs. Jones said that having her husband
home all the time was quite an upsetting experience for her.
"I can tell you what a husband does when he is home all day,"
she said. "He supervises the kitchen, he supervises the cleaning of the house, and he frequently says to the wife when she
gets ready to go out to visit someone, 'Why don't you sit
down, you don't have to go there now. Stay and keep me
company.' " [50]

Some of the ways in which business executives near the top
react to failure to be chosen for the presidency of their corporation, a position that they wanted very much, have been
depicted by Eugene E. Jennings.[51] His orientation is primarily
psychological; he acknowledges that some executives are able
to accommodate themselves smoothly to such disappointment
but dramatic cases of personal frustration are analyzed in his
books. In many of these cases, crises induced by failure to be
promoted led to major changes in life-style and behavior with
undesirable consequences for themselves, their families, and,
in some cases, for their corporations. The severe emotional
problems encountered by these thwarted executives led Jennings to suggest that many of the men who climb to the top
of big business corporations are warped by what he calls the
success habit.[52] In his words, "Many are neurotic, immature,
unstable, terror-stricken, and irresponsible." [53]

The personal adjustments of one whose upward mobility
stops when he is in the middle layer of management may not
be as severe as those reported by Jennings. Kurt Tausky and
Robert Dubin found evidence in a 1962 survey of men who
were middle-level managers and specialists in five north-
western business firms that only about one in ten of the managers and only about one in twelve of the specialists aspired

50. A case from the writer's file.
51. See E. E. Jennings, *Executive in Crisis* (East Lansing, Mich.:
Bureau of Business and Economic Research, Michigan State University,
1965); and *Executive Success: Stresses, Problems and Adjustment* (New
York: Appleton-Century-Crofts, 1967).
52. Ibid., p. 22.
53. Ibid., p. 202.

to reach the top.[54] Age was found to be a major factor in explaining the upward career orientation. The younger men tended to have great expectations, whereas most men over forty-five had scaled their aspirations downward. The reference point of the older men tended to be the bottom. They counted the number of steps that they had advanced upward from the time they started, rather than the number of steps that remained between them and the top. This is a very interesting finding. It helps us to understand how managers who fail to attain their objectives are able to adjust their aspirations to reality. Most people judge their accomplishments by comparison with others and those who look downward toward their humble beginnings are doubtless comparing themselves with persons who have been less successful than themselves. Success is a comparative matter. Furthermore, it is easy to rationalize. Few upwardly oriented executives who have stopped rising will admit that they are not competent to rise further. Rather they are likely to say that the prize is not worth the effort.

There are probably fewer truncated careers in colleges and universities than in the administrative career line in business or in the officer career line in the armed forces. Most men who obtain a Ph.D. and make a career commitment eventually reach the rank of full professor. The operation of the tenure policy in universities removes from consideration and from the staff of the particular institution those who are not considered to have promise as members of the professional staff of the particular institution of higher learning. Nevertheless, those who follow scientific occupations in universities and elsewhere may still experience the feeling of relative failure.

Among scientists and probably also among other professionals, satisfaction with the progress one has made in his occupational career is based to a major extent upon comparison with role models or colleagues. Even eminent scientists may have a feeling that they are comparative failures. Accep-

54. Kurt Tausky and Robert Dubin, "Career Anchorage: Managerial Mobility Motivations," *American Sociological Review* (vol. 30, no. 5, October 1965). pp. 725–734.

tance of a Nobel laureate or of one of the great historic figures as a role model may inspire a scientist to great effort, but because the scientist is likely to compare his own achievements with those of his role model, he may feel that his own achievements have little importance. As Barney G. Glaser has said:

"The feeling of comparative failure that may result when the average scientist judges his lesser success by the considerable success of his 'great man' model will tend to occur for many scientists within the context of a stable-promising career. . . . [but] A comparative failure can still be successful; an absolute failure is through." [55]

Moving from Professional to Administrative Careers

Scientists widely believe that younger people make the outstanding contributions, especially in physics, mathematics, and chemistry.[56] The rapid increase in scientific knowledge poses a special problem to the older scientist or engineer because much of his own store of knowledge may be superseded.[57] To remain productive as a research scientist throughout the entire span of a long work life demands unusual persistence and effort. It is possible for some to prolong their creative work life by switching to somewhat less demanding specialties, but relatively few are able to make a successful transition to a completely new academic discipline. Many, however, do shift into administrative positions, department chairmanships, deanships, and university presidencies. Once a transfer has been made to the administrative career line, it can seldom be reversed. As Reif and Strauss have said:

55. Glaser, *Organizational Scientists*, p. 131.
56. Fred Reif and Anselm Strauss, "The Impact of Rapid Discovery upon the Scientists Career," *Social Problems* (Winter 1965), pp. 302–305.
57. P. H. Abelson, "Revitalizing the Mature Scientist," *Science* (August 1963).

"It is very unlikely that the scientists will after several years of outside activities, return to research; under the present conditions of rapid discovery, he will have lost contact with the main stream of his science. The transition requires thus an adaptation to a permanently new pattern of life, one which makes demands on the scientist's administrative and political abilities. It also requires a reorientation of values and aspirations. The scientist, raised in a tradition of science where the great discoverer is preeminent, does not find it easy to abandon his ego-ideal as active researcher and is prone to internal conflicts in his new role. The older eminent scientist, although filling some key position important to the development of science in his country, may yet not feel his office deeply satisfying." [58]

These comments seem particularly relevant in connection with the really eminent scientists rather than those who do not reach the commanding heights in their disciplines. The latter have adjusted their expectations downward earlier, sometimes while still in graduate school, if, in fact, they ever had expectations for great accomplishments.

Some professors regard a transfer to the administrative career line within a university as continuation of upward mobility. However, a substantial and probably increasing number of professors do not regard movement into the administrative career line as a promotion. Not every professor is interested in becoming a department head or even a dean. In many universities, administrative positions carry little, if any, additional salary, and they always involve duties that are distasteful to some professionals. The administrator is obliged to deal with the professional staff, with secretarial personnel, and with other administrators. He has to be concerned about property and about relationships with students and others. In fact, the working day of a department chairman or a dean is so filled with these activities that he finds it extremely difficult to engage in scholarly research or creative writing, the activities that bring professional recognition.

Many professors, particularly those who are members of

58. Reif and Strauss, The Impact of Rapid Discovery upon the Scientists Career, p. 309.

what Everett Hughes has called "the home guard" and Alvin Gouldner has called the "locals," nevertheless make a career commitment to a particular university and its community rather than to a specific academic discipline. Many of them are keenly interested in administrative positions and regard appointment to such positions as promotions.

A definite etiquette is present in many universities concerning the manner in which administrative posts may be sought. The usual norm is that the job is supposed to seek the man rather than vice versa. One who systematically studies public administration and overtly seeks administrative positions in an institution of higher learning is quite likely to be passed over rather than appointed. At the same time, there are some things that a person can do to attract "the lightning." The approach considered acceptable in many faculties is the organization-man approach, typical of what David Riesman has called "the other-directed person."

Prospects for administrative positions are frequently identified through successful performance on university committees. My hypothesis is that this is a normal route to a deanship. A person seeking administrative preferment would be wise if he avoided identification with unpopular causes. The "safe man" is almost always chosen in preference to one who has expressed his views on controversial issues. In view of the importance of the work imperative in our society, the candidate for administrative position would do well to work hard, or at least to give the appearance of doing so. Working hard on committees evidently is an acceptable substitute in the administrative career line for working hard on scholarly research or creative writing.

While it is doubtful that physical appearance or style of presentation of self makes very much difference for advancement in the career line of professor, the situation is otherwise in relation to the administrative career line in the university. Large handsome men of Anglo-Saxon ancestry who are also articulate, tactful, and well groomed are much more likely to be chosen for administrative positions than those who do not possess these qualities.

As suggested earlier, in most universities, tenure is conferred only in the professional career line. In the University of California at Santa Barbara, and perhaps in other universities, administrative service is now limited to a specified period.[59] This results in motivating those who accept administrative positions to maintain their scholarly productivity and interests and thus facilitates their return to the career line of professor. In most colleges and universities, however, those successful in administrative career lines tend to remain in them. Those who return to the professional career line after long service as administrators may have very grave problems of readjustment. Their salaries may be reduced, they lose many of their contacts with other administrators, they are no longer consulted concerning issues in which they were involved as administrators, and they do not receive the same type of deference from colleagues who were previously their administrative subordinates. In addition, they are usually out-of-date in their professional knowledge, and find it difficult to perform professional roles adequately.

Many engineers move into administration. A recent nationwide study sponsored by the American Society for Engineering Education shows a substantial shift from technical work into administration with advancing age. The proportion whose duties were primarily or entirely administrative increased from about 6 per cent with three years or less of work experience as engineers to nearly 40 per cent of those who had worked twenty-four years or more.[60]

Concluding Remarks

Looking to the future, we may well ask whether a more satisfactory work life may be expected by those who develop a relatively rational approach to career planning. The answer is "yes." Furthermore, I believe that social science concepts,

59. Personal communication from a dean at the University of California at Santa Barbara.

60. Robert Perrucci, William K. LeBold, and Warren E. Howland, "The Engineer in Industry and Government," *Journal of Engineering Education* (March 1966), p. 246.

theories, and empirical findings will prove more useful than folklore even at present.

Some of the ideas from social science that seem to be relevant are:

1. There is the idea, developed and tested by psychologists, that individuals differ in ability, and the companion idea that each individual ordinarily has the capacity to succeed in more than one occupational role.[61]

2. Probable changes in occupational structure, especially the long-term trend away from manual work toward mental work, should be taken into account. This trend emphasizes the need for formal education.

3. The movement away from manual work toward work with people and ideas places additional emphasis on the need for the development of communication skills in addition to proficiency in technical fields.

4. Although the general shape of the future may be in the directions indicated, detailed occupational requirements are unpredictable. Most people will probably need to undergo retraining at least once and maybe several times during the course of their work life. Therefore, a broad rather than a narrow base in terms of educational preparation would permit retraining for new occupational roles.

5. Most desirable occupational careers will continue to be found in organizations, especially large organizations.

6. Because occupational careers are pursued within social systems, knowledge of the importance of clique groupings, peer and power relationships, and occupational ideologies is relevant, especially to one who expects to establish effective relationships with others.

Selected References

Caplow, Theodore, and McGee, Reece J. *The Academic Marketplace.* New York: Basic Books, 1958. This book presents

61. See Anne Roe, *Psychology of Occupations* (New York: John Wiley & Sons, 1956), and Donald E. Super, *The Psychology of Careers* (New York: Harper and Bros., 1957).

details concerning recruitment and job hunting by professors during the early 1950s when academic positions were less plentiful than they were in the middle 1960s.

Fichter, Joseph H., S.J. *Religion as an Occupation.* South Bend, Ind.: University of Notre Dame Press, 1961. This is a scholarly discussion of career patterns among priests, nuns, and other religious functionaries of the Roman Catholic Church in America.

Glaser, Barney G., ed. *Organizational Careers. Chicago*: Aldine Publishing Co., 1968. Contains a substantial number of articles that provide useful insights concerning various aspects of careers in organizations.

Glaser, Barney G. *Organizational Scientist: Their Professional Careers.* New York: Bobbs-Merrill Co., 1964. This is an interesting report of the study of career patterns of scientists in a large government research organization devoted to health research.

Janowitz, Morris. *The Professional Soldier.* New York: Free Press, 1964. Paper. This monograph presents an analysis of the social backgrounds and career patterns of a large number of generals and admirals supplemented by questionnaire data from approximately 550 staff officers on duty in the Pentagon and interviews with 113 officers.

Lieberman, Myron. *Education as a Profession.* Englewood Cliffs, N.J.: Prentice-Hall, 1956. A critical review of the occupation of teaching at the elementary and secondary levels.

Smigel, Erwin O. *The Wall Street Lawyer.* New York: Free Press, 1964. This is a fascinating report of recruitment and other aspects of career mobility in large Wall Street law firms.

Warner, W. Lloyd, and Abegglen, James C. *Big Business Leaders in America.* New York: Harper and Bros., 1955. This monograph presents information from a questionnaire study of more than 8,500 top executives (presidents and board chairmen) of large American corporations, supplemented by information obtained through personal interviews with a smaller sample.

Warner, W. Lloyd, Van Riper, Paul P., Martin, Norman H., and Collins, Orvis F. *The American Federal Executive*. New Haven: Yale University Press, 1963. This monograph presents information obtained by questionnaire from 12,929 civilians and military officers, approximately 70 per cent of those to whom the questionnaire was sent. Chapters 10 and 11 dealing respectively with career lines and the careers of women are of special interest.

Name Index

Abegglen, James C., 94, 184, 223, 295, 315, 342
Abelson, Philip H., 205, 336
Ackerman, W. C., 243
Adams, Sexton, 315, 316
Ahmad, M. T., 271
Akhtar, Jamila, 271
Anderson, C. Arnold, 191
Anderson, Dewey, 227

Barber, Bernard, 38, 73, 167, 169, 182
Bates, Frederick L., 12
Beal, George M., 102
Becker, Howard S., 165, 167, 182, 201, 330
Bell, Alan P., 259
Bell, Daniel, 29
Bendix, Reinhard, 126, 137, 220, 230
Berelson, Bernard, 200, 292, 293
Berg, Ivar, 186
Berkner, L. V., 43
Blau, Peter, 10, 107, 112, 221, 237, 239, 292
Blauch, Lloyd, 199
Bloomberg, Warner, Jr., 26
Bogue, Donald J., 31, 143, 148, 150, 153, 164
Bordin, E. S., 279
Borow, Henry, 139, 298
Bowles, Roy C., 244
Box, Steven, 269
Brawer, Milton J., 223

Brookover, Wilbur, 206, 208, 209
Brown, David G., 325, 326
Brown, James S., 100
Buckingham, Walter, 62
Burchinal, Lee G., 261, 264
Burck, Gilbert, 116
Butler, Alfred, 52

Campbell, Angus, 243
Caplow, Theodore, 90, 203, 294, 295, 310, 325, 328, 330, 340
Carlin, Jerome, 166
Carlsen, Gösta, 223
Carnes, E. F., 281
Carper, J. W., 201
Carr-Saunders, A. M., 166, 168, 170, 176, 181, 182
Chapman, Brian, 310
Chinoy, Eli, 50, 217, 253
Churchill, Betty C., 319
Clark, Burton K., 185, 193, 209
Cogan, Morris L., 166
Coleman, James C., 194, 266
Collins, Orvis F., 318, 322, 342
Collins, Randall, 186
Cowhig, James D., 249
Crane, Diana, 324
Crockett, H. J., Jr., 216
Cubberly, Elwood, 116

Dalton, Melville, 294
David, Fred, 166
Davidson, Percy E., 227

Davis, James A., 249, 250, 251, 265
Davis, Kingsley, 271
DeFleur, Lois B., 267
DeFleur, Melvin, 90, 325
de Grazia, Sebastian, 32, 36
DeJong, Peter Y., 223
Diebold, John, 63, 68, 69, 74
Dionne, David, 316
Drabick, Lawrence W., 244
Drucker, Peter F., 1, 62, 75, 185
Dubin, Robert, 31, 108, 335
Duncan, O. D., 10, 132, 133, 221, 237, 239, 292
Dunkelberger, John E., 253
Dunlop, John, 185

Edwards, Alba M., 126, 136
Eichhorn, Robert, 22
Elder, Glen, 292
Eldridge, Eber, 261
Ellis, Robert A., 265
Ellul, Jacques, 74
Empey, LaMar T., 245
Erickson, Edsel, 206, 208, 209
Etzioni, Amitai, 91

Faris, Robert E. L., 185
Fichter, Joseph H., 341
Field, F. L., 282
Flanagan, John C., 242, 244, 298
Flexner, Abraham, 166
Floud, Jean, 191, 210
Ford, Julienne, 269
Form, W. H., 167, 223, 231, 239
Friedman, E. A., 26
Fyffe, Don, 315, 316

Garfinkle, Stuart, 139
Gasson, R., 291
Gilbreth, Frank, 109
Ginsberg, Eli, 275, 282, 285, 298
Glaser, Barney G., 123, 294, 323, 336
Glass, D. V., 223
Glick, Paul C., 188, 189, 194

Goldner, Fred H., 93, 331
Goldstein, Berniece, 22
Good, H. G., 117
Good, William J., 93
Gordon, Chad, 241
Gottlieb, David, 201
Gouldner, Alvin, 106, 107, 329
Grant, W. V., 188, 198, 200
Greenwood, Ernest, 167, 168, 169, 177
Gross, Edward, 167, 169, 170
Gusfield, Joseph, 233
Guzzardi, Walter, Jr., 315

Haller, A. D., 244, 261, 268, 291
Halsey, A. H., 191, 210
Harbison, F. H., 185
Hart, Hornell, 58
Harwood, Edwin, 147
Hatt, P. K., 127
Hauser, R. M., 291
Havighurst, R. J., 26
Herr, Edwin L., 274, 275, 278, 298
Herrington, Ronald E., 316
Hightower, Jim, 61
Hodge, Robert W., 135
Holland, J. L., 274, 279
Hoos, Eda Rusakoff, 71
Hoppock, Robert, 268
Howland, Warren E., 339
Hughes, Everett K., 25, 165, 171, 178, 183, 329

Iffert, Robert E., 276
Illich, Ivan, 186, 187

Jackson, Elton F., 216
Jacobsen, Lenore, 208
Janowitz, Morris, 166, 205, 311, 341
Jennings, E. E., 334
Jensen, Arthur R., 206, 207
Jewkes, John, 57
Johnson, Donald, 285

Johnson, Lyndon B., 146, 147, 196, 213, 215
Johnstone, J. W., 255
Jordaan, J. P., 281
Joslyn, C. S., 184

Kahl, Joseph, 293
Kaldor, Donald J., 261, 264, 269, 279, 285
Katona, George, 281
Kehas, C. D., 282
Keller, Richard L., 82
Kennedy, John F., 140, 142
Kerr, Clark, 185
Kornhauser, William, 295
Kowarski, L., 41
Krause, Elliott A., 176
Kuhn, Thomas S., 38, 39

Lane, W. Clayton, 265
LeBold, William K., 339
Lerner, Max, 29
Lieberman, Douglas C., 57
Lieberman, Myron, 341
Lipset, S. M., 126, 137, 220, 223, 228
Lipstreu, Otis, 65, 67
Loomis, C. P., 76
Love, Robert E., 304

Mannheim, Karl, 299
Marcson, Simon, 74, 89, 110, 120
Martin, Norman H., 106, 113, 114, 123, 294, 322, 342
Matlin, N., 281
McGee, Reece J., 90, 203, 294, 295, 325, 328, 330, 340
McGill, Ralph, 72
McGrath, Earl J., 184, 205
Menke, Ben A., 267
Merton, Robert K., 11, 42, 182, 293, 329
Michael, Donald, 63, 195
Miller, Delbert, 231
Miller, Herman P., 189, 194
Miller, Stephen J., 166

Mills, C. Wright, 25, 172, 175
Mills, Donald L., 183
Miner, John B., 24
Moore, D. G., 318
Moore, Wilbert E., 8
More, Douglas M., 93
Morse, Nancy C., 24
Moynihan, Daniel P., 20
Myers, Charles A., 185
Myrdal, Gunnar, 205

Nachman, Barbara, 279
Nam, Charles B., 135, 137, 249
Nosow, S., 167, 223, 239
Nunalee, T. H., 244

O'Brien, M. P., 43
Orenstein, Alan, 259
Orzack, Louis H., 32
Osipow, Samuel H., 274

Parsons, Talcott, 110
Pavalko, Ronald M., 183
Perrucci, Robert, 339
Phillipson, Morris, 73
Powers, Mary G., 135, 137
Presthus, Robert, 106, 107, 112, 123, 254

Rainwater, Lee, 328
Randolf, Senator Jennings, 68
Reed, Kenneth A., 65, 67
Reich, Charles, 34
Reif, Fred, 294, 327
Reiss, Albert J., Jr., 126, 131, 137, 236
Riesman, David, 26
Rivera, Ramon, 255
Robin, Stanley S., 223
Roe, Anne, 274, 340
Rogers, E. M., 102
Rogoff, Natalie, 223
Rosenberg, Morris, 262, 288
Rosenthal, Robert, 208
Rossi, Peter A., 135

Sahi, Abrar Fatima, 271
Salz, Arthur, 176
Samuelsson, Kurt, 19
Sawers, David, 57
Schein, Edgar H., 76
Schiffman, J., 144
Schon, Donald A., 44, 319
Scott, William, 107, 112
Segal, S. J., 279
Seligman, Ben B., 49
Selznick, Philip, 108
Sewell, William H., 9, 259, 268,
    291
Sexton, Patricia, 206
Shah, Vimal P., 9, 268, 291
Shaycroft, Marion F., 291
Shils, Edward B., 63
Sibley, Elbridge, 250
Siegel, Paul M., 135
Simon, Kenneth A., 67, 108, 188,
    198, 200
Slocum, Walter L., 20, 59, 71, 90,
    96, 101, 104, 118, 211, 244,
    251, 259, 261, 264, 265,
    266, 268, 269, 288, 291,
    292, 294, 325
Smelzer, Neil, 46
Smigel, Erwin O., 10, 86, 87, 89,
    166, 175, 319, 341
Sorokin, Pitirim, 211
Stareshevsky, R., 281
Stillerman, Richard, 57
Straus, Murray A., 268
Strauss, Anselm, 113, 114, 166,
    174, 294, 328, 336, 337
Super, Donald E., 274, 281, 282,
    340

Taeuber, Conrad, 148
Taeuber, Irene B., 148
Tausky, Kurt, 335
Taussig, F. W., 184
Taves, Marvin J., 261
Taylor, Frederick W., 109
Taylor, Lee, 293
Teare, B. R., 204

Thatcher, Virginia S., 56
Tiedeman, D. V., 282
Tilgher, Adriano, 17
Tumin, Melvin M., 26
Turner, Ralph H., 193, 262, 268,
    290
Tyler, Leona, 257, 283
Tyler, Ralph W., 166

Ullah, Inayat, 271
Unwalla, D. B., 318

Van Riper, Paul P., 322, 342
Venn, Grant, 210
Vetter, Harold G., 264
Vollmer, Howard M., 183

Warner, W. Lloyd, 106, 123, 189,
    223, 295, 315, 322, 342
Weber, Max, 19
Weiss, R. S., 24
Wheeler, Charles L., 281
White, Harrison C., 79
Whyte, William F., 91
Whyte, William H., Jr., 89, 91,
    174
Wilensky, Harold, 19, 167, 168,
    171, 172, 173, 178, 182,
    234
Wilkening, E. A., 285
Will, Robert E., 264
Williams, Robin, 262
Wilson, Logan, 118
Wilson, T. A., 166, 170, 176, 181,
    182
Wolfbein, Seymour F., 139, 140,
    141, 148, 194
Wood, Arthur L., 320
Woofter, T. J., Jr., 102
Worthy, James C., 112

Youmans, E. Grant, 265
Young, Michael, 12

Zuckerman, Harriett, 41
Zytowski, Donald G., 269, 279, 285

Subject Index

Achievement, determinants of, 289
    educational, 290
Administrative careers of professionals, 336
Age and occupation, 153
Agricultural revolution, 59
Application, job, 305
Aptitude theories of decision-making, 278
Aspirations, determinants of, 256
    economic factors, 264
    general factors, 260
    interpersonal relationships, 258
    occupational information, 267
    personal variables, 256
    reference groups, 260
    school experience, 265
    work experience, 266
Aspiration, levels of, 240
    adults, 252
    college undergraduates, 249
    high school students, 242
    school dropouts, 245
Attainments, early occupational, 292
Automation, 62
    influences on employment, 67
    influence on workers, 69
    outlook for, 64
    trend of, 62

Behavior norms, 85
Boundaries of work organizations, 83
Business executives, careers of, 313

Business, family-operated, 104

Career,
    administrative, 336
    arrested, 331
    definition of, 5
    entrepreneurial, 317
    executives, 313, 321
    lawyers, 319, 320
    lines, 6, 78
    military, 311
    mobility, 309
    paradigm, 295
    professors, 323
    progress, 293
    rewards, management of, 91
    scientists, 222
Chemistry, industrial, 53
Colleges, 118
Corporations, 105
    occupational requirements of, 110
Culture, 7, 13

Decision-making, occupational, 269
Decision-making theories, 274
    aptitude, 278
    developmental, 274
    economic, 279
    need, 278
    rational, 285
    self-concept, 281
Demotion, 92
Developmental theories of decision-making, 274

Economic theories of decision-
  making, 279
Economic factors and aspirations,
  264
Education,
  and income, 188
  continuation, 203
  scientific and professional, 199
  technical, 197
  vocational, 198
Educational attainments,
  of nonwhites, 189
  of workers, 187
Educational organizations, 115
Educational preparation for
  occupational roles, 194,
  196
Electronics, 51
Elementary schools, 116
Employment trends, 144
Entrepreneurial careers, 317
Entry into work organization, 306
Esteem, personal, 124

Factory, 46
Family farms, commercial, 100
  self-sufficing, 96
Family-operated retail business,
  104
Farms, commercial, 100
  corporation, 103
  large, 102
  self-sufficing, 96
Federal agencies, 114
Federal executives, careers of, 321

Inept, protection of, 93
Interpersonal relationships and
  aspirations, 258
Invention, 57

Job hunting, 304
Job security, 308

Lawyers, careers of, 319, 320
Linkages between organizations,
  86

Mass production, 48
Mechanization, 46
Medical technology, 55
Meritocracy, 12
Military, 120
Military careers, 311
Mobility, occupational, 211
  and migration, 212
  intergenerational, 217
Monograph, occupational, 303

Norms, informal behavior, 85

Occupational attainments, early,
  246, 247, 292
Occupational decision-making,
  269
Occupational information and
  aspirations, 267
Occupational mobility, 211
  intergenerational, 217
  individual, 225, 228
Occupational monograph, 303
Occupational outlook by industry
  agriculture, 158
  construction, 158
  finance, insurance and real
    estate, 162
  government service, 162
  manufacturing, 159
  wholesale and retail trade, 160
Occupational outlook by
    occupation
  clerical, 156
  craftsmen, 157
  managers, officials and
    proprietors, 156
  professional and technical, 155
  semiskilled, 157
  unskilled, 157
Occupational prestige, NORC
  scale, 129
Occupational status, census
  classification, 126
Occupations, income differences
  in, 133, 134

Occupations, number of, 2, 17
Organizational relationships, 76

Paradigm, 39, 40
Part-time workers, 142
Personal variables and
    aspirations, 256
Personnel processes, 87
Peter principle, 93
Plantation, 102
Positions, 76
Product champion, 44
Professional,
    associations, 176
    autonomy, 174
    careers, 177
    client relationships, 173
    community service, 172
    intellectual base, 170
    occupations, 177
    values and behavior norms, 171
Professions, definition of, 166
    characteristics of, 168
    and universities, 181
Professors, careers of, 323
Promotion, 92
Protection of inept, 93
Protestant ethic, 19, 22, 23
Puritan ethic, 20, 29

Rank, social, 125
Rational theories of decision-
    making, 285
Recruitment, 87
Reference groups,
    and aspirations, 260
    definition of, 260
Rules, formal, 85

School experience and
    aspirations, 265

Science, 38
Science and technology, 42
Scientists, careers of, 322
    number of, 39
Screening function of education,
    190
Secondary schools, 117
Selecting an occupation, 302
Self-concept theories of decision-
    making, 281
Social ethic, 23
Socialization, 11
    organizational, 307
Status index, Duncan's, 132
Subculture, organizational, 84

Tenure, 94, 308
Training new employees, 90
Transportation, communication
    and public utilities, 161
Transportation revolution, 54
Triple revolution, 35

Unemployment trends, 144
Universities, 118
Upgrading skills of the
    uneducated, 205

Women, employment of, 141
    occupations of, 150
Work, attitudes toward, 29
Work experience and aspirations,
    266
Work, functions of, 26
Work histories, San Jose, 227
    Oakland, 230
    Ohio, 231
    Midwestern, 223
Work life, length of, 138
Work systems, structure of, 76

Occupational Careers, Second Edition
by Walter L. Slocum

Publisher, Alexander J. Morin
Manuscript Editor, David Etter
Production Editor, Georganne Marsh
Production Manager, Mitzi Carole Trout

Composed by Wolf Composition Co.
Reading, Massachusetts
Printed by Printing Headquarters, Inc.
Arlington Heights, Illinois
Bound by Brock and Rankin,
Chicago